E. T. Booth, E. Neale

Rough notes on the Birds observed

During twenty-five years shooting and collecting in the British Islands

E. T. Booth, E. Neale

Rough notes on the Birds observed
During twenty-five years shooting and collecting in the British Islands

ISBN/EAN: 9783742864918

Manufactured in Europe, USA, Canada, Australia, Japa

Cover: Foto ©Andreas Hilbeck / pixelio.de

Manufactured and distributed by brebook publishing software
(www.brebook.com)

E. T. Booth, E. Neale

Rough notes on the Birds observed

ROUGH NOTES

ON THE

BIRDS OBSERVED

DURING TWENTY-FIVE YEARS' SHOOTING AND COLLECTING

IN THE

BRITISH ISLANDS

BY

E. T. BOOTH.

WITH PLATES FROM DRAWINGS BY E. NEALE,

TAKEN FROM SPECIMENS IN THE AUTHOR'S POSSESSION.

VOLUME I.

LONDON

PUBLISHED BY R. H. PORTER, 6 TENTERDEN STREET, W.

AND

MESSRS. DULAU & CO., SOHO SQUARE, W.

1881–1882

TEMPORARY INTRODUCTION.

A few words by way of a temporary introduction appear to be necessary. It is hoped that those who take up these pages will bear in mind that the title leads them to expect nothing beyond "rough notes."

I have stated simply what has come under my own observation, with the addition of a few facts picked up from those whose occupations have brought them constantly into contact with all kinds of wild life. I am well aware that naturalists have so frequently drawn attention to what they have been pleased to style the ignorance displayed by gamekeepers, that they would utterly condemn all information acquired from such sources. During my wanderings by sea and land I have, however, learned much concerning the habits of many scarce species, that I have subsequently proved to be correct, from keepers and foresters, as well as from fishermen and coast-gunners. As these pages do not profess to diffuse scientific knowledge, I consider there is no harm in giving any information gained in this manner that tends to describe the habits of birds, so long as the sources from which it was obtained are plainly made known.

Except where it readily strikes the eye, any attempt at the description of minute details of plumage has been omitted; and those who desire such particulars as the relative lengths of the first and second primaries, the number of feathers in the tail, or the construction of the internal organs had better not waste their time over 'Rough Notes.'

The Plates, on which great care and attention have been bestowed by my friend Neale, are taken entirely from subjects in my own collection. Occasionally I have come across specimens, recently killed by others, showing various interesting stages of plumage that have never yet been depicted; but, owing to the difficulty of knowing where to draw a line if my original idea was once broken through, I have decided (as in the case of the collection, where every bird now figured may be seen) to limit the drawings in these 'Notes' solely to specimens I have myself obtained.

It is, I consider, presumptuous to state one's intentions with regard to the future; if, however, 'Rough Notes' should be continued to further Parts, the description of the various species (with the exception of certain classes) will be somewhat curtailed; and possibly eight or ten Parts, with between sixty and seventy Plates, will suffice to give an account of the species (about 230) that I have met with up to the present date.

I have devoted the greater portion of my time to studying the habits of the larger Birds of Prey, Highland Game, Waders, Wildfowl, and Sea-birds. Concerning the remaining families my experience is comparatively limited, and many will have to be treated with simply a few passing remarks.

I take this opportunity of tendering my best thanks to those gentlemen and sportsmen who have so kindly assisted me by granting permission to explore their estates or shooting-ranges; without their help my collection would have been small indeed.

In conclusion, I must beg my readers to make due allowance for the productions of one who is but little accustomed to indoor work.

E. T. BOOTH.

September 1881.

[At the last moment (too late for insertion in Part I.) I have decided to add a drawing of the adult male Kite. This Plate will appear in a future Part.]

INTRODUCTION.

More years than I anticipated have been spent in describing the habits of the birds procured and the production of the coloured Plates for 'Rough Notes.' During the time which has elapsed several other birds have been obtained, and it is now necessary that twenty-five years, instead of twenty as at first stated, should be given as the period over which my observations extend.

The assistance of the men well trained in the use of ropes, from the Bass Rock in the Firth of Forth and other quarters, whom I took with me, rendered the work of reaching the nests of the Golden Eagles on the mainland, and the White-tailed Eagles on the Western Islands, remarkably easy, all our attempts to descend the rocks or cliffs being made without a mishap. While in pursuit of Skuas, Fulmars, and other Gulls in the North Sea, I was luckily able to hire some of the most powerful double-engine tug-steamers employed at Yarmouth, and we met with very good sport, shooting and obtaining specimens. We also caught exceedingly heavy cod, and the largest silver whiting that have come under my observation, for several years during the fishing-season, when the immense flocks of birds were collected about twenty miles off the land, where the luggers from the harbours on our southern and eastern coasts, and the Scotch craft (numbering in those days about sixty or seventy), were following the course of the herrings. It is a remarkable fact that the commencement of all the gales and bad weather we encountered assisted in bringing us more rapidly towards the harbours for which we were making.

To search thoroughly over the high tops of the Highland mountains where the Ptarmigan pass the winter months is by no means easy. Being, however, well acquainted with the parts of the hills they frequented, no accidents occurred, though, no doubt, we had some rather narrow escapes.

Little beyond what has come under my own observation is given in 'Rough Notes'; much information, however, is recorded that was picked up from those whose occupations have given them opportunities for making observations on the birds frequenting the hills in the most remote parts of the Highlands, on the marshes and low grass-lands in the fens, and also at sea in the fishing-luggers. A few extracts are made from two or three of our old ornithological authors, who described the habits of

British Birds to the best of their ability. The quaint and old-fashioned Bewick is the most amusing of these writers, and his woodcuts and the type employed in his work are sure to attract attention and afford entertainment to those who study his productions. Under the heading of the Capercaillie several extracts have also been made from Mr. J. A. Harvie-Brown's work on 'The Capercaillie in Scotland,' published in Edinburgh in 1879. I am aware that naturalists have so frequently drawn attention to what they are pleased to style the ignorance displayed by gamekeepers, that they would utterly condemn all information acquired from such sources. During the time passed searching over the moors and also knocking about in stormy weather at sea I have, however, learned much concerning the habits of many scarce species, that I have subsequently proved to be correct, from keepers and foresters, as well as from fishermen and coast-gunners.

Few remarks concerning the changes of plumage through which the various species pass are given, unless the birds are several years in assuming their last attire. As most carefully coloured drawings of the soft parts * and plumage of Eagles, Ospreys, Kites, Harriers, Goosanders, Gannets, Skuas, as well as a few other species, were made for this work, having been taken either from life or at the time the birds were obtained, Mr. Neale has been enabled to give the most accurate representations of the various stages through which several species pass.

I take this opportunity of returning thanks to those who have so kindly rendered great assistance by granting me permission to explore their estates or shooting-ranges; without their help my collection would have been small indeed. In conclusion, I must beg those who study the contents of these pages to make due allowance for the productions of one who has been but little accustomed to indoor work.

E. T. BOOTH.

May 1887.

* This refers to the fleshy elevations on the beaks, the prominent circles round the eyes, and the size and colouring of the legs and toes, all of which rapidly contract and fade after death.

CONTENTS OF VOL. I.

CONTENTS OF VOL. I.

LIST OF PLATES TO VOL. I.

ERRATA.

Kestrel [Vol. I.], page 3, line 1 from bottom: *for* trays *read* traps.

Grey Wagtail [Vol. I.], page 1, line 2: *for* Alnaharra *read* Altnaharra.

Cirl Bunting [Vol. I.], page 1, line 25: *for* edges *read* hedges.

Woodcock [Vol. II.], page 5, line 18. "One Woodcock," *instead of* "A couple of Woodcocks," should have been inserted in the description of the second Plate.

Great Black-backed Gull [Vol. III.], page 2, line 23: *for* Durnoch *read* Dornoch. On page 2, line 36: *for* Hickley *read* Hickling.

GOLDEN EAGLE.
FEMALE

GOLDEN EAGLE.
MALE

GOLDEN EAGLE.

AQUILA CHRYSAETUS.

For years we have been told that this species was rapidly disappearing from the British Islands; but those who are well acquainted with the Highlands of Scotland will easily call to mind scores of glens where the bird may still be found as wild and untamed as were his ancestors before the rage for excessive game-preserving set in and drove the survivors to the forests and the more remote ranges. So long as deerstalking remains as a sport, and the quiet and solitude of the forests are guarded as jealously as they now are, there is no fear that the Golden Eagle will become a scarce bird. The crow of the Grousecock, or a startled hare bounding up the mountain-side, pausing again and again to watch the cause of its alarm, have given warning to many a noble stag of the approaching stalker; and as the increase of both species is supposed to be checked by the Eagle, care is taken that his eyrie in the forest be not disturbed. Where the hillside is under sheep the case is totally different. The shepherd in nearly every district in the Highlands is the worst enemy to the Eagle; perhaps for the protection of his flock, but more probably for the sake of the money he can make by the sale of the eggs to dealers or collectors, he will contrive by some means or other to rob every nest that is placed on his beat. Active and surefooted as a mountain-goat, there are few precipices he will not succeed in scaling, though, should the rock prove too steep for him to climb unaided, there are always ropes kept at the large farms for rescuing sheep from the dangerous and almost inaccessible ledges to which they may have picked their way in search of grass when food is short; and by means of these, and with the help of one or two hands from a neighbouring beat, securely placed indeed must be the nest that escapes him.

I should be of opinion that it is seldom a straggler is now found on this side of the border, though hardly a season passes without attention is drawn to the fact, in some county paper, that a magnificent specimen of the Golden Eagle has been obtained in the district; this, in every case I have investigated, has turned out to be the Sea-Eagle. On more than one occasion I have brought down on my head the indignation of the "fortunate possessor" for daring to hint that his specimen was not what he fondly believed it to be.

Although his greatest admirers cannot deny that he will occasionally carry off a lamb, the Golden is in many districts considered far less destructive on a sheep-farm than the White-tailed Eagle. I do not think this species does any very great amount of damage to Grouse where hares or rabbits are plentiful. In one or two instances I have known him to take such a fancy to the newly-dropped fawns of the roedeer, that no young were reared in the district for a couple of seasons; but, as a rule, I am convinced that Grey Crows and Peregrines are far more destructive to all winged game. Now and then, when grouse-shooting, I have had a wounded bird that was falling at a distance carried off in front of me; but to my mind the loss was amply atoned for by the sight. I also remember, after a heavy shot at Wigeon with a punt-gun, one winter, on a river in the north of Scotland, seeing an Eagle dash down from the sky after a bird that had separated from the flock and was blindly making its way uphill; before being overtaken it fell dead into a patch of long heather. After circling two or three times over the spot, the Eagle settled on a stone close by; and here his majesty remained so long, apparently considering how to extricate his prey from the thick cover, that I was forced to remove the glasses and attend to the work I had in hand.

Those who have only noticed an Eagle leisurely sailing across the sky can form but a very faint idea of the irresistible swoop he is capable of making when in pursuit of his prey. It is, however, to descend from the sublime to the ridiculous to describe the actions of the "king of the air," when pressed by want, vainly attempting to capture a mountain-hare in broken ground among large stones.

It is now fifteen or sixteen years ago, but I still have a perfect recollection of being witness to a most amusing scene of this description in Glenlyon, in Perthshire. The ground was deeply covered with frozen snow; and a white hare, which had been down on the low ground during the night in search of food, was again making his way uphill just as the early rays of the sun were catching the hills to the north of the Lyon. My attention was first attracted by an Eagle rising a short distance in the air and settling again on the large stones. Here he would, with apparently more haste than speed, hop clumsily from one rock to another, occasionally fluttering upwards and then alighting with outstretched wings, and dislodging once or twice great flakes of snow as he brushed against the sides of the stones. It appeared that the Eagle was unable to seize the hare as it dodged backwards and forwards amongst the rocks, while, owing to the frozen snow, the hare was unable to escape into any of the crevices or holes which would otherwise have afforded it shelter from its pursuer. Every time the Eagle rose to any height in the air, the hare made a dart for fresh cover, and kept gradually working its way uphill, the Eagle again and again returning to the attack, but apparently without success, as at last I lost sight of both over the brow of the hill. The length of their wings, which, while moving on the ground, they frequently spread, seems to render their actions extremely awkward. I noticed particularly that the wings of the Eagle when in pursuit of the hare appeared on more than one occasion to strike against the stones; and again a few years later I observed another instance of the same circumstance occurring.

The keepers had noticed two or three young birds frequenting a rough hillside; and as they were generally seen within a short distance of the same spot, we placed a bait (a setter which had recently died) at the foot of a rock on which one of these occasionally rested, and set two or three traps on the nearest stones, one of them being on the rock itself. On visiting the spot on the following day, two of the traps were sprung, and in one were left a couple of the longest quill-feathers from the wing of an Eagle. From the manner in which the stones were scored, it was evident that the bird had been held for a considerable time before he effected his escape.

While observed soaring high in the heavens, or perched on a pinnacle of rock standing out in bold relief against the sky, the Eagle is certainly what he has always been described—a grand and noble-looking bird. When, however, he descends to the low ground, he leaves (to my mind, at least) his nobility behind him, and shuffles about with no more dignity, and far less ease, than a Carrion-Crow. It is, nevertheless, a fact that although in the air he is frequently attacked and buffeted by various species of birds, any number that may be feeding on or gathered round some prey they have discovered at once give way and withdraw when his majesty appears on the scene.

To see an Eagle to the very greatest disadvantage, he ought to be watched when sheltering himself from the force of the elements during a storm of wind and rain. As I am well aware that it has been stated by some writers (good sportsmen, too) that the Eagle is utterly regardless of the storm, that he, indeed, defies the hurricane, it may be as well to remind my readers that I simply give my own experience. I never yet had an opportunity of watching an Eagle or, indeed, any other bird that appeared particularly to appreciate the effects of wind, together with rain or sleet and snow. A steady downpour seems often acceptable to many species, and even the cold and wintry blast will scarcely affect them; but let the weather be only what a Highland Gillie would describe as "coarse" (which means all the disagreeable properties of our British climate combined together and let loose at once), and then I fancy, if the observant naturalist was in a position to minutely examine and publish a bulletin concerning the state of the royal bird, he would scarcely be justified in stating that, judging by external appearances, he defied the elements.

A few years ago I was crossing the hills on a fearfully rough and stormy day; although late in May, the weather was bitterly cold, the tops were covered at least a foot deep with newly-fallen snow, and squalls of sleet and rain were drifting with blinding force along the mountain-side. Our track was through a gorge in the hills; and while picking our way in single file over the stones that encumbered our path, my attention was attracted by an exclamation in Gaelic from one of the keepers, and on looking up I discovered an *Eagle* perched on a slab of rock in the face of the cliff on the opposite side of the pass. At the first glance it was difficult to make out any thing through the downpour beyond an indistinct brown mass; but on further inspection this gradually resolved itself into the shape of the most dejected-looking representative of the species Eagle I have ever beheld. With his head drawn down between his shoulders, his plumage apparently thoroughly soaked, and the water dripping from his feathers, he seemed so entirely engrossed by his own misfortunes as to be utterly regardless of our presence. I examined the spot as carefully as I could (considering the rough state of the weather), but I was unable to perceive any manner in which the bird could be stalked and shot, so inaccessible was his perch, except by means of a rifle. Few and far between were the passers-by in this wild glen; and I think most likely that the ledge was a favourite resting-place. Eagles often have certain stations, sometimes at a considerable distance from their breeding-quarters, to which they resort after feeding, where they may quietly digest their meal and arrange and clean their plumage.

One such spot I discovered on a grassy slope near the summit of an island in a large loch at no great distance from the west coast. Here for a space of six or eight feet the grass was worn quite short, and pellets and feathers were scattered in all directions. Although there are no nests in the immediate vicinity, the hills on which three or four eyries are placed are plainly visible from the spot. The lower portion of the island (which is at the distance of at least a mile from the nearest shore) is thickly wooded and the ascent by no means easy; but those who scramble to the summit will be rewarded by the sight of some of the finest scenery in the Western Highlands. The surrounding moorland within five or six miles of the loch, though crossed by several rough and stony ridges, contains no hills of any commanding height; consequently in clear weather an unbroken view can be obtained of several of those lofty mountains whose fantastic outlines are always an object of interest to those who visit this wild and deserted region.

Another of these resting-places is on a steep hillside in one of the central districts of the Northern Highlands. This spot appears to have some particular attractions to these birds: though only one or possibly two may be noticed frequenting it, should they be captured, it will again be tenanted in the course of the next few days. It is now some years since the locality was first pointed out to me; but I am well aware that it still continues a favourite resort. A few feathers and some down clinging among the tufts of heather that sprung from the face of the slabs of rock below the ledge first led to the discovery. There are along the same ridge within half a mile no less than three or four other moss-covered stones or grassy slopes that bear evidence of being at times used by the Eagles. This their head quarters is overshadowed by a couple of thick birch bushes and a mountain-ash. The worn turf at the roots of the trees and the moss themselves, together with a mass of pellets and dried and dirty feathers, bear witness to the frequent visits to the spot; while the lower branches of the trees that come within reach of where they sit are entirely cut off by their beaks. The birds had in fact formed a regular arbour to shelter themselves, removing all the boughs that interfered with their comfort, as neatly as if the work had been carried out by a woodman armed with a chopper. The ends of the twigs that were left were perfectly dead and scored with hundreds of marks, showing that the result had not been accomplished in a day. When first I went to examine the place I was in search of specimens, so I at once proceeded to set traps on the ledge. Within a few feet of one another there were three spots on which the birds rested; and placing a carefully-covered trap on each, we made them fast round the roots of the trees. On our way downhill, and within a quarter of a mile of the ledge, we came across a mountain-hare half consumed, which had evidently only been recently killed, and had probably just furnished a meal for the Eagle. The following day, having delayed looking at the traps till after it was likely the birds had fed and then retired to rest, we again passed over the same ground, and after having observed that the remains of the hare had been carefully picked, we were by no means surprised to find one taken. The trap was again carefully reset, and before a week had passed a couple more had shared the same fate. As I was then leaving the district, the traps were removed; but in less than a fortnight I learned that another pair of birds, both immature, were noticed frequenting the spot; and, again, a year later I found others still there.

The first Eagle taken had but one foot; and as the bird was a male in almost adult plumage, I thought that the ledge would probably have been his nesting-place had it not been for his mutilated condition. The next two captured were a young male and female only in the second year's plumage; and this at once put an end to my supposition that it was a pair that frequented the spot. It was not till the others were noticed that I had any idea how extensively the place was used; and it appears strange that the birds should have such a fancy for this particular ledge, as they could with but little difficulty be stalked from three different quarters.

It is by no means an uncommon occurrence to take an Eagle that shows signs of having at some time or other suffered from the effects of a steel trap. To hold a bird of the size and strength of an Eagle with any certainty requires a large and heavy trap; they may at times be captured in one of the common size used for rabbits or Crows and other small vermin; but for a single bird that is taken several most probably will make their escape, leaving behind them either toes or claws. If the traps could be visited regularly, the birds might possibly be secured; but on the high moors snow is liable to fall at almost any time of year, while in some parts mist and fog for days may render crossing the hills and searching the ground utterly impossible.

The Eagle may without fear of contradiction, I think, be termed essentially a lazy and indolent bird, unwilling or unable to capture for himself any prey that would require much exertion on his part. Hares or rabbits when surprised in the open most probably fall easy victims, while lambs or fawns are far too feeble to cause him any great amount of trouble. I cannot call to mind a single instance where I have observed him in pursuit of any winged game that was not partially crippled by shot, while I have noticed scores of times that he has contented himself by making an ignoble meal off some wretched Crow or other vermin that was struggling in a trap. A keeper in the north related to me the following incident; and as it helps to illustrate the character of the bird, it may not be out of place.

He was on his rounds visiting the traps, when his attention was attracted by an Eagle which was rising a short distance in the air and again dashing down. On carefully approaching the spot (a rough and stony gully, where he was easily able to obtain a view) he discovered a wild cat held by a claw, and the Eagle swooping down, as he imagined, attempting to seize the cat. Every time the bird approached with outstretched talons the cat sprang forward to the fullest extent of its chain, and the Eagle sheered off. Crawling still nearer, he was at last observed, and the bird reluctantly sailed away to a range of hills above the spot where the encounter had taken place. Making sure that the Eagle would speedily return, he killed the cat and left it as a bait; then, resetting his trap, he threw the rabbit which had been his former bait on one side, and rapidly left the spot. Returning after a few hours quite confident of finding the Eagle in the trap, he was greatly surprised to discover every thing apparently untouched. It was only when he had removed the cat, whose skin he required, and looked out for the bait previously used, that he noticed the rabbit had disappeared from where he had flung it in the morning, and was nowhere to be found. Had he only thought for a moment, it ought to have been clear to him that the Eagle would never have attempted to interfere with the cat (a true wild cat is far too rough a customer to be tackled with impunity), and the hungry bird was simply endeavouring to reach the rabbit; even this proceeding the cat most forcibly resisted; and it was not till he returned and found every thing quiet that he managed to search out the prey he was originally in quest of and then make off.

There can be but little doubt that Eagles are able to take Grouse and other birds should they be forced to make the necessary exertion. I have seen remains of Grouse and Blackgame within a short distance of their breeding-quarters; while, if all the stories that I have heard from shepherds and others are to be believed, so plentifully do they stock their larder, that the nest at times must bear a resemblance to a well-furnished stall at a poulterer's.

While the young are small and helpless they are probably supplied by the old bird with partially digested food. I have watched the female shortly after her arrival at the nest apparently disgorging something; but I was unable to get a view of the young at the same moment. I have also observed a young one calling continually, evidently needing food, but perfectly unable to help itself to a mountain-hare and the remains of a lamb which were both close at hand on the side of the nest.

Should any accident happen to one of the old birds, the survivor has hard work to procure food for the nestlings and keep watch at the same time. I observed an instance where the female having been shot shortly after hatching, the male brought food and regularly attended to the young one; before many days had passed, on visiting the spot, I discovered the nestling dead and partially eaten. This, I conclude, must have been the work of Grey Crows. I did not catch them in the act, but I noticed one flying along the hillside croaking loudly within about a quarter of a mile of the spot.

The situations chosen by the Golden Eagle for breeding-purposes vary considerably. I have never seen their nests so open and exposed to the storm and wind as those of the Sea-Eagle; they appear, in most instances, to seek a more sheltered and hidden position. At times the eyrie may be in the face of a precipitous range of rocks, utterly inaccessible except to those well acquainted with the use of ropes; but more frequently it requires but little skill to scramble within a few feet of the spot, and, with the assistance of a single line from above, to reach the nest itself. Numbers of ledges showing more or less of the old and weather-beaten nests have been pointed out to me, where, without the slightest help, a very moderate climber might easily make his way to the spot. These localities, with the exception of those in the strictly preserved deer-forests, are now nearly all deserted. I have, however, during the last few years frequently heard of Eagles taking up their quarters and nesting in districts where their presence formerly, except during an occasional flying visit, was entirely unknown.

The most curious and striking nest of this species that I ever came across was placed just above a sloping bank that was a perfect bed of primrose-roots. A stunted holly-bush formed a background and broke the dull appearance of the dark and sombre slab of rock that rose straight from the back of the ledge. The primroses were a mass of bloom, but the holly looked as dried and uncomfortable as if it was struggling for existence in the smoky atmosphere of some London garden.

It is seldom, I believe, that the nests are now to be found on trees. The old and decaying remnants of the deserted structures may still be seen, but the tenants have long been evicted. I am aware of but two eyries so placed which are still used in the Northern Highlands; in both instances a large Scotch fir is the tree resorted to. The materials used for building by the Golden Eagle vary according to the district; I have seen the foundation formed of the dead branches of the nearest trees (pine or birch as a rule), while heather, coarse grass, and the roots or leaves of any strong-growing plant are worked round the upper portion.

I am quite ignorant how many years scientific authors are in the habit of allowing to this species before it arrives at maturity. My own opinion, formed entirely from specimens I have obtained or watched in a state of nature, is that the bird is at least five or six years of age before it gains the perfectly adult dress. The first feathers on the back, breast, and wings are a dark brown, with a rich deep plum-coloured tint or bloom. It is a strange fact that in the Golden Eagle the tail is at first almost white, with only a black band round the lower part of the feathers; and it is not until the bird is adult that the white entirely disappears. In the case of the Sea-Eagle it is just the reverse; the tail of the immature bird is dark, and it is only after several moults that the feathers become perfectly white. At about a year old there is but little change in the plumage; the tail is considerably more white than black, and the feathers on the legs or tarsi (the part that is bare on the Sea-Eagle; and this is the best distinguishing mark for those who are not well acquainted with the two species) are nearly all white or shaded very slightly with a dark brown. The feathers on the crown of the head, I believe, vary considerably; in some specimens they may be scanty and worn, but in others I have observed them thick and in good condition; they have not, however, the tawny hue so strongly marked as in the adults, but appear of a paler or more washed-out colour. This stage of the bird is shown in Plate I. At the age of two years the tail shows but little difference; the feathers on the back and wings have changed from the uniform brown tint and have a more mottled appearance; the tarsi are much the same, or, if any thing, rather warmer in colour. This is the stage shown in Plate II., the drawing being taken from a female obtained in April. The Eagle figured in Plate III. is probably in the last stage before assuming the adult dress. The tail shows only a small portion of white near the base, and the tarsi are of a warmer brown tint. Plate IV. gives the male in the perfectly adult plumage. The white has entirely disappeared from the tail, the tarsi have turned a uniform fawn-colour, and the breast has also become a rich dark warm brown (in some cases almost black); the feathers on the head also are more tawny. The tint of these feathers I fancy fades slightly after the bird has been dead some time. I have never seen on any specimen alive or fresh-killed the bright golden hue with which they are at times depicted. The Gaelic name for the bird signifies "the Black Eagle;" and this appears to me far more appropriate than that of Golden Eagle.

WHITE-TAILED EAGLE.

HALIAETUS ALBICILLA.

It is not an uncommon occurrence for this Eagle, while in the immature stage, to make its appearance even in the south.

The whole of the eyries that I am acquainted with in Great Britain are placed in the Northern Highlands and on some of the adjacent islands; this species, however, seems to be of a more roving disposition than its relative the Golden Eagle; and hardly a season passes without specimens being either noticed or captured in various parts between the Tweed and the English Channel. There are few maritime counties, I believe, in England that cannot claim the Sea-Eagle as an occasional visitor; but I have only had opportunities of observing it in Yorkshire, Norfolk, and Sussex. In the two latter counties I have noticed it at least half a dozen different times; though in not one instance could I do more than simply recognize the species, the distance being far too great for closer observation. I have also examined specimens that have been obtained in these districts: in every case the birds were in the immature state, and in all probability under the age of twelve months. This is the plumage in which they are frequently described in local publications as magnificent specimens of the Golden Eagle.

Although at the present time rather beyond their usual range, I have now and then seen immature birds that have taken up their quarters for a few months on the moors near the east coast of the Highlands; and I have also met with several in the north-west of Perthshire. In this part they are noticed almost every season during autumn, winter, or spring; as they are usually observed frequenting the ground for a few days only, it is probable that they are on their passage from one part of the country to another. While on a shooting-expedition in the neighbourhood I was informed by some of the keepers and gillies that years ago the woods in the Rannoch district, especially those to the north-west of the loch, had been a favourite resort for these birds. Whether they nested or not in this part my informants were unable to tell; but two old men remarked that, on several occasions while crossing the country, about forty or fifty years ago, on their way from the north (travelling by the rough track from Fort William to the upper part of Glenlyon that runs along the west side of Loch Rannoch), they had seen as many as a dozen or more sitting about on the stumps of old trees on different parts of the moor as they passed along. I also lately learned from an old forester, a native of the braes of Rannoch, that in his younger days he remembered having seen packs of White-tailed Eagles, numbering twenty and upwards, frequenting the moors from the west end of the loch on towards the county march. He fully called to mind the fact that they nested in large numbers in the old trees, mostly birch, that were then standing on the islands in the small lochs that are scattered over the country in that direction. In different parts I have at times come across the remnants of old nests in such situations. There are no residents now in the district; and those that are seen are probably driven from the west coast by stress of weather to seek a refuge for a time from the wintry blasts, where food and shelter are more readily obtained than on their own bleak coasts.

The nature of this species and its indolent habits have the effect of rendering it less destructive to game than the Golden Eagle. I have never noticed the latter making a meal off any thing but moderately fresh prey; while on more than one occasion I have disturbed the Sea-Eagle from a banquet of braxy mutton that I should almost imagine was too far gone to suit the taste of even a Highland shepherd. Whether it is only prejudice that sets us degenerate southerners against mutton in this form I am unable to state from personal experience, as I never, to my knowledge at least, sat down to a dish. The peculiar and unpleasant odour, however, that pervades a dwelling in which a store is hanging is particularly striking to a stranger. It is now many years since I first became acquainted with the fact; but I still retain a vivid recollection of the scene and the scent as well. I had gone on a visit to a large sheep-farmer in the west of Perthshire. No sooner had I entered the door than I became aware of an indescribable change in the purity of the atmosphere. I was not sufficiently new to the district to imagine the drains were out of order; but for a long time I could find no clue to the mystery, and I hardly imagined it would be in accordance with good manners to seek an explanation from my host. At last I determined, on the first chance that presented itself, to examine the premises myself; and, following a more than usually powerful whiff, I drew on towards the back regions, and eventually found myself in a large and what ought to have been an airy kitchen; but here the all-pervading and oppressive odour was stronger still, though every thing looked bright and clean, from the bare-legged lassies to the utensils they were scrubbing. Casting my eyes upwards at a number of curious-looking joints hanging from the beams, I was proceeding to continue my investigations, when the farmer appeared on the scene. "Fine stock of hams," he remarked; and, noticing I hardly comprehended his meaning, he added, "aye, grand braxy hams." Need I say that when the hospitable board was spread I was particularly watchful to look to what dishes I was helped? and on the earliest opportunity urgent private affairs demanded my presence elsewhere. I subsequently discovered I need not have been under the slightest apprehension, as the braxy was the property of some of the shepherds who lodged in another part of the establishment.

These Eagles are also in the habit of searching the shore for any thing that may be cast up by the waves; dead fish or almost any refuse proves acceptable, while now and then the carcass of a seal that has been wounded and escaped for a time is washed up; and this affords the material for a most substantial feast. Gulls, Ravens, and Crows are also attracted to the spot; but each and all are forced to give way when his majesty appears on the scene. That the Eagle will satisfy his hunger with food of this description I have not the slightest doubt; but to state that I have seen him feeding on it is hardly in accordance with the facts. Once, while watching a mixed party that were gathered round the carcass of a half-grown seal, I noticed the arrival of a fine old Sea-Eagle. After circling two or three times over the spot, and putting the whole of the assemblage to flight, he settled on a rock close by, and, shaking his feathers and folding his wings in the most careful manner, he took up his position where he was enabled to keep the whole of the hungry birds at a distance. Although I remained some time, in order to see with what sort of an appetite his majesty would commence his repast, I was doomed to be disappointed. An hour went by without his making the slightest movement: at one time his attention appeared to be attracted by another Eagle which was slowly circling over the loch on his way to a distant range of hills; but he shortly relapsed into his former condition; and as there was no knowing how long he might remain in that state, I was compelled to leave the spot, as many a long and weary mile over rough hillsides and marshy glens had to be passed before I reached a place of shelter. It is probable that the Eagle had made a meal earlier in the day, and having noticed the attack that was being made on what he had intended to supply his future wants, he had simply taken up a position to preserve his larder from utter ruin. I have frequently noticed birds driving others less powerful than themselves from food they did not appear to stand the least in need of. On my next visit to the locality an Eagle, probably the same, was making his way from the spot, having evidently been in some manner disturbed by our approach; and I again lost an opportunity of watching him feeding.

Mutton, I think, in one form or another is the usual diet of this species, and for lamb it has without doubt a great partiality. It, nevertheless, exhibits its cowardly nature in procuring even such a helpless prey, as it is seldom that an Eagle will swoop down and carry off a lamb that is not separated from its mother.

On some of the large sheep-farms, where these birds are forced to be kept down by trapping in order to preserve the flocks from their attacks, but few are captured in seasons when the grass is backward. The baits used by the keepers or shepherds who undertake the business are for the most part lambs and sheep that have died. When after a protracted winter and a dry cold spring the herbage is scarce, so many dead carcases may be found in all directions scattered over the moors that there is little chance that the traps will be touched. In search of food in marshy spots many sheep get bogged, and, unless speedily rescued, their struggles cause them to sink into the soft ground and they soon die; others also frequently attempt to make their way to some small green patch in the face of a precipitous cliff; here they will remain for days till discovered by the shepherds and reached by means of ropes; or else in endeavouring to effect their escape they loose their footing and are dashed to pieces in falling. Numbers also come down on the shore at low water to nibble the seaweed; and these are almost invariably swept away by the flowing tide, as they appear to have not the slightest notion of retreating from the advancing water by the way that they came, but allow themselves to be overtaken by the flood and carried away. They swim for a short distance, but are soon drowned, their bodies being afterwards cast up on some part of the coast. From these causes in bad seasons there is always a plentiful supply of food for the Eagles.

It has so frequently been stated that it was dangerous to approach an Eagle's nest, that I suppose there must have been some foundation for these reports. I am afraid if this was ever the case that the Eagles of the present day are a sadly degenerate race. An old bird on the nest is not easily driven from her post; but when once disturbed, she sweeps out from the cliffs, and either entirely takes her departure or remains circling over the spot at such a height as to be perfectly secure from gun-shot. This is my own experience, and it coincides exactly with all that I have heard from keepers, shepherds, and others who have had more opportunities of observing the habits of these birds than have fallen to my own share.

I have never met with any recently-occupied nests of this species except in the face of cliffs either overhanging or at no great distance from the sea or salt-water lochs. Their nursery is generally a large clumsy structure of twigs and sticks, with a slight inclination to a cup-shaped resting-place for the eggs. The upper portion is finished off with finer materials, a few strands of long coarse grass and some small heather-stalks: there is generally also a quantity of the roots or stems and leaves of a bright green rush or flag-like plant that grows plentifully among the rocks near the shore; when gathered it soon fades to a brown tint, and in this state is seen in the nests.

Some eyries are so placed beneath the shelter of overhanging slabs of rock that to reach them appears almost impossible; others are simply in the face of steep cliffs, and offer no insurmountable difficulties to those well acquainted with the roping business; while now and then this species will choose a spot where the very roughness of the ground (coarse heather springing up among large uneven blocks of stone, together with the twisted branches of old and weather-beaten stems, and the roots from tough and wiry bushes of mountain-ash or holly) renders the feat of climbing to the nest a work of very little risk even without the slightest assistance. I have also seen a few localities formerly used (with the remnants of the old structure still plainly visible) where the nest was placed openly in the slope of a hill by no means dangerously steep. It is little wonder that the tenants had long ceased to occupy any situation so easily assailed.

It is a common occurrence to hear those who have visited the Highlands, and explored what they imagine all the wildest districts, make remarks on the scarcity of Eagles. In order to see this species in its native haunts the usual routes followed by tourists and sightseers must be avoided. To many parts of the coast where the Sea-Eagle is generally to be found there is not even the roughest track within miles of the spot, and the travelling is a work of no little difficulty owing to the inaccessible nature of the country. The hills are steep and rocky, the valleys and low-lying flats in many parts impassable during wet and stormy weather, being intersected in every direction with marshy pools and waving bogs.

The various changes undergone by this species in its progress towards maturity would require a series of coloured drawings to illustrate them accurately: and as I confine the plates and descriptions in these pages * entirely to those birds I have myself obtained, I must defer for the present, till I have had the opportunity of procuring the necessary specimens, any attempt to enter into the full details of each succeeding stage of plumage. As I have, however, frequently observed and taken notes on the immature birds I have watched on the hills, I shall not be breaking through my rules by simply stating that the whole of the first plumage, including the tail, is a uniform dark brown, striped and mottled with lighter shades. As the bird increases in age the pale brown feathers appear on the head and neck, and the tail gradually becomes a pure white.

I have no means of judging with any certainty, but should imagine that the perfect adult dress is not assumed till the bird has attained the age of five or six years. The old female from which the Plate is taken is as fine a specimen as it would be possible to procure. All signs of immaturity have entirely disappeared, the beak has turned a clear yellow tint, and the feathers of the head and neck, having lost all traces of darker markings, are become a uniform pale brown; the tail also is perfectly white.

In this species the tarsus (that part of the leg between the knee and the foot) is always bare of feathers. This is the best distinguishing mark (to those who are not perfectly acquainted with the birds) between the two British Eagles, the Golden being feathered to the foot †.

The eye during life showed little difference in colour from the surrounding feathers on the head, except by its brightness. On close inspection the iris was a pale fawn tint, rendered still lighter by being marked with lines like crystals radiating from the pupil, which added both depth and brilliancy to its appearance. I had a good opportunity of thoroughly examining this specimen when first recovered from the loch into which it had fallen wounded, and was greatly struck by the sparkle of its wild and flashing eyes.

A few words on the capture of this fine old bird may not be out of place. An extract from my note-book for 1877 will give all necessary particulars, together with a short account of the locality, as well as a few remarks on the natives of the soil.

"April 29th. After a three-days' journey by easy stages from Inverness we reached the lodge on Loch Uisge, which had been kindly placed at our disposal by the tenant. The travelling on the last day was over an exceedingly wild and desolate country; the road, which here and there skirted the sea-lochs, was rough and narrow, but, except in a few parts, far better than would have been expected from the scanty amount of traffic that must pass over it. Two or three small villages were seen, as well as a few scattered shealings, most of the buildings being placed at no great distance from the shores of the salt-water lochs. The dwellings of the natives are miserable in the extreme; the walls are built up with stones and mud, and the roof composed of straw, grass, and turf. Windows they have none, unless sometimes a small piece of glass is let in with mud. Chimneys are unknown: the peat-fire burns on the ground, or, it may be, on a small heap of stones, and the smoke finds its way out at the door if open; at other times it forces its way through the thatch or the cracks in the wall.

"On our arrival the keepers informed us there were at the present time several Eagles frequenting the

* A few remarks in the Introduction explain my reasons for adhering to this resolution.

† I mentioned this fact in my notes on the Golden Eagle, and I repeat it here, as it is such a frequent occurrence for the two species to be confounded.

ground; a nest of the White-tailed had been already discovered, and this they were anxious that I should proceed to on the first opportunity. Being several miles from the lodge, it was quite possible that it might be robbed by the fishermen from some of the adjacent islands, who occasionally visited that part of the coast in boats in search of seaweed, which they gathered for manure to put on their small pieces of cultivated ground. This weed and the roofs of their houses, which they are forced to remove once a year when the thatch is completely rotted by smoke and soot, form the only dressing that their land ever gets.

"Sunday, 29th. Luckily, although cold, the morning was fine, the minister having arrived the night before and put up at the lodge on purpose to preach in the district to the fishermen and crofters who lived in the small villages on the coast. A sail was spread over three oars on the bleak hillside opposite the lodge, and beneath this shelter, which much resembled the wigwam of an Indian chief, the minister held forth, first in English and then in Gaelic, to a congregation of nearly one hundred persons, who mostly arrived in boats, only a few crossing the hills on foot. For at least a couple of hours they sat on the damp grass and heather, exposed to the biting cold east wind and a drifting rain that set in some time before the service was concluded, evidently listening with the greatest attention to the exhortations of the preacher. The minister himself afterwards told me that wet or fine, hail, snow, or sunshine, the people would be there if possible; and although several were at times laid up by the exposure, and some not unfrequently died from the effects of the cold, they would never miss a chance when he came into the district two or three times a year. The only absentees, he stated, were a few of the poor old bodies, who were kept away by the absolute want of clothes to appear in.

"30th. We did not make a particularly early start for the Eagle's nest, as the minister was returning home today, and I stopped to take leave of him. Before our departure he gave a short farewell service inside the lodge to the inmates and some of the men: This unfortunately received an unexpected and somewhat protracted interruption. It had, I suppose, been imagined that the minister would confine the service to reading portions of the scripture and prayers: to conclude, however, he gave out a hymn, and as no preparations had been made for moving the dogs of the establishment, it caused a slight delay while 'Scamp,' a roguish terrier basking in front of the fire, was hustled from the room, and two stout serving lassies were despatched to the kitchen to help 'Athol,' a magnificent retriever, to sustain himself under the trials in store for him.

"All went well during the first verse; with the exception of a stifled whimper from 'Scamp' there was not the slightest interruption. This, however, was but the calm before the storm: after a short pause the second verse was commenced; then a sound like a smothered groan was heard, and next a prolonged and melancholy howl proclaimed the fact that 'Athol' refused to be pacified. Large as a donkey and powerful as a bull his voice was perfectly deafening, and a stoppage was made while a couple of men were told off to assist in preserving order. No sooner was a beginning again attempted than it was obvious that further reinforcements were necessary. 'Scamp' had now broken loose, and having taken to the stairs, he resolutely refused to be either caught or comforted. At last he was driven to some remote corner, where his miserable yells were scarcely audible; then, with a congregation sadly reduced in numbers, the singing was recommenced and continued to the end."

I should not have mentioned this incident, only it tends to show how peculiarly devout and reverent is the disposition of the people, and how deeply impressed they are by the sanctity of all matters connected with religion. Had such an interruption taken place during prayers in most English households, I am afraid the solemn nature of the proceedings would have been sadly interfered with; but, although the pauses were long and somewhat trying, not the slightest signs of a smile were visible on the countenances of any of those assembled.

"At last we were off, our impediments (consisting of ropes, traps, and provisions) furnishing loads for about half a dozen keepers and gillies. It was past midday before we reached the neighbourhood of the nest; the weather, although dull, having been fine, a part of the journey had been performed by boat.

"Considering the rough character of the country the walking was by no means bad; owing to the recent dry weather the low ground was in most parts fairly hard and fit to cross. A continuation of rain for a few days would, however, have rapidly converted many of the marshy spots into waving bogs. About a mile from the nest we were joined by a couple of shepherds, who reported that the Eagle had been seen sitting soon after daybreak. When we arrived within the distance of a few hundred yards a halt was called, and all arrangements were made, so that there might be no unnecessary noise to disturb the bird. The nest was placed on a small ledge about sixty or eighty feet from the summit of an almost perpendicular cliff, the distance down to the water being about three times that height.

"As the only means of obtaining a shot at the Eagle, either on the nest or while flying out, was by firing from above, it was settled that I was to go down with a rope till I could obtain a view of the sitting bird. Owing to the ground above the cliff being steep for some distance and the turf too slippery to afford safe holding-ground to the men paying out the rope, they were forced to take up a position on a higher flat, and would be consequently unable to see what line I required; being encumbered with the gun, and in momentary expectation of a shot, I should have enough to do without passing signals up the hand-line. In order that they might be acquainted with what I required, we posted one man on a rock where he could command a view of the whole of the operations and signal my position to those with the rope. A keeper was next sent back to make his way down to the foot of the rocks with the retriever 'Athol,' so as to be prepared in case the bird should fall into the water.

"All things being now arranged, we made our way with the ropes slowly and silently to a point on the hillside right above the nest. While the lines were being uncoiled I had a good opportunity to look round and observe the wild and desolate appearance of the country. The nest was in a rugged and uneven range of rocky cliffs overhanging a small salt-water loch; to the north and west the barren hills increased in height, and the summits were lost in mist and fog. Owing to the dull and cloudy sky the view was more cheerless than it would otherwise have been; but even under the most favourable circumstances of bright weather and sunshine the whole scene was dreary and desolate in the extreme. A single White-tailed Eagle, probably the mate of the sitting bird, wheeling high in the air above the loch, and a Great Northern Diver on the water almost below the nest, were the only signs of life. The mournful cry of the Diver alone broke the oppressive stillness, the monotonous roar of the surf breaking on the open coast being almost lost in the distance.

"A signal from the man on the look-out informed us that the keeper with the dog had reached the appointed spot, and, every thing being ready, with the ropes made fast in such a manner that I could use the gun with freedom, I prepared to descend. The rocks in the face of the cliff were soon reached; and with only one hand on the ropes for a guide, I managed to scramble on to a small ledge. Looking down from this point I was able to discern the edge of the nest, and crawling further out, the white tail of the Eagle came in sight. So far I could have easily gone without the slightest assistance from the ropes; but to have fired a shot would have been utterly impossible. I tried several spots, but soon discovered that I should have to shoot from the ledge. Signalling my intentions to the man on the look-out, I knelt down on the edge of the rock, and the rope was most carefully paid out; inch by inch, slowly but surely, I was able to stretch over the face of the cliff, till at last I could make out the back of the bird; and as my position was hardly comfortable, I did not wait to make any further observations, but fired at once, and with a tremendous flutter the Eagle fell backwards over the precipice, receiving the contents of the second barrel as it disappeared from sight. The rope was next carefully brought back so that I was enabled to regain the ledge. Being here unable to see what had happened to the bird, I gave the signal to lower away for the nest; this being a straight drop was easily effected, and, crawling to the edge, I had a good view of a most animated scene below me. The Eagle was still alive and apparently strong, although with both wings broken close to the body. Having fallen on the water the wind had carried her against a small rock about a dozen yards from the shore; here, with her head turned towards her foes, she defied the attempts of the dog, who was swimming round, awaiting a favourable opportunity for an attack, having apparently but little fancy for facing the terrible beak and talons of his antagonist. At last a sudden gust of wind carried one of the broken pinions over the head of the Eagle, and the dog, seizing the point of the feathers in his mouth, swam off towards the shore; the poor bird then drifted on its back, and, impotently clutching at the air, was dragged to land. On examining the nest (which was composed of dead heather-stalks and pieces of fir, lined with coarse grass and the roots of a broad-leaved rush) I found the eggs unbroken, and one large feather from the wing-coverts cut by a shot alone bore witness to the murder that had taken place. While climbing back with the assistance of the ropes I discovered an old stump of mountain-ash almost concealed by heather. When I reached the ledge above no signs of it could be discerned; and this, I expect, had taken off the greater part of the first charge, and prevented the bird from being killed on the spot.

"By the time I gained the point from which I started the Eagle had been brought up from the shore. With its beak tightly bound up with a leather bootlace, and its powerful legs and claws made fast by some dirty white material that bore a suspicious resemblance to a pair of garters, the poor bird was utterly incapable of mischief, and its bright and flashing eyes alone gave signs of life.

"It was quite possible that the male might soon return; and having found the nest unoccupied, I imagined he would most likely take his place on the eggs. On this account we deferred setting traps till after we had rested and taken our lunch. Concealing the ropes under some heather, we retired to a sheltered gully, where we were perfectly hidden from view. The whole of the arrangements had been carried out without a hitch; the signals had been conveyed and the ropes payed out with the regularity of clockwork. The latter part of the business had been rather ticklish work, as an inch or two more than was required when I fired the shots would have pitched me headlong off the ledge. 'Athol,' notwithstanding his objection to hymn tunes, had done his work right well. Sitting now demurely awaiting his share, he hardly liked to trust the Eagle from his sight, but ever and anon he turned his eyes towards the slab of stone on which was laid out the body of his fallen foe.

"Cautiously returning an hour later, we found the nest untenanted; a villainous Grey Crow flying croaking past was the only bird in sight. As it seemed useless to remain any longer, a couple of traps were soon set in the nest; and having securely covered up the ropes for use on the following day, we left the spot and made our way homewards across the moors.

"Before leaving the coast we followed the shores of the loch a short distance further west, in order to examine with the glasses a small bay that was concealed from sight by a projecting ledge of rocks. Here a number of Gulls and Crows were collected round the carcass of a dead seal. While watching this assemblage the arrival of a White-tailed Eagle put most of the party to flight; and I particularly noticed a pair of Grey Crows making a straight course towards the cliffs in which the Eagle's nest was placed. The journey before us was long and the way was rough, or I should certainly have turned back to learn if possible the object of their visit to this locality.

"May 1st. On reaching the nest the following day I discovered the eggs had been sucked; this was, without doubt, the work of Crows, although in some manner the robbers had managed to avoid the traps and make their escape. As the shells were almost dry, it was evident that they had been broken for some considerable time; and it is most probable that the damage was done shortly after we quitted the spot the previous evening, and before the male Eagle had a chance of returning to the nest."

Another extract from my notes will show that even when the eyrie of the Eagle has been discovered, the work of procuring specimens is not always so easy as might be imagined; and the slightest accident or a moment's forgetfulness may frustrate the best laid plans. I may as well here state that I was using one of the newly invented hammerless guns; and to this cause the Eagle was probably indebted for a slightly longer lease of life than it would otherwise have enjoyed. The mistake I made in this case (attempting to shoot with a gun from which the charges had been extracted) was of but little consequence, and shortly after atoned for. Far more serious results, however, are likely to occur should a gun of this description containing cartridges be handled by some inexperienced sportsman who believes the weapon to be what he would term "empty." The gun of the future ought, in my opinion, to possess indicators that show plainly whether or not the barrels contain cartridges.

"On arriving at a spring within a quarter of a mile of our destination we halted for a few minutes, and, with the help of the glasses, made a thorough examination of the nest, which was now in view, placed in the face of a steep and overhanging cliff. It was evident that the female was absent; but the male was at length discovered, at the distance of nearly a mile, perched on a detached rock out on the open moor. As he sat with his head drawn back and facing the full blaze of the sun, which was now getting low, it appeared as if he had not yet observed us. After carefully scanning the intervening space with the glasses, we came to the conclusion that, if I could manage to reach a long broken ridge of rock that ran in the direction of the slab on which he had taken up his position, I should probably be able to obtain a shot. The track I was forced to follow was far steeper than I had anticipated; owing to the dry weather the turf was slippery as glass, and I had the greatest difficulty in getting foothold. At last I reached the summit, and I now discovered that our suppositions were correct, as if able to keep myself low enough to gain the shelter of the ridge, the travelling would be comparatively easy. The air was oppressively hot, and the heat in the gully up which I had climbed had been almost unbearable. Just as I had advanced about halfway over the eighty or one hundred yards of open moorland that separated me from the ridge, and which I was forced to cross in serpentine fashion, crawling flat on the ground, and shoving the gun in front of me, I encountered a delightfully cool and pleasant breeze. The sudden chill, however, put a stop to my advance, as it brought on such a fit of sneezing that I was compelled to bury my head in the moss for several minutes for fear of disturbing the bird. While working the gun along through the rough grass and among the tangled heather-stalks, I discovered that, owing to the absence of hammers, I could make my way with far greater freedom than with the old-fashioned weapons. At last I was able to proceed, and once well under the shelter of the ridge I was no longer obliged to adopt such an uncomfortable mode of progression. On starting again after a short rest, I was not long in reaching the marks I had taken as the nearest spot from which I should have to shoot. Here I was delayed a few minutes in order to thoroughly examine the muzzle and barrels of the gun; and while preparing to look over my attention was attracted by a harsh scream high in the air above me, and on rising suddenly up I discovered the bird just disappearing from sight over the brow of the hill, having probably only spread his wings a second or two before, when the alarm-note of the female gave him warning. As both Eagles were now on the watch and evidently disturbed, it was useless to wait; so I made my way slowly back towards the spot where we had halted. Slightly altering my course I avoided the steep gully up which I had scrambled, and returned by a longer but easier track, rejoining the men a short distance from the nest. After examining some time surveying all approaches and places for concealment, we retreated a few hundred yards to a grassy hollow, from which, under the shelter of some stunted bushes and moss-grown stones, we could obtain a view of the whole range of cliffs in which the nest was placed, and at the same time refresh ourselves with lunch. With the exception of a wee nip taken at a well near the foot of the hill, neither bit nor sup had passed our lips for over eight hours, and rest and food were most acceptable. While repacking the baskets after satisfying our hunger, I first noticed that the gradually increasing gloom was not entirely caused by the disappearance of the sun behind the hills, and a distant roll of thunder shortly after warned us that a tempest was approaching. One of the men, who, while I was absent in pursuit of the male, had been as near to the nest as he was able to crawl, stated that he had plainly heard the young birds calling; if this was the case, I was of opinion that I should be sure of a shot by waiting for the return of the female. Before many minutes had elapsed the western sky was entirely overcast with dense black clouds, and the loudness of the peals of thunder indicated that the storm was rapidly drawing nearer. While I was still undecided whether it would not be wiser to beat a retreat and make for some place of shelter for the night, we caught sight of the female Eagle flying along the face of the cliffs, and, after a single turn in front of the nest, she disappeared under the shadow of the overhanging rocks. I was well aware that it was impossible to reach the Lodge or even the nearest shealing before the storm would break, as eight or ten miles of rough travelling lay before us, to say nothing of a burn, which, although crossed almost dry-footed in the morning, would, if the storm passed over its upper waters, be coming down in spate and quite impassable. Under these circumstances I thought I might as well endeavour to get a shot if possible before the darkness closed in. We had previously discovered a rough tract that ran down the face of the cliffs a short distance to the east of the nest, and by following this to the bottom we should be enabled to gain a footing among some large stones about twenty yards below the ledge on which the eyrie was placed. Leaving the rest of the men and the baggage where we had lunched, Sandy (the head forester) and myself started at once for this spot, making the best of our way over the broken ground. A few drops of rain were commencing to fall as we reached the steepest part of the track; here the rocks and stones were piled one above another in most fantastic disorder, and, being forced to crawl with the greatest caution, it took us several minutes to get over the last few yards. Just before we reached the bottom of the pass the full fury of the storm burst over us. It was now utterly impossible to advance farther with any hopes of success; the rain fell in blinding torrents, the lightning flashed incessantly, and the peals of thunder echoing back from hill to hill appeared like one continued roll. For a few minutes we attempted to shelter ourselves beneath an overhanging crag of rock; then a sudden shift of wind carried the squalls of rain from an opposite quarter, and we retreated a short distance up the pass to a spot we had examined on our visit in the earlier part of the day. A terrier which had followed one of the keepers led to the discovery: his persistent barking and hunting among the slabs of stone induced his master to follow; and at last he came upon a number of small caves, formed by the cracks and crevices of the fallen rocks. Some of the larger openings extended a considerable distance underground, all appearing to communicate with another below the surface; and from the excitement shown by the dog, it was evident that this subterranean retreat was either a fox-cairn * or the den of a badger. Creeping on hands and knees I made my way cautiously into one of the larger caverns, while Sandy betook himself to another, a few yards farther up the pass. Once past the entrance, which was somewhat contracted, the space was by no means confined; and snugly ensconced on a bundle of dry grass and heather, which we had previously collected in case I had to wait for the birds, I felt decidedly thankful at having reached so secure a shelter. The storm, which had lulled for a few minutes, again broke out with increased violence, flash after flash lighting up the inmost recesses of my hiding-place. As the lightning appeared to play about the bright barrels of the gun, I imagined that such an efficient conductor would be safest at a distance; so crawling outside I withdrew the cartridges, and placed it under cover of the first stone I came to, and again retired towards my den. Just as I was returning a blaze of light, which illumined the whole scene for several seconds, revealed the familiar features of Sandy peering from an opening among the rocks. The forester is as fine a looking Highlander as one would meet in a day's march; but he certainly presented a most spectral and uncanny appearance under the influence of the flickering gleams and the grim and rugged surroundings. Then retreating to the farthest corner of my quarters I spread out the rough litter, and making myself as comfortable as circumstances permitted, I prepared to wait till the storm cleared off. Before long I became aware of a dull oppressive sensation in the atmosphere coupled with a faint unpleasant smell; but whether it was caused by dampness and the mildew collected on the stones, or was merely a slight reminiscence of the usual tenants of the establishment, I was unable to determine. Tired with the long day's work and lulled by the distant rumble of the thunder, I soon fell asleep, and it was not till some hours after daybreak that I woke

* A "cairn" usually signifies a heap of stones; it is also frequently the name given by keepers and foresters in the Highlands to the earth in which foxes rear their cubs.

up. For several moments I was unable to realize the situation or collect my scattered senses; at last I comprehended the state of affairs, and crawling to the entrance of my burrow the first object that met my eyes was the ever watchful Sandy, in the same position that I had last seen him during the height of the storm. The sun was now shining brightly, the air was cool and pleasant, and all signs of the tempest had passed away. As soon as I made my appearance the forester crept stealthily forward, and stated that the male Eagle, carrying a lamb in his claws, had once been in towards the rock, but whether he had proceeded as far as the nest he had been unable to discern, as an angle of the cliffs shut out the view in that direction. The female had not shown herself, and we at once decided that not a moment should be lost for fear she took her departure in search of food. Hastily snatching up the gun we made our way, as rapidly as the roughness of the track would allow us, to the lower part of the pass; and having selected a position with firm standing-ground from which I could shoot, Sandy proceeded a yard or two further and gave a low whistle and, after waiting a second or two, a loud shout, neither of which had the effect of starting the bird. A small stone was next pitched on to the ledge, but still no signs; and I was beginning to think she must have slipped away unperceived, when, with a mighty spread of wing, out she swept, presenting a magnificent chance. No sooner had I pressed the first trigger than it flashed across my mind that I had omitted to replace the cartridges extracted during the storm of the previous night. Two dull clicks were the sole response; and the Eagle sailed away without appearing to have taken the slightest notice of our presence."

OSPREY.

PANDION HALIAETUS.

In England, during spring and autumn, the Osprey may generally be observed in certain localities in the southern and eastern counties. The western division of Sussex and the east of Norfolk appear to have particular attractions for these birds. At different times I have seen three or four in the neighbourhood of Shoreham, in addition to several others reported by local gunners; while in the broad-district near Yarmouth I occasionally have noticed as many as half a dozen in the course of a few weeks, and some years back a gamekeeper obtained three immature specimens in a couple of days on one piece of water.

From the number observed at these seasons, it is probable that our southern coasts are visited at the time of migration by stragglers from the continent, as well as our native birds, that are on their way to and from their breeding-quarters in the Highlands. The great majority of the specimens obtained are, as a rule, in immature plumage; and more than once I have seen them in Norfolk all through May and as late as the first week in June. These, of course, must have been birds that would not have nested that season.

Several pairs of Ospreys still resort to the central and northern districts of the Highlands, and take up their quarters for the summer months. Though their natural food is everywhere abundant, and the whole face of the country is wild and deserted, they are but seldom observed among the Western Islands. I never noticed a single specimen in the Outer Hebrides; and, after many inquiries of keepers and shepherds (who were, I discovered, well acquainted with the species from having seen them on the mainland), I could hear of but one bird having been met with in the district, and that was passed at sea during a fresh breeze of wind halfway between Loch Shell and the Shiant Islands. It is probable that, owing to the absence of trees or rocky islets* and old buildings on the freshwater lochs, they may be unable to find suitable nesting-quarters. To the same cause their scarcity in Caithness may be ascribed: trout are to be found in every loch and burn, while solitude reigns supreme over the northern and western parts of the county; still it is only on rare occasions that an Osprey makes it appearance.

Formerly they often frequented the mountain-lochs among the bleak and barren moors, where a few stunted firs or dwarfed birches were the only timber. At the present time their favourite resorts, with but few exceptions, are the more open parts of dense pine-forests that cover either steep hill-sides or rough marshy low ground. In one or two instances the journey to their eyrie is an undertaking of no slight labour. It is necessary to force a way through tangled heather of gigantic growth, entwined in places with matted bushes of juniper or bog-myrtle, while here and there waving bogs of green and treacherous moss are intersected by stagnant pools or streams concealed by luxuriant rushes and rank water-plants. At not unfrequent intervals huge rocks and crumbling precipices or gullies, cut by winter torrents and blocked by fallen trees with sharp

* I was told of a small island, in a loch at a short distance from the coast, where formerly some large bird of prey (possibly the White-tailed Eagle) had nested. I started to visit the spot; but a heavy storm, accompanied by blinding squalls of snow, rendered our journey, which had partly to be made by boat, utterly impossible.

and pointed limbs, may bar the passage, and a circuitous course will have to be taken in order to avoid such impracticable obstacles. Being screened from nearly every breath of wind, the atmosphere in sultry weather is almost stifling: clouds of poisonous midges and flies in myriads buzz and hum around one's head; to rest is utterly impossible, the incessant attacks of the insects preventing all attempts at peace and quietness. Those who have struggled to the haunts of the Osprey in these localities will, I am afraid, bear away few pleasing memories of their visit to the district.

As a rule, these birds return to some old and weather-beaten nest, which is generally put slightly into repair on their first arrival, before the eggs are laid. This is not, however, always the case, as I once observed a female on a nest, which, when examined, appeared to have been untouched for at least a twelvemonth. The eggs were on a soft carpet of moss, green and perfectly alive, covering entirely in one mass the whole foundation of sticks, and showing plainly that no additions could have been made that season.

In some of the forests and on the strictly-preserved estates they may still be found so numerous, that two, or even three, breeding-stations might be visited in the course of a single day. In the more open districts, where strangers are allowed to wander as they think fit, the poor Osprey has either entirely disappeared, or is only an occasional visitor to those regions where formerly, during the whole of the summer season, he was sure to be found "at home."

The fact that the present species holds its own simply where its safety is guarded by foresters or keepers, is one answer to the arguments of those ranting sentimentalists who preach against all preserving, urging that every living creature is sacrificed to make way for game, and strongly recommending that keepers should be abolished and the balance of nature restored. No sane person, however, can have the slightest doubt, if such an undesirable state of affairs ever came to pass, that not only game, but every species of bird that at present adds such a charm to the wildest scenes would speedily disappear before what these purveyors of twaddle would term the advance of civilization. Notwithstanding all that has been written or said against him, the gamekeeper and his assistants are the greatest protectors to the whole of the feathered tribe.

The nests in the more northern districts were, with few exceptions, formerly placed on rocks or large slabs of stone in the freshwater lochs. I have visited at different times several of these localities; but in every case the eyrie was deserted, and at most only a few sticks remained to mark the spot. In one instance, on an island in a loch in the midst of a very wild and desolate stretch of country, I found on a low bush, or rather, if I remember right, an old twisted birch-stump, at the height of not more than four or five feet from the ground, a very large nest, which was said to have been formerly built by these birds. Although the structure still held together, it was evident it had not been used for many years; but the size of the sticks and the substantial manner in which it had been put together prevented it from falling to pieces. I have frequently observed the remains of other old nests, almost similarly placed, in various stages of preservation, when I have visited the islands in some of the remote hill-lochs. In several cases I think it was doubtful whether the former occupants had been of this species or the Sea-Eagle.

Those who have ever read the graphic account given by the late Charles St. John of his adventures in the Northern Highlands will readily call to mind the description of how his friend Dunbar gallantly swam out to the rocks on which the Ospreys' nests were placed. To reach the islands in this manner was entirely beyond my powers; so I used for this purpose, and also to search the shores, which were in many parts quite unapproachable from the marshy character of the ground, an india-rubber boat, which is a most handy invention, being easily carried in a small pack, and taking barely five minutes to get ready to go afloat. The labour of dragging the ordinary boats of the country to some of the required spots, many miles from even the roughest tracks, would be an undertaking of the greatest difficulty. On freshwater lochs I have never met with the slightest mishap; and by carrying a life-belt, one ought to be safe if by any chance the air escaped.

How its extreme buoyancy would enable it to withstand a heavy squall, I cannot state from my own experience; but I only just missed an opportunity of satisfying myself on this point on Loch Maree, in Ross-shire, while rowing out to look at the islands, on which were stated to be a couple of trees formerly resorted to by one or two pairs of Ospreys. The birds themselves had long been banished, and the object of my visit was only to inspect the locality, and compare the trees with others that I had seen used by this species. I was within a stone's throw of one of the islands, when, happening to cast my eye to windward, I noticed that, at the distance of about a mile, a regular whirlwind had caught up the water into a cloud of spray, which with irresistible force was rapidly drifting across the loch. In less than a dozen strokes I was ashore; and lifting the boat on to the bank, I made the painter fast round a tree, and bringing it back lashed it round the seat. Before I could gain a place of shelter the storm had burst; and the first force of the squall carried the boat straight out from the tree to the full extent of the line, and dashed it to and fro till one of the lashings parted, when the wind fortunately lulled almost as rapidly as it had risen. In the larger lochs among the hills there is always a chance that such storms may arise; and what their effect upon the boat would be, I can only conjecture. I, however, always console myself by the reflection that even although capsized, if one can but hang to the boat by means of the life-lines (which are rigged round the sides after the manner of a lifeboat), sooner or later one must be blown to land. The only danger in this case would be the chance of a rocky shore. I have noticed that large slabs of stone and sharp and jagged rocks, extending a considerable distance into the water, surround some of the islands among the inland Highland lochs; and if driven on such a coast, I fancy both boat and crew would suffer a heavy amount of damage before a landing could be effected. One hundred yards or so farther north of the point where I came ashore there is much such a spot.

The ruins of an old castle on Loch Assynt, which were stated formerly to have been on an island, although now joined to the northern shore, were pointed out as having been used as a breeding-station by the Osprey; but the greater part of the nest had disappeared, even at the time of my first visit to the locality, now nearly fifteen years ago. While passing along the shores of the loch only a few months back, I noticed a single Osprey, apparently an old bird, flying in a westerly direction along the water-side. Many miles further south, on the old castle on Loch an Eilan, a nest in a tolerably good state of repair may still be observed; but although a bird or two now and then alights and rests for a short time on the building, it is some years since it has been resorted to for breeding-purposes.

All the nests now occupied that I have visited during the last few years have been placed on trees, and, without a single exception, the birds had chosen Scotch firs. In two or three cases the nest was placed on the highest branches, which were twisted and growing downwards towards their extremities, giving almost the impression that the growth of the tree had been influenced by the weight of the nest. If the same spot was resorted to for many seasons in succession, such a result might possibly be brought about. In one instance I believe the tree has been made use of regularly, while another is only one of several different eyries to which the birds occasionally return, some years taking up their quarters at one spot, and the next changing to another. For the last twenty or thirty years they have never been known to choose an entirely new situation. Within a distance of twelve or fifteen miles nearly a dozen nests in various stages of repair may still be seen; but it is seldom if ever that more than a couple of pair will be found breeding over the whole range. In one instance an immense spreading fir is resorted to (one of the largest and finest trees in the forest); here the nest is placed among the lower branches, at a height of about fifteen feet; it is seldom that I have seen them at a much greater elevation—twenty or twenty-five and (in two instances only) about thirty feet, the latter being the highest I have ever noticed.

The manner of building seems to vary considerably. I have seen some nests only about a foot and a half or, at most, two feet thick, and nearly nine or ten feet across. I never measured one accurately, but well remember that, after having climbed up the tree and stretched out my hand, I discovered, when bending over the nest, that I could not reach within a foot of the eggs without scrambling on to the structure itself. In many instances the nest is heaped up to a height of three or even four feet, gradually growing smaller towards the upper part. In all cases the foundation consists of good-sized sticks, finer materials being used to complete the upper portion.

The Fishing-Eagle (or rather Water-Eagle, as I have heard this species termed in the north) ought apparently to prove an ugly customer to all aggressors and thoroughly able to protect its own. Once when examining a nest I discovered the female sitting on a single egg, with the shell of another, which was but recently broken and sucked, lying beside her. In this case both male and female were alive, and could never have suffered from any intrusion of visitors, as, besides being close to a keeper's lodge, the eggs were evidently quite fresh laid. It is difficult to understand how the Crow (and this robber was without doubt the culprit, as I saw two pair within half a mile of the spot) had managed to get a chance to approach the nest.

I never remember having seen it stated that this species was nocturnal in its habits; but on more than one occasion, when in the neighbourhood of their nests, I have heard the old birds calling loudly during the night. Owing to the darkness it was impossible to tell whether they were on wing or perched, although I have stopped and waited some time in order to make sure.

Unless molested the Osprey is always a most unsuspicious bird. I have seen one alight on a beacon (marking the course of the Norwich river across Breydon mud flats) and allow two or three wherries to sail past within fifteen or twenty yards without paying the slightest attention. These beacons (large flat-headed stakes, a foot or more in diameter) appear to be favourite resting-places for this species, both in the tideways and in the freshwater broads. I have also observed one pitched on a small pole, driven into a mud-bank to hold a net, that was no larger at the top than a good-sized walking-stick. Here the bird remained apparently at its ease, though how it managed to retain its position was by no means clear. This specimen was particularly confiding, turning its head and watching all our motions while I closely examined it with the glasses from a punt at the distance of little more than half a gunshot. At a Highland lodge I have frequently visited it is no uncommon sight to notice one sitting on the boat-sheds close in front of the buildings. The female, like many other birds of prey, is by no means easily scared from her nest. While passing near an eyrie one spring, and being uncertain whether it was occupied that season, we left the track and proceeded a short distance into the forest in order to examine it. After walking round the tree and noticing that the nest (which was not above fifteen or, at most, eighteen feet from the ground) did not appear to have received any fresh additions, we came to the conclusion that the birds had chosen some other spot. One of the keepers at last happened to strike the tree with his stick, and I then noticed the white head of the female rise up a short distance, but immediately drop out of sight again. The large size of the nest had entirely hidden the sitting bird; and it was only when she sprang up for a moment that we became aware of her presence. Four or five of us walking about and talking loudly within a few yards of where she sat had not caused her to move.

The young birds of this species appear to be quite fearless, and exhibit not the slightest shyness, eagerly attempting to take food from their captors almost as soon as they have been removed from the nest. I have never taken but one pair that I required as specimens, although I might possibly have endeavoured to rear one or two in confinement, had it not been, from some cause or other (most probably on account of their fish-diet), that they proved so abominably offensive to the nasal organs that the occupation of feeding or even visiting them could hardly have been agreeable.

What fish these birds obtained while frequenting the fresh water in the south, I was always unable to discern, though I have heard, from marshmen and other natives in Norfolk, that they appear to have a preference for the rudd. On one occasion on Breydon I distinctly observed one, by the aid of the glasses, making a meal off a butt, the local name for the flounder. Most authors describe the manner in which this species seizes its prey, dashing down at times with great force and clutching it with its powerful talons. This without doubt is its usual method; but under certain circumstances, I imagine, it is forced to change its tactics. I have watched one or two, while searching for flounders in the muddy creeks on Breydon Water, following the course of the channels, and fishing in exactly the same manner that Gulls may be noticed when picking up the floating refuse in a tideway, the only difference being that a Gull seizes the food with his beak, while an Osprey grasps it in his claws. The thickness of the water renders it impossible for any fish to be detected at a depth below the surface; flounders, however, may frequently be seen working their way close to the edge of the stream; and from the manner in which the birds proceeded, I have not the slightest doubt they were in pursuit of this description of fish. After hovering round for a second or two, I have noticed one dip down close to the mud-bank, and, although appearing scarcely to have touched the water, sail off to some quiet spot, where it could leisurely devour its prey,—a favourite resting-place in that locality being the sweeps of an old mill standing within a short distance of the flats, from which a good view of approaching danger might be obtained. Mullet are very plentiful in the upper parts of Breydon Water, and to these the Osprey is stated to be particularly partial when observed in the south of England. I have never as yet (though, of course, that is no proof that the bird does not) seen one attempt to capture any of these fish on this water. Possibly it may be owing to the fact that the only part where they can be seen below the surface is, during summer, almost choked by a green slimy weed, which would probably hinder the bird from taking its prey. On several occasions in the Highlands I have noticed that small trout, a quarter of a pound or less, were brought to feed the young; and the male I have also observed carrying fish of about this size to the female while sitting. Although it has been frequently remarked that large and heavy fish are captured, I have but once or twice seen a trout in their talons that could have been a pound in weight. This species of fish, the common lake or brown trout, appears to be their favourite prey in the north, as I have noticed no other members of the finny tribe taken. I was rather surprised on one occasion to see a wounded Osprey disgorge some portions of an exceedingly small trout. Although the whole fish could not have been above an ounce or two (about the size of a sardine), it had been bitten into two or three pieces, appearing to have been divided straight across, and looking as clean cut as if chopped with a knife. On examining the remains it seemed strange how so small a fish could have been grasped by the foot of the bird.

Now and then I have come across paragraphs in different publications stating that this species had been observed attempting to capture both fowls and rabbits. If any faith can be placed in these reports I should imagine the birds must have been much reduced by want before they would resort to such unnatural food. Had not the robber in one instance been shot, I should have been of opinion that some other bird of prey had been mistaken for the Osprey.

Collectors and gamekeepers are not alone responsible for the annual diminution in the numbers of this species. A wandering bird, while on its passage across the country, no sooner takes up its quarters for a short time in the neighbourhood of some well stocked pond or river, than the custodian of the water becomes alarmed for the safety of the fish committed to his charge; a strict watch is kept, and before many days have elapsed the unfortunate stranger falls a victim either to misplaced confidence or the temerity caused by excessive hunger; and a paragraph in the county paper duly records the capture of the depredator.

Two or, more commonly, three eggs appear to be the usual number. When all the young birds have been reared, I observed that by the time they were full-fledged there has been considerable difference in the size, the largest being, as nearly as possible, double the size and weight of the most backward. By the end of the second or third week in July the young birds are generally fit to leave the nest. For some time after they are well able to fly they will remain about the spot, returning every night to roost upon the nest; and here the old birds also bring them food.

The Plate shows the plumage of a young bird when fully fledged and shortly before being able to quit the nest. I particularly noticed the manner in which all the young, that I have had an opportunity of watching, carried their wings. The shoulders are drooped and brought far forward; and this position, to the best of my knowledge, they usually retain while standing. The younger and weaker birds but seldom rise on their feet. The colours of the soft parts were—iris deep chrome-yellow; beak black; cere blue-black; legs and feet a pale livid flesh, claws black.

The adults are so well known that there is not the slightest necessity for illustrating them. What age the bird may be before it assumes the perfectly mature dress, I am unable to state, except from conjecture; but I should imagine it is not put on before the third or possibly the fourth year.

A specimen I shot on May 20 on Breydon mud flats showed less white about the head, and considerably more dark feathers among the markings on the breast, than any of the birds I have seen at their breeding-quarters. From the date of its capture, it evidently could not have paired and nested that season, and I should imagine it was a bird in the second year. The back had lost all of the light-coloured edgings that appear on the feathers of the young in their first plumage; and the only difference I could detect from the adults was, as previously stated, on the head and breast. The legs and feet were more deeply tinted with greenish blue than I ever observed on any other fresh-killed specimen. In a pair shot at their nest the feet and legs of the male were of the very palest livid white, with only the slightest tinge of bluish green; while in the case of the female the colour was a pale fleshy white, almost the same that I have observed in the nestlings. The tint of the legs and feet must, I should be of opinion, if any faith is to be put in the coloured plates in most works, vary considerably in different individuals. Here is the description of the above-mentioned pair, taken from my note-book:—"The male and female were alike in plumage, and only differed in the male being by far the smallest. Iris bright king's yellow; beak black; cere cobalt-blue: legs and feet by no means so bluish green as usually depicted; in the female especially the colour was a pale livid flesh."

[illegible]

MALE

COMMON BUZZARD.

BUTEO VULGARIS.

The only parts of the country where I have had a chance of observing this species in any numbers have been a few remote glens in the wilder districts of the Highlands. Here the Common Buzzard may still be found as a resident, breeding in any rough precipice or broken range of rocks sufficiently removed from intrusion.

In all the northern counties I have met with opportunities of watching a few specimens either circling slowly over the moors, or perched on some commanding eminence on the hill-side from which a good view of the surrounding country could be obtained. During the early part of winter I have on several occasions noticed a bird or two, apparently immature, which had taken up their quarters in the big woods near the coast in East Lothian. At times they might be seen sailing over the rabbit-warrens among the sandy links, the prey they were able to pick up in such situations being probably their attraction to the district. On the fells of Cumberland and among the Yorkshire moorlands I have now and then come across a single specimen; and in some parts of these counties the rocks they formerly nested in were pointed out. In Norfolk and Sussex a few stragglers now and then make their appearance. Those I observed in Norfolk were near the sea-coast in the neighbourhood of the Denes, where rabbits were plentiful; some of these were probably Rough-legged Buzzards, as I seldom obtained a view sufficiently close to identify the particular species. In Sussex, although I never heard on any reliable authority of this bird nesting in the county, I have known several to show themselves early in the autumn, frequenting the wooded districts and hunting over the furze-covered fields and downs. Not a few of these, I am well aware, have been, as in Norfolk, Rough-legs; but I plainly distinguished the Common Buzzard, and have also seen several that have been shot or trapped by keepers, as well as others whose dilapidated remains graced either the end of the dog-kennel or the vermin-pole.

I can well remember being present about thirty years ago (when a school-boy) at the death of a large Hawk which was nesting in a high tree in a densely timbered part of East Sussex. Several gamekeepers were summoned to surround the spot so as to prevent all chances of escape. The sitting bird was shot. Its size was large, its colour brown, and it was called a Buzzard by the keepers: these are the only particulars I can now call to mind. The eggs, two in number, however, fell to my share, and remained for some years in a collection I had formed with the assistance of the keepers of the district. They were of a dirty white tint, and, to the best of my recollection, corresponded exactly with eggs of this species that I have since taken in the Highlands.

Though cautious and wary in most instances when approached with the gun, the Buzzard is by no means difficult to capture by means of traps, if set with only ordinary skill; the young during their first season are still less suspicious, and are almost certain to blunder into the first trap they meet with. A few years back I noticed early in the autumn several immature birds frequenting a rough and stony moor that was well stocked with rabbits. Having placed a trap baited with a blue hare on a small pile of stones, a watch was kept; and in twenty-four hours three young Buzzards were taken, in addition to a cat and a stoat.

This species, I am of opinion, does but little harm to game. It has been stated by some writers who are considered good authorities that it will take young Grouse and Partridges; but, according to my own experience, the damage caused in this manner must be exceedingly slight. When in the neighbourhood of their breeding-quarters I always carefully searched the ground in order to discover on what they had been feeding. Scattered over the grassy slopes and on the nearest ledges I have found the remains of hare- and rabbit-fur, and at times some portions of skins that appeared to have belonged to moles and mice. In no single instance have I detected feathers, either in the vicinity of the nest or in their castings. A wounded or diseased bird, I have but little doubt, would prove acceptable; but that they would tackle a strong and healthy Grouse, or even the young that were not deprived of the protection of either one or both of their parents, must, I should imagine, be of rare occurrence. In most districts where the Buzzard still survives, blue hares or rabbits are numerous, and in some cases so abundant as to be a nuisance; in these parts, at any rate, it is a pity that the bird should be exterminated. Scientific naturalists condemn keepers for destroying this species; it ought, however, to be borne in mind that these men are bound to set traps, in order to keep down Crows, stoats, and other vermin; and, whether they desire it or not, the Buzzard, owing to the manner in which it procures its food, is almost sure to offer itself as the first victim. It is, I am aware, possible to conduct the extermination of vermin, by judiciously placed traps and the occasional use of the gun, in such a manner that none but the guilty are destroyed; but such accurate knowledge of the habits of all birds and beasts of prey is, I am afraid, more than can be reasonably expected of the majority of gamekeepers.

I am ignorant of the age at which this species acquires the perfect adult plumage. The difference between the young and the mature specimens I have obtained is not striking; and the Plates will show the two stages far better than I am able to describe them. The immature bird was trapped in September 1865, and the adult male shot at its nesting-quarters a few years later, both specimens being obtained in the Highlands. The old male, when fresh killed, was remarkably brightly coloured, parts of the breast and flanks being deeply tinted with reddish brown. I noticed after a few years that its plumage had faded considerably; and the artist has been forced to rely somewhat on a rough sketch I made myself, in order to produce his drawing. The female was by no means so richly marked, and much resembled the immature specimen.

Though none have fallen to my own exertions, I have seen many young birds, in very curious stages of plumage, that have recently been shot or trapped by keepers. Several specimens were of a uniform dark-brown or chocolate colour, in others a pale red or cinnamon was the pervading tint. During the last few years these varieties appear to have occurred more frequently. I never remember to have seen a single specimen, either old or young, on wing in the Highlands that approached these birds in colour; and from the fact that all I examined were procured in either Norfolk or Sussex or the adjoining counties, it is possible that they are all foreign bred. Should, however, dark-coloured birds have been obtained breeding in some parts of the British Islands, my supposition that these varieties are all from the north of Europe at once falls to the ground.

An extract from my notes referring to the capture of the male represented in the Plate will supply some information as to the unsuspicious character of the bird and the rapidity with which a mate is at times procured when one is lost. On this occasion, in little over half an hour after the death of the male, the female was calmly seated on her eggs, with a fresh partner quietly perched on a stump within a few feet of her nest.

"May 30.—Started early from the inn, in a downpour of rain, to make our way to the glen where the Buzzard was supposed to be breeding. I have had many a tramp through dull and dreary wastes; but I scarcely ever remember a journey so long and uninteresting. Thick drifting mist obscured the view on all sides; and after leaving the low ground not a glimpse of the surrounding country was obtained beyond the distance of a few hundred yards on either side, until we descended from the high moors into a grassy valley shut in by steep and broken cliffs. The heavy rain now cleared, and was succeeded by occasional showers, while the clouds rolled further up the hills. Being uncertain about the exact spot where the nest was situated, we kept, close below the rocks, on towards the northern extremity of the glen, in which part the shepherd who had brought the information had noticed the birds. At length, during a heavy squall of sleet and rain, a Buzzard was noticed to leave the cliffs; but, although we closely examined the whole face of the rocks both from above and below, we could detect no signs of a nest. In order to give the bird a chance to return, we retired to the cover of a broken bank in a gully, at a distance of three or four hundred yards from the spot we required to watch. Scarcely five minutes had passed when the pair of birds were seen flying in circles at some height in the air; then, gradually extending their flight towards the north, they were lost to sight in the mist. A few moments later, one suddenly returned, and, sweeping close under the cliffs, at once disappeared onto one of the ledges we had previously examined. Leaving one of the keepers in the valley to mark the exact spot where the bird came out, we took a circuitous course, and again made our way to the top of the rocks. On reaching the summit, and crawling cautiously to the edge of the cliffs, the bird left the ledge, which was within the distance of a few feet, so rapidly that it was impossible, owing to my cramped position, to obtain a shot. I was able to detect the situation of the nest; and, the ropes being produced, there was but little difficulty in reaching the ledge. Though the distance was so slight, the rock proved to be dangerous for roping-work. If it had been necessary to descend far, the risk would have been considerable, as numbers of loose stones were detached. The nest was placed on a small grassy ledge, partly sheltered, and almost obscured from view by a projecting slab of rock. It was not a particularly neat structure, being roughly put together, and consisting of heather stalks and roots, with a few pieces of that coarse-growing rush so commonly seen in nests of Eagles, and lined with fine twigs entwined with strands of grass. As I had previously obtained specimens of adult birds, the nest and eggs were the main objects of my visit; and, owing to the crumbling nature of the rock, I was afraid lest a second descent might prove destructive to them. We consequently removed the nest and eggs, which were securely lifted to the top of the cliffs; and then, in order to decoy the old birds, I constructed a fresh nest from dead heather, and also two imitation eggs made up of balls of heather tied tightly in pieces of rag cut from my dirty pocket-handkerchief. About a foot and a half of turf with fine short grass separated the nest from the edge of the precipice; and here we placed a trap, concealed with the greatest care. I imagined that one of the old birds might possibly settle on the ledge and be taken, but never calculated that they would be sufficiently imposed upon to venture on the nest. When completed, the whole affair had a most natural appearance. Looking down from above, it was impossible to detect the changes that had been effected. On our way back we discovered a projecting rock at a slightly higher elevation, from which a far better view could be obtained of the ledge where the nest was situated. From this point I was satisfied the birds could have been easily killed at the time of our first visit, if we had been acquainted with the exact position of the eyrie. Tired and hungry, and but little inclined to wait for the chance of a shot till after a rest, I turned downhill to where we had left the man to keep watch. He reported that during the time we had been employed about the rock he had been unable to make out either of the birds. A short distance further up the glen the mist was still thick; so it was quite possible that they might have been within a quarter of a mile without having been discerned. Lunch was now brought out; but a commencement had scarcely been made, when one of the Buzzards was noticed to skim rapidly under the shadow of the cliffs, and at once disappear onto the ledge. Two or three glasses were turned to the spot by the time the nest was reached; but the bird apparently avoided the trap, and alighted at once on the eggs, as not the slightest disturbance was noticed. After waiting about half an hour longer, as the bird gave no signs of leaving, I determined to try and obtain a shot from the higher ledge we had lately discovered. Taking with me only the head keeper, I followed the same track by which we had returned from our last ascent. On nearing the edge of the cliff, Duncan secured a good grip of my coat while I cautiously stretched over so as to command a view of the ledge. The Buzzard was evidently covering the imitation eggs; and it needed a whistle to induce it to fly. Being well prepared, as soon as it spread its wings I fired; and the bird, just clearing the ledge, fell to the foot of the cliffs. By the help of the glasses I was able to make out that the aspect of the nest, eggs, and covering of the trap was in no manner changed; so we returned at once to the spot where we had been lunching. By the time we arrived the dead bird had been picked up, and proved to be, as I at first imagined, the male. We had not regained our position above ten minutes when the remaining Buzzard came in sight, and, after circling three or four times over the nest, it sailed away back to the north. In less than a quarter of an hour it again appeared in view, and, following the exact course pursued by the bird already killed, it settled at once on the nest. We had just come to the conclusion that this one also had managed to escape the trap, when our attention was attracted by a third Buzzard which was flying immediately over the spot. After two or three turns, it alighted on a dead stump of mountain-ash, within a few feet of the sitting bird. I should have started at once to endeavour to obtain another shot; but the commanding position taken up by the latest arrival rendered it unlikely that we could get within range before warning of our approach would be given. For over an hour we waited, in hopes that the bird might take its departure; but it showed no signs of moving. As a last resource, I despatched a couple of men to walk a short distance up the glen, and return again close below the nest, directing them on no account to pause while in the immediate vicinity, but to keep steadily on their way. This manœuvre had the desired effect; the bird left the tree without giving the alarm, and, after circling a few times over their heads, made a straight course towards the north, where it was speedily lost in the mist. As soon as it disappeared, we started again for the rock; and on this occasion I had some difficulty to force the bird to move. I was unable to get a shot while she sat; and for several moments she refused to stir. At length spreading her wings, I fired at once, and she fell dead into the trap. It was necessary to go down to the ledge with the ropes in order to recover the dead bird; and on examining the imitation nest and eggs it was discovered that neither the male nor the female had made the slightest alteration in the arrangement of their domestic affairs. The difference in the nest was certainly slight; but it was strange how the birds had been imposed upon by the texture of the eggs."

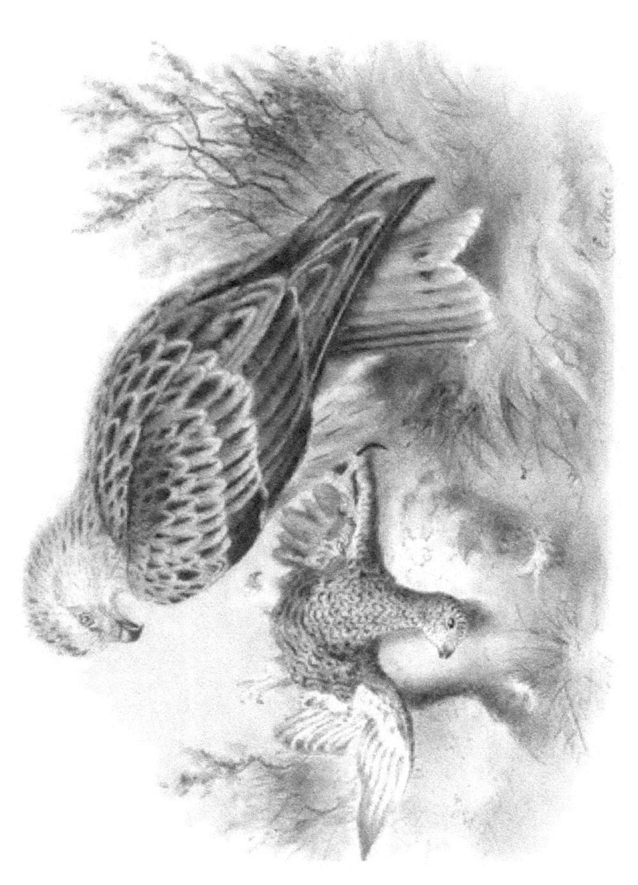

E. Neale

KITE.

MILVUS REGALIS.

The citizens of London would at the present day open their eyes with amazement to behold a Kite constructing its cumbersome nest among the branches of their grimy trees, or soaring over the river-banks in quest of prey; yet, if we are to put faith in old records, such sights must have been of common occurrence in days gone by.

It is seldom now that a Kite is observed in the south, though forty or fifty years ago they appear to have been numerous. The only one that ever came under my own observation in England was while shooting in the neighbourhood of Brighton during the autumn of 1878; I then noticed one passing west at a considerable elevation. On mentioning the fact to the farmer on whose land I was, he told me that when he was a young man, over sixty years previously, he had known both Kites and Buzzards plentiful in a large wood near Canterbury. He stated he had frequently robbed the nests of the Kites, and that it was always considered the safest plan to mount first higher up the tree, so as to get a good view of the interior, as the birds were in the habit of carrying snakes and vipers to feed their young; these reptiles having at times sufficient strength left to hiss and strike if touched, rendered it necessary to take care when making an inspection.

Some works I have consulted give "reptiles and carrion" as forming part of the diet of these birds; but I must say, from my own experience, that the Kites of the present day appear to be decidedly more refined in their tastes. In some of their nests I have found a few squirrels and rabbits, numbers of Grouse and Peewits, and, on several occasions, the young of Curlew, Duck, and Pigeons. Grouse seem to be their favourite food. The last nest I had a chance of observing I passed several times, and on every occasion the young birds had a fresh-killed Grouse lying beside them.

The old birds usually have some particular spot to which they carry their prey to partially pluck and break up before taking to the young. Sometimes it is the stump of a tree, a large moss-covered stone, or a bare mound of earth; at other times, if the immediate neighbourhood of the nest is covered with long and coarse undergrowth, they prepare the food on the branches of a tree. Once, while passing a nest belonging to this species, an old forester pointed out one of these spots (in this instance a clear space among long tufts of heather and dead and rotten branches) where he had recently trapped an old bird. He had only needed some feathers for flies; and having plundered his captive of all he required, the poor wretch was released, a thinner clad but possibly a wiser Kite, as I judged by the wide berth he gave us while we remained in his neighbourhood. In addition to the place where they prepare the food for the young (which I have heard keepers style "the Kite's dressing-table"), I believe these birds, like Grey Crows, occasionally have some spot to which they carry their prey to consume at their leisure. I once counted the remains of over thirty Grouse under the branches of a large fir; some were only bleached and weatherbeaten skeletons, and probably had laid for many months. This stock could hardly have been brought together for the benefit of the young, as the nest of the pair of birds frequenting the tree was within the distance of one hundred yards, and contained, at the time I discovered the remains of the Grouse, only eggs at the point of hatching and a single nestling with its eyes as yet unopened.

The Kite appears by no means a powerful bird; and how it manages to possess itself of so strong and heavy a prey as an old Grouse, I am at a loss to understand. In most instances I have noticed that young birds were brought as food to the nest; and where I have seen the remains plentiful, they were in many cases so old and decayed as to be past judging at what age they had been captured. Still I well remember that most of the feathers scattered about belonged evidently to young birds; I also particularly remarked that the only old cock Grouse I ever found on one of their nests (perfectly fresh-killed and in a fit state to examine) was minus the head. This bird I fancy, from the manner in which the neck was lacerated, had been struck down by a Peregrine (these Falcons frequently kill more than they require, leaving their victims lying where they fall), and afterwards picked up and brought in by the Kite. Probably the greater part of the Grouse destroyed by this species are wounded or diseased birds, with the exception of the young that they take when their own nestlings are in the most ravenous stage. The squirrels must, I should imagine, have been surprised on the ground, while on their way from one tree to another in some open part of the country, as among the branches so active an animal would, I fancy, have been more than a match for its captor.

Formerly the Kite was stated to be remarkably easily taken by means of traps. During the last ten years, however, I have only known about half a dozen captured in this manner. This species appears to have been entirely banished from the woods in the more open and cultivated parts of the country, and those that are left have, in most instances, taken up their quarters in wild and remote districts where little or no trapping is carried on, also in deer-forests, where, of course, vermin are never molested. I was told by an old keeper, in one of the glens in the Northern Highlands, that about forty years ago, when these birds were common, he used to trap numbers in the spring by using old rags instead of bait, the birds being in the habit of taking these materials for constructing their nests. I am also well acquainted with a forester's lodge in another district where, even at the present time, it is useless during the nesting-season to put out any small articles of wearing-apparel to dry unless a close watch is kept, as they are sure to be carried off by the Kites before the day is over.

All the nests of this species that I have seen have been placed in trees, and in every instance a Scotch fir has been resorted to. The position of the nest varies considerably—sometimes in the very topmost twigs of a small bending pine that is scarcely able to bear the weight of even the lightest climber, occasionally among the higher branches of some large and spreading fir, conspicuous by its size among the giants of the forest, and at times at only the height of fifteen or eighteen feet, placed close to the main stem, where even the immense collection of rubbish that is used as a nursery by this species is scarcely noticed, a situation having been chosen where several large limbs branch out from the trunk.

I have never yet had the opportunity of visiting a nest that was placed among rocks or cliffs; but I was informed by a keeper on the west coast of the Highlands, in a wild district where large timber was scarce, that he had the previous season destroyed the greater part of a brood of Kites which had been reared in a nest among some large and broken slabs of rock on a steep hill-side. He described the birds accurately; but on searching the spot we could find no traces of their having visited the locality for breeding-purposes again, although one of the old birds had escaped the massacre of the previous season. I would not hazard an opinion as to what species of Hawk it could have been, as not even a feather was preserved; and I know by past experience that it is useless to trust to the memory of any person who is not thoroughly well informed about the bird they attempt to describe.

The difference in size between the male and female, which is so conspicuous in many of our birds of prey, is scarcely to be noticed in this species. My own opinion was that the male when on wing appeared slightly the largest; the naturalist, however, who prepared the specimens I shot stated otherwise. The colouring of the sexes is almost identical; in the male perhaps the head is lighter and the markings more clearly defined; the reddish brown on the breast, flanks, and wings is also slightly brighter. The tail is certainly longer and considerably more forked. The tints of various specimens differ somewhat remarkably; but it is impossible to form a judgment from old skins, as the colours are certain to fade unless great care is taken to prevent exposure to strong light.

I believe that in pursuit of prey for their young the old birds will at times roam over an immense extent of ground, as many as fifty or sixty miles being covered during a single foray. As they usually proceed in large circles, and seldom in a straight course, the distance actually passed over must be considerably greater.

Some years back I used to notice (most frequently a few hours after daybreak, but now and then at all times of day) a single Kite sailing slowly along over the low ground adjoining the banks of a large river in the Central Highlands. The track followed was almost identical on every occasion; the bird appeared to be making its way straight up the valley, but it always paused to take three or four circles over certain patches of rough ground, and also regularly examined some straggling plantations of birch that fringed the sloping hill-sides.

On reaching the large fir-woods, a mile or two further up the glen, it would search round more closely; but, although often watched, I never observed it capture any prey. Once it appeared to be carrying some small object in its talons; but the height at which it kept rendered a good view impossible. I concluded that there was a nest somewhere within a few miles, and made several inquiries, but without any result. At length, a year or two later, I discovered by chance that the bird that followed this route belonged (in one instance at least) to a nest fully twenty-five miles distant *.

Having only visited the glens frequented by this species during the summer months, when they were engaged in their nesting-operations, I have never met with a chance of studying their habits during the depth of winter. The greater part of the birds, I believe, remain in the neighbourhood of their usual haunts; but I can state nothing concerning the manner in which they procure their prey during that season. The small numbers (compared with the young of the White-tailed Eagle and the Osprey) that are observed about the time of migration would lead one to suppose that but few change their quarters on the approach of severe weather †. I was informed by one of the Trinity men who had passed many years on different portions of the coast, and was particularly well acquainted with birds of prey, that he had never seen a Kite during his time of service. Numbers of Peregrines, a few single Owls (and on one occasion a flight of forty or fifty), an Eagle or two, and several Ospreys had come under his observation; but not a Salmon-tailed Gled had he recognized since the days when he had robbed their nests in his native glen. Visitors from the continent are by no means numerous; and as our stock of Kites is far from large, I am afraid that, with the exception of two or three forests where the survivors are strictly guarded, these interesting birds will, before many years have passed, have entirely disappeared from the British Islands.

I am not acquainted with above four or five districts where this species may still be found breeding; in some of these localities but one or two pairs are usually observed, in others as many as three or four nests might possibly be found scattered over the woods within a distance of twenty or twenty-five miles.

The shy and wary habits of the Kite, as well as the nature of the country in which it is now found, can, I think, be best described by giving a few extracts from my note-books, written at the time I was in search of specimens.

"1870, June 19th. Having previously made arrangements, drove up the glen and met the keepers, who

* This circumstance is referred to hereafter.

† While these pages were in the press I again (September 22nd, 1881) observed a Kite in Sussex within a few miles of the channel; I also heard from a friend of a specimen procured in Suffolk during the same month. I conclude that a few at all events make a move towards the south in the autumn migration, unless these are stragglers from across the German Ocean.

were awaiting our arrival. They had discovered where one pair of Kites were breeding, though they had been unable to detect the exact part of the forest in which the nest was placed. The resort of the birds was a large fir-wood covering both sides of a steep gorge in the hills. The ground was so broken up with masses of rock and dry and stony gullies, as well as rendered almost impassable from fallen and rotten timber, that it was a work of no little difficulty to reach the spot where they had been observed. As we advanced, the birds, which were both flying in circles above the wood, came down nearer; but not above once or twice did they venture within even a long gunshot. After scrambling a considerable distance, we stopped a few minutes to rest in a rather more open part of the wood, and, happening to look up, discovered a nest in one of the smallest trees just above our heads. Then examining the ground below it, we could easily see that it was now used; and on proceeding thirty or forty yards farther up hill, we were able, by the help of the glasses, to thoroughly inspect the contents, and made out that it contained two young Kites, just commencing to show a few feathers through the down. The old birds were now flying at a great height, with no signs of approaching closer; so a few dead boughs were collected, and placed in such a manner as to form a small hiding-place, about forty yards from the nest, under which I might await their return, while the keepers left the spot and retired to a safe distance, where they would be perfectly concealed from view. I had not long been in the shelter before my attention was attracted by a number of small stones rattling down the hill-side; on looking up I discovered a goat standing on a small ledge, regarding me intently. After a few seconds he made a start, bounding over some loose rocks, two or three of which were dislodged, and came dashing down towards where I was hiding. I did not make a move to save myself, as I knew not which way to turn; and luckily I did not stir, as a couple of pieces, neither of them weighing less than a quarter of a hundredweight, crashed past within a few feet of where I was stationed. I remained for between three and four hours, but without success, as neither of the old Kites returned to the nest, and, indeed, disappeared entirely from sight during the last hour I waited.

"28th. Returned to the nest shortly before daybreak. One old bird left the tree just as I got within range; there was, however, not light enough to shoot, with any certainty, at the momentary glimpse I caught of the bird as it skimmed swiftly and silently through the dark shadows thrown by the trees. After waiting a couple of hours without either bird appearing, we went back to the Lodge for breakfast, and later on returned with a small Bantam cock, which was taken up the tree and made fast in the nest, the young having been first secured, so that he could not get at them. I imagined that when the Kites came in sight and found the intruder in possession of their nest, they would immediately come within range in order to turn him out. No sooner, however, did one of the old birds appear than the little cock, who had previously salked and remained laying on his side, raised himself up and, with a shrill cock-a-doodle-doo, bid defiance to the Kite, which instantly turned tail and rapidly disappeared from view, leaving the Bantam in possession. Although I waited for a considerable time, I only caught a distant glimpse of one bird, which retired again as soon as it came near enough to make out the state of affairs in the nest. As it appeared useless to wait any longer, we removed the cock and, having set loose the young birds, returned to the Lodge.

"Great was the rejoicing among the members of the keeper's family at the safe return of the Bantam. The plucky little fellow, however, fully deserved the welcome he received.

"Any cock, the saying is, will crow on his own dunghill; but seldom has one of his race thrown down a challenge to an unknown foe under more adverse circumstances.

"The nest was composed of dead twigs of fir, and lined with sheep's wool, hair, rags, dirt of every description, and bits of old scraps of newspaper. The food provided for the young consisted of a fresh young Grouse and a squirrel; there were also the remains of a Curlew or two, with plenty of old bones and feathers laying about, showing that Grouse, Pigeons, and Peewits were frequently taken."

As I was of opinion that after the fright the old birds had got it would be best to leave them quiet for some days, I did not return till the 20th, when I again drove up the glen to make another attempt.

"26th. The weather was fearfully hot, and, where the cool breeze was excluded by the denseness of the timber, the persistent attacks of the midges were almost unbearable. While we were advancing towards their quarters, the Kites did not seem by any means shy; and just before we reached the nest, one of them sailed over our heads, apparently within range. In hopes of a shot, I steadied myself against a rock (the ground was excessively steep and, owing to the dry weather and total absence of herbage, was slippery as glass), and awaited its approach on the following circle. The next time it was hardly so close; but when I fired it fell, as if dead, into the top of a fir, and then giving a flap or two with its wings, freed itself from the branches, and went over the precipice into the gorge below. When the bird struck the tree I did not fire the second barrel, as it was within twenty yards, and would have been blown to pieces. Expecting but little trouble to find it, we turned back, as the rocks just below were almost perpendicular, and made the best of our way to the spot where it appeared to have lodged. While descending the rocks, a couple of dogs we had with us started two fox-cubs from a cairn, and this caused an interruption that hindered us for some time. At last we reached the bottom of the gorge, just below where we lost sight of the bird; but, though we hunted for at least a couple of hours, we could find no trace of it, not even so much as a feather. The number of dead and decaying stems of trees, together with the cracks and crevices among the broken slabs of rock and stone, rendered our search any thing but easy.

"The remaining bird kept circling round at an immense height, and gave not the slightest signs of returning to the nest. As it seemed of little use waiting for a shot at the present time, we retired to a bothy on the opposite side of the gorge, from which, with the glasses, we could overlook nearly the whole of both sides of the glen. Here we resolved to make ourselves comfortable till about midnight, when I settled to crawl as near the nest as possible, and then wait till daybreak for a chance of a shot. Shortly before dark we observed the remaining old bird pitch in a tree near the upper part of the wood, and, after shifting its position three or four times, we at length lost sight of it close to the nest.

"27th. Soon after midnight I started from the bothy, and cautiously making my way down hill, I ascended the opposite side of the gorge, till I got some distance above the nest. Although we had previously marked a track by placing dead branches against the trees, I had no little difficulty in finding my way owing to the darkness. The night was perfectly still, without a breath of wind, and extra caution was needed as I drew near the spot to avoid making the slightest noise. At length, after a long and tedious crawl, I reached my station, about thirty or forty yards from the nest, and almost on the same level, as the tree on which it was placed stood lower down the hill. I could plainly make out the heads of the two young birds against the clear sky; and, by the help of the glasses, I could see them snapping at the insects, which caused a great annoyance to them. It was evident that the old bird was not near the nest; and while slightly moving my position, so as to obtain a better view of the surrounding branches, I snapped a dead twig, and in an instant I noticed a dark shadow glide from the further side of the tree and immediately disappear from sight. As there was now but little chance that the bird would return for several hours, I called up the keepers, and we set a trap on the nest, making fast both of the young birds. Then leaving the glen, we did not revisit the spot till the middle of the day, when the trap was unsprung. As no food had been brought, and there were now no signs of the old one, I was of opinion that, owing to having been so much disturbed, it might have deserted the nest. We accordingly took the two young ones, and left the trap which we had previously set.

"The nestlings differed considerably in size; one was almost full-fledged, while the other only showed about half its feathers just sprouting through the down. The eye was dark hazel, beak black, cere king's yellow, legs and feet a pale yellow. As I imagined they would make more interesting specimens if slightly more fledged, we kept them alive for a few days before sending them to be preserved. They were at first remarkably shy and sulky, hiding their heads, and evidently disliking to be noticed. For the short time they remained under our care, their diet consisted of raw beef; and on this they appeared to thrive well, though they resolutely refused to swallow a morsel unless placed in their mouths and forced half down their throats.

"July 3rd. On again visiting the glen, I found the trap in the nest untouched; neither had any food been brought.

"We observed a single Kite hovering over an open moor a few miles distant; but although the keepers while on their rounds had several times passed within sight of the nest, they had noticed no bird in that locality."

"1877, May 19th. Having sent a man the previous day to Glendhu, in order to learn if the Kites were breeding this season in their old quarters, I to-day received word that a pair had nested in a Scotch fir marked to be cut down. Among the rubbish in the nest, which contained three eggs, were the usual amount of old rags and, in addition, a perfectly new pair of lady's cuffs. I heard, however, of another pair or two of birds which had been observed about twenty miles further up the glen.

"21st. Reached the lodge early in the afternoon, and shortly after set out through the forest to search for the nest.

"On starting we were able to drive along a rough track, within about a mile and a half of the spot where the birds had been usually seen. After leaving the trap, the ground was by no means easy travelling, being covered with long coarse heather, interspersed with stunted bushes of juniper and bog-myrtle, and cut here and there with small watercourses leading towards a stretch of marshy pools, that could be plainly seen through the trees, at the distance of a mile or so to the north. The timber, which grew in small patches, three or four or, possibly, half a dozen trees together, and occasionally an open space for a hundred yards or more, consisted of large Scotch firs, and here and there a birch. Owing to the open nature of the wood, it would be impossible for the Kite to get on wing without being observed; consequently we were able to examine the ground thoroughly without taking any very great amount of time for the work. We had not proceeded above a quarter of a mile from where our search commenced, when I caught sight of an old bird just leaving the upper part of a large thick fir. Before we could reach the spot, which was not above the distance of a couple of hundred yards, the pair of Kites were circling high in the air, right above our heads. As soon as we stopped below the nest, which was among the topmost branches of the tree, both birds sailed right out of sight. Long spreading limbs, almost down to the ground, rendered the work of climbing easy; and on mounting to the nest, it was found to contain one young bird just hatched and two eggs. Thinking that the female would be likely to return as soon as possible, the nestling being so helpless, we collected a few rough branches, and quickly constructed a shelter against the stem of a large fallen tree, about five and thirty or forty yards distant. Then directing the men to take the most open track, I sent them back over the brow of the hill to wait where the machine had been left.

"It was just 7 P.M. when I took up my station, and I had not long lost sight of the keepers when I observed the two Kites coming from the direction in which they had disappeared.

"Having been built into my place of concealment almost too securely, I could only command a view towards the tree containing the nest; occasionally, however, I caught a glimpse of one or other of the birds soaring round and round at a considerable height above the wood. At last one settled on the far side of the tree; here it remained for some time, turning its head in every direction, and apparently unwilling to approach the nest too closely. I was just on the point of crawling from my shelter, in order to obtain a better chance of a shot, when the bird changed its position, exposing the whole of its breast; at this I immediately fired, and down it fell, as if perfectly dead, to the foot of the tree. Just before I reached the spot, however, it rose again, and flapped slowly away, requiring another barrel before it was secured. In the course of a few minutes the keepers appeared on the scene; and as the sun was now low, we set a trap in the nest, as I thought it possible that the male bird might not come in till after dusk. The men then returned to their former station, while I remained as long as I could see, and finally joined them, just as a cold drifting rain, which eventually increased into a heavy downpour, set in. I had but little doubt that this would soon kill the young bird in its present weak state.

"22nd. As the trap had been set in the nest, and was so placed that the male could not possibly gather the eggs or young together without being taken, I did not think it necessary to be very early on the spot, and it was nearly 11 A.M. before we reached the tree. On mounting to the nest we found the young one, as I had expected, quite dead and the trap unsprung. Having this morning more time to examine the locality, I discovered, within the distance of seventy or eighty yards, a large dead fir that was evidently a favourite resort for the old birds. It is, I think, very probable, since I had only a few moments previously lost sight of the male before shooting his mate, that he had by that time settled on this tree; being so close at hand would account for his having deserted the nest. Beneath the branches I found the remains of over thirty Grouse, a few quite fresh; but the great majority were only bare and weatherbeaten skeletons, and had evidently laid for many months. Feathers, feet, wings, and bones were scattered in all directions; and the heather was, in some parts, quite white with the droppings of the birds. There were no other remains or feathers (except, of course, those plucked out by the birds while dressing their own plumage) besides those of Grouse. The tree, which was somewhat singular in shape, must have been one of the oldest in the wood: at the height of about ten or a dozen feet the huge stem divided into several large and widely-spreading limbs; in various parts of the branches, and also in the trunk itself, were numbers of marks of Woodpeckers, the holes having apparently been bored for many years. While we were waiting, I caught sight of a large bird settling in a tree, at the distance of three or four hundred yards, in a dense part of the forest. Imagining it might possibly be the Kite, I crawled, by means of a small gully, within range. On reaching the spot, however, it turned out to be only a Heron, which had pitched on its nest; a few of these birds are now and then found breeding singly in the large woods in this part of the country.

"As there seemed no chance that the male would now return, we removed the young bird and eggs, taking also a portion of the upper part of the nest; this, as usual, was constructed with dead twigs and small branches of fir, while the lining was composed of moss, sheep's wool, a few pieces of old rag, and a quantity of scraps of paper. In addition to numberless torn and crumpled slips from various publications I could not make out, there were several pages of a 'Bradshaw,' portions of the 'Field,' 'Times,' 'Scotsman,' and some west-country paper, as well as a packet of tissue-paper neatly folded. Not the slightest remains of food were on the nest.

"The two eggs varied considerably, one being a dirty greenish white, and the other marked with several blotches and streaks of reddish brown; the latter was just on the point of hatching, while the former was addled.

"The young bird had a long hairy tuft of white down on the top of the head; on the back the down was of a dirty-brown hue, and on the underparts white. The eye was not opened, but what could be discerned was of a dull grey colour; bill black, lightish towards the point; cere pale yellowish flesh; legs and feet pale flesh.

"The female shot the previous day was a fair specimen, in the usual summer plumage. Eye very pale lemon-yellow, circle bright yellow; cere yellow; beak light horn, darker (almost black) towards point; legs and feet chrome-yellow, nails black."

The Plate showing the nestling and eggs is taken from the above-mentioned specimens. The taxidermist who preserved this interesting juvenile informed me that it was impossible to skin a bird so young and tender in the usual manner; the work of removing the perishable portions was, I believe, somewhat complicated.

"1878, June 27th. Drove up the glen and met the foresters, according to previous arrangements; then proceeded several miles further north to a bothy on the hills, where the horses and trap were put up. The road we followed was particularly rough and uneven, and the country we passed through wild in the extreme.

A dull and sultry morning had been followed by excessive heat, and after midday the weather gave every indication of an approaching storm. Shortly after one o'clock the gloom and darkness increased, and heavy thunder was heard rumbling among the hills both north and south of us. On leaving the bothy, we walked about three miles on towards the wood in which the Kites were breeding—a long straggling belt of timber composed entirely of Scotch fir. The nest was placed in a fork, where three limbs branched out from the main stem, about twenty-five or thirty feet from the ground, and was a rather larger structure than I had previously seen. It contained one young bird and a bad egg, and, when last visited by the keepers, the larder provided for the nestling consisted of a Grouse, a Duck, and a Peewit. The men had already put up a small shelter of fir-boughs, to screen me from the sight of the old birds, within about thirty yards of the tree; and here I took up my position about half-past six, when the keepers retired to a burn about a mile distant, so as not to hinder the approach of the birds. I had not been waiting above half an hour when a single Kite passed over at a great height, evidently being aware that something was wrong. After circling two or three times over the nest, it took its departure, without making any attempt to come down to the young bird; and although I was able to watch it by means of the glasses, I could see no signs that it carried any prey. As might naturally be expected, the midges gave me good cause to remember them, and before it got dark I was nearly driven wild by their attacks.

"Owing to the heavy thunder-clouds, it was so dark by a quarter to ten that I could no longer make out the nest; so I left the shelter, and made the best of my way to where the men were waiting. As the country was strange, I had no little difficulty to discover the road, and, in the end, I had to fire off my gun to draw their attention. As we proceeded on our way homewards the storms, which had been round us all day, again drew near, and our track through the forest was lighted up by the flashes of lightning which followed one another in rapid succession.

"For a couple of miles our course lay through a wild and rugged glen, where the whole of the timber had long been dead; by far the greater number of the trees were fallen and lay rotting on the ground; while here and there a grim and weatherbeaten stem remained, and gave a ghastly appearance to the scene, its bare and twisted limbs standing out plainly defined by every flash against the inky blackness of the surrounding hills. On reaching the bothy shortly before eleven o'clock, as the atmosphere of the interior was perfectly stifling, we sat down to our supper outside the building. The flickering gleams of the sheet or summer lightning almost continuously illumined the smallest objects, and, although the night was dark and overcast, gave sufficient light for all our requirements. Hardly a drop of rain had fallen, and the air was close and sultry, without a breath of wind. As the heaviest of the storm was some miles distant and appeared to work round us instead of approach, we had ample leisure, after our hunger was appeased, to admire the grandeur of the scene. At times a vivid flash would strike the summit of one of the distant hills, and, bursting into a thousand sparks of flame, would fall, like a cascade of fire, into the valley below. For a second or two we might be enveloped in murky darkness, the hollow roll and echo of the distant thunder would die away for a moment, the silence being only broken by the murmurs of the water in the adjacent burn, when again a blaze would shoot across the heavens, and instantly mountain-side and heathery brae, the dark pine-forest and glassy surface of the loch, would each in turn be lighted up for a moment and again disappear from view. After watching the progress of the storm for at least an hour, the horses were put to; and, having settled to meet the keepers the next night to try for the Kites at daybreak, we started for our twenty-mile drive through the forest to the lodge where we were stopping. The fitful gleams of the lightning as they flashed through the shadows thrown by the dark and gloomy fir trees were just sufficient to guide us on our way and to enable the driver to avoid the hidden dangers in our course. As we emerged from the cover of the woods and pulled up for a few moments at a keeper's house, the first streaks of dawn were just struggling through the storm-clouds, which were now rapidly disappearing. A few miles farther, when the light had increased, we could plainly discern, by the swollen burns and the channels scoured across our track, how heavy had been the force of the storm.

"Before we reached our journey's end the sun was shining brightly; but on arriving at the lodge we learned that the tempest had been so severe in the early part of the night that the inmates had been half frightened to death, and had all retired to bed as being the safest place.

"28th. The storm of the previous night had cooled the air, and the day was beautifully clear and fine. As I was expecting a hard night's work, I rested during the day, and starting in the evening reached the bothy, where the keepers were waiting, by half-past eleven. Our walk through the forest to the nest was a contrast to the last time we passed over the ground. The night was lovely and the wind a trifle chilly, which, after the weather we had recently experienced, was by no means unpleasant. We reached the plantation in which the nest was placed soon after one o'clock; and, owing to the darkness, it was some little time before I was securely packed into my shelter and provided with all the rugs, waterproofs, provisions, and other necessaries (I had also a bottle of vinegar, by which I hoped to keep off the attacks of the midges, which was, however, an utter failure). By about half-past one my arrangements were all completed, and the men retired to their waiting-place in the barn. Owing to the shadows thrown by the trees, it was at first so dark that I could not even make out the whereabouts of the nest. Soon after two o'clock I discovered the young bird stretching himself and flapping his wings, having apparently just woke up. Half an hour later the old female pitched suddenly on one of the lower branches of a fir, within fifteen yards of my hiding-place; she had in her talons a Peewit, which she partially plucked (every feather on her head being thrown up on end during the operation), and then flew to another branch about forty yards away; here I could hardly watch her movements, owing to the denseness of the timber. After some time she disappeared without my noticing her departure.

"Nothing more was seen of either of the birds for about an hour, when the female again flew from a tree right over my head, and it is quite possible that she might have been sitting there the whole of the time. She then continued flying in circles over my head for more than three hours—at times sweeping down to within twenty yards of where I was concealed, and, after hovering for a second or two, evidently trying to make out what was amiss, shooting up to a great height and sailing round and round the wood till she gradually diminished the circles and again came to close quarters. Almost incessantly she kept uttering a most mournful cry, which ended in a long-drawn plaintive whistle. Till nearly seven o'clock I had seen but one bird, the female, easily recognized by her ragged plumage, a couple of feathers being deficient in one wing. She had as yet never attempted to settle to the young one; indeed, since her first appearance with the Peewit, which was soon dropped, she had no prey with her. I had been in no hurry to fire, as I was certain that, by leaving my shelter while she was out of sight on one of her longer circles, I could, if I wished, at any time have an easy shot, and I was in hopes that the male might show himself.

"At last the attacks of the midges, which I had patiently endured for the last six or seven hours, became almost unbearable; and I was preparing to start from my hiding-place (from the interior I could only take a pot shot at the nest) when I recognized a slightly shriller scream, and, waiting a moment, a much finer bird passed over.

"He turned in an instant, and was back before I could get out; the next time he passed out of sight, he seemed to be sweeping farther off; so creeping from under the boughs, I had ample time to get ready before he reappeared. I could plainly see his shadow thrown through the upper branches of the trees before he came in view; and as there was an open space round the nest, he afforded the easiest possible shot, and fell as dead as a stone at my feet. The female, who was at the time at a great height, immediately sailed away to the north without turning round to see what had happened to her mate or young."

This is the specimen from which the Plate of the adult male is taken.

"I had ordered the men to come up if they heard a shot, and a very few minutes had elapsed before they made their appearance. As I did not care to wait for the return of the female, we took the young bird and also removed the upper portion of the nest, which, as usual, contained a quantity of old newspaper and rubbish of all descriptions. There were no signs of eatable food, and the only remnants were a few bones of a Plover and the cleanly-picked skeleton of a Pigeon.

"It is, I think, very likely that, in the absence of the old birds, Crows at times pay visits to the larder of the nestlings in quest of food. Shortly before daybreak, I had noticed a couple of Crows fly silently through the trees just above the nest, and after hovering over the spot for a moment or two, they quickly returned in the direction whence they came, croaking loudly as they went: another that was approaching turned back at once, and the whole party departed together. I had no idea what could possibly have been the object of their visit or the cause of their speedy return till I became aware of the empty state of the larder.

"The young bird was slightly larger than those I had taken a couple of years before. He was remarkably sulky, and so persistently hid his head underneath him in the basket in which he was carried, that I was afraid he would be stifled.

"I had noticed that while the old birds were about the young one was ever hardly quiet, shuffling round and round his nest, stretching himself and flapping his wings, and occasionally pecking at the old bones that were lying beside him. On the first signs of the approach of the old birds, long before I had made out their note, he would drop down on the nest, and puffing up his feathers would quietly await his food, only occasionally answering their continued cries by a low whistle.

"After packing up a portion of the nest which I wished to examine, making a sketch of the tree, and collecting the luggage from my shelter, we made the best of our way to a burn with steep and well-wooded banks, where we had our breakfast. It was a splendid morning; the sky was cloudless, and I must confess I found the shade of an umbrella by no means unpleasant: only the previous night I had blown up an English servant who was with me for bringing such a cockneyfied invention on to a Scotch hillside; but this morning I was by no means above availing myself of its shade. For the future, when making out the list of articles to take on the hills in summer, I shall never omit the homely gingham. While getting ready to start again, a Golden Eagle passed within a couple of hundred yards of where we had been resting, sailing slowly over the forest, barely clearing the tops of the trees. The keepers pointed out a couple of eyries of these birds—one in the face of a steep cliff, which they stated to be still used (although I happened to have seen the green grass growing through the bottom of the old nest), and the other on the opposite side of the glen, and some miles farther south, in a large Scotch fir. This had been, in days gone by, a grand locality for birds that have now become rare. During our morning's walk we had passed the deserted breeding-places of three pairs of Kites, and I had examined no less than four trees on which there still remained the foundations of old nests that had been built by Ospreys. After watching the Eagle, which had settled on a rock at no great distance (apparently perfectly ignorant of our presence), for a considerable time, we proceeded slowly on our journey, stopping a few minutes to examine two or three small rushy lochs, where the keepers had seen some birds, which from their description I could hardly make out. I have no doubt that the strangers were Red-necked Phalaropes, which had rested for a short time on the pools; there were no signs of them to-day, and I expect it had been but a flying visit on their way to the far north.

"On arriving at the bothy we started as soon as the horses were put to, and reached the lodge by midday, after a pleasant drive through the forest.

"The young Kite was quite safe on his arrival, although he had apparently attempted to smother himself, and it took no little persuasion to induce him to swallow a meal of fresh-killed Pigeon.

"During the afternoon, while fishing in a burn about a couple of miles from the lodge, I was rather surprised to see the old female Kite (easily distinguished by her ragged plumage) fly over my head, within half a gunshot. She was about twenty-five miles distant from her nesting-quarters, and was following the same course under the hills that I had on several occasions seen taken by these birds while passing up and down the glen.

"20th. This morning the captive was decidedly more tractable; during the day he consumed the most of three Pigeons. The beak was very dark horn-colour, almost black; cere king's yellow; feet and legs a pale orange-chrome; eye pale lavender tint, which turned a deeper grey with age.

"July 11th. The young Kite had now reached the stage in which I wished to have him preserved. All signs of down had disappeared and he was perfectly full-fledged, although the tail had not attained above half the length of an adult and showed hardly any signs of the fork. He was getting by degrees more tame and sociable than when we first obtained him; but at times he was terribly sulky, and no description of food we could provide him with would be to his liking. He was supplied, as a rule, with the flesh of Pigeons and young rabbits. When, however, these dainties were not procurable, he was obliged to put up with raw beef or mutton. This change of diet he evidently looked upon as an insult, and it required considerable care to induce him to retain his meals. As it did not seem that he would ever become perfectly reconciled to confinement, I had much less reluctance to sign his death-warrant than that of a pair of young Ospreys the previous week. After I had taken his portrait in several different positions, he was executed this morning and forwarded to the south for preservation.

"Considering the pains that had been taken to rear this troublesome customer, the people of the inn we were stopping at were greatly surprised at his death. 'What!' exclaimed one of the attendants, 'is the puir wee beastie to be killed the noo, and twelve and sax pence paid for his meat! Well! well!'

"Having quite accidentally heard of another Kite's nest in a different locality, we left our present quarters, and drove as near the wood as the state of the road would allow us. On this occasion the Kites had taken up their residence in an extensive fir-wood, covering a steep hill-side sloping down to a large loch. While approaching the breeding-place we proceeded with great caution, in case the old birds might be near at hand. The nest was placed about five and twenty feet from the ground, near the top of a small Scotch fir. The men had stated there was but one young bird; we could, however, plainly make out a pair when we examined the nest through the glasses, and both sat perfectly quiet when we drew near the spot and stood on a rocky knoll, from which we could look right down upon them.

"There were apparently no signs of the old birds, so we retired a few hundred yards in order to avail ourselves of the shade of the large trees by the loch-side and give time for them to return with prey for the young, as, while examining the nest, we had been unable to detect any food. After waiting about an hour I returned towards the nest, and, while cautiously descending the steep brae that overlooked the tree, I noticed that one of the birds had shifted its position; and as it now sat with its forked tail in full view, I discovered that instead of two young ones, the old female had been all the time on the nest. While searching for an opening among the branches for the best chance of a shot at her as she flew off, my foot slipped on the sloping ground, which the dry weather and the fallen spines of the firs had rendered like glass, and down I came, flat on my back, luckily just missing by less than an inch a frightfully broken and jagged stump of a dead tree. Before I could scramble up, being considerably shaken, but nevertheless exceedingly thankful when I discovered my narrow escape, the old bird, probably startled by the fall, left the nest, and, gliding rapidly below the branches of the trees, was out of sight in a moment. Before many minutes had elapsed, both male and female were sailing round and round at a great height over the spot, and, gradually extending the circles when the keepers came down to see what had happened, they at length disappeared entirely from view. The young bird now fully showed itself; and as it appeared quite capable of flying, I took up a position below the tree while one of the men went up to drive it off. He had not mounted above halfway to the nest when it spread its wings and made an attempt to escape. I had now picked out more secure standing-ground, and as easy shot was the result. This young bird proved on examination to be in precisely the same state of plumage as the one killed and sent off in the morning."

The Plate showing the advanced stage of the young Kite is taken from this specimen. The tint of the feathers on the cheek was considerably lighter than in the young one that had been kept in confinement; the plumage on the crown of the head was also slightly paler. In other respects there was no perceptible difference between the two birds, the colours in both being exceedingly bright.

"As there was still an hour or two of daylight, I determined to wait and try for a shot at one of the old birds. A slight shelter of branches, with dry heather to sit on, was soon put up under an overhanging bank within forty yards of the tree, and under this I crawled. For at least an hour I patiently endured the attacks of the midges; but as I had as yet, since entering the place of torment, seen neither of the old birds, I could bear it no longer. Owing, I suppose, to the low marshy nature of the ground where the tree stood, these horrible pests were more persistent in their attacks, as well as more venomous, than in any other locality where I have ever had the misfortune to meet with them. Leaving my shelter, I followed the track along the loch-side to the gully where the keepers were waiting. The cool breeze off the water, with the assistance of a cigar, helped to keep my enemies at bay, and after remaining till the daylight began to fail, I quietly made my way back to the nest; but neither of the old birds had returned. As I did not care to stop any longer, we removed the food on the nest (a fresh-killed young Grouse, partly eaten) and set a couple of traps. Although we visited these traps at regular intervals for the two following days, the wind was so high that all covering was blown from them almost as fast as it was rearranged. The old birds, however, occasionally came into the nest; but, owing to the traps being exposed, they dropped the food they brought (consisting of young Grouse and Pigeons) on the extreme edge. As I was anxious to pay a visit to another district, we removed the traps and left the poor birds in peace."

Since the above was written, I have again been through the various districts inhabited by the Kites. In most of the glens the birds were still present; but a pair or two appeared to be wanting. Having no occasion for procuring specimens, I never molested them in the slightest degree; but the observations I was enabled to make with regard to their habits and food, as well as their manner of procuring their prey, were simply a repetition of what has been recorded above.

PEREGRINE FALCON.

FALCO PEREGRINUS.

Notwithstanding the number of young that are taken for Hawking-purposes, the quantities slaughtered by keepers, and the constant attacks both on eggs and birds by collectors, the Peregrine may still be found by no means sparsely scattered over the country, from north to south.

In the Highlands of Scotland this species has numberless breeding-stations on the inland mountains and along the rocky portions of the sea-coast, as well as on the adjacent islands. To the south of Perthshire, though I have watched the birds as roving visitors in most counties where I remained for any length of time, I met with no nesting-quarters, with the exception of those in the cliffs overhanging the sea. I have heard as an old tradition, in more than one part of the country, that these Falcons nested formerly in the towers of churches; but I can give no more trustworthy authority. I noticed one circling round the dome of St. Paul's a few years back; but here, I believe, it is well known that a pair at times take up their residence for some months, being attracted by the Pigeons frequenting the edifice. In certain localities it seems as if no amount of persecution would drive them from their favourite haunts. If one of the parents be destroyed, another shortly after joins the survivor; should the young be removed, the following season eggs are sure to be laid either on the self-same spot or else at no great distance. Ever since I have known the Bass Rock, now over twenty years, I believe it has been regularly resorted to as an eyrie, though I cannot speak with certainty as to the last few seasons. Possibly the young may have flown on one or two occasions; but every year that I have been in the district I learned that the nest had been robbed. I frequently observed the old birds on the adjacent islands of Craig Leith, the Lamb, and Fidra, and heard from the North-Berwick fishermen that eggs had been taken from them; but I never caught a glimpse of any spot that seemed to have been used as an eyrie. The May, at the northern entrance to the firth, is likewise a well-known station; I have repeatedly seen the birds flying above the gloomy caves on the south side of the island. The chalk cliffs between Rottingdean and Beachy Head during autumn and winter harbour a large number of Peregrines; and a pair or two now and then breed in the eastern portion of the range. They are, however, so well looked after that but few young birds are left long enough to take their departure. I have observed a stray bird or two round the Isle of Wight; and on two or three occasions on the Cornish coast a pair appeared to frequent the rocks between Trewavas and Porthleven; and, again, it was seldom that I visited the neighbourhood of the Land's End without noticing one or two within a short distance of the cliffs.

During the last week of October 1880 I witnessed a rather curious performance between a pair of Peregrines in this district. I was on the brow of the hill above the duck-pool near the Tol-Pedn-Penwith (the funnel hole), when I caught sight, as I at first imagined, of a Peregrine in pursuit of some smaller Hawk coming from the direction of the Land's End. The larger bird was continually rising above the smaller, and then dashing down as if attempting to strike it; the latter, sharply altering its course by a downward and sidelong movement, avoided every swoop; and their flight, the whole time they remained in sight, was simply a repetition of these evolutions. They must have been in view for at least a couple of miles, as they made a curve right round the hill on which I was standing, passing within the distance of fifty yards—so close, in fact, that the rush of their wings as the attacking bird swooped down and suddenly checked itself were plainly audible. I then discovered them to be a pair of Peregrines, the female in pursuit of the male. They continued their course in the same manner right out of sight, disappearing from view in the line of the Lizard. From the regularity of their movements I imagine they were simply engaged in sport. I have watched the male and female White-tailed Eagle flying in somewhat the same style; only the latter pursued their course in regular overlapping circles; there was nothing approaching the rapid mount and dashing swoop of these two Peregrines.

There is not the slightest doubt that this Falcon is most destructive to game. Grouse are perhaps the greatest sufferers from its attacks, but every other member of the family, with the exception of the Capercaillie, which is probably too heavy, is carried off by this dashing robber. The damage he effects would not be so extensive or conspicuous if he merely contented himself by satisfying the cravings of his appetite or the requirements of his brood. There is, however, no denying the fact that, in addition to those he needs as food, he strikes numberless victims for the mere pleasure of slaying. This unfortunate propensity has, I believe, been contradicted by naturalists and falconers; it is nevertheless well known to those who have studied the habits of the bird in a wild state. I have watched Grouse struck down on more than one occasion, and not the slightest notice taken of their fall, the Falcon continuing his flight after the retreating pack with undiminished speed. This has taken place both during a Grouse-drive and also when a pack has simply incurred the displeasure of the tyrant by passing within a short distance of the crag of rock on which he was resting. Falconers, I am aware, when a charge of this description is brought forward, argue that the Falcon was prevented from following its prey to the ground by the presence of witnesses. If this were invariably the case, why does the Hawk make a second attack except for the sake of slaughter? I once observed two Grouse struck within a distance of a few hundred yards, both birds being entirely disregarded and left where they fell. In order to ascertain if the Falcon ever returned to these remains, I visited some of them repeatedly; but although Grey Crows and Ravens were occasionally attracted to the spot, I have seen no signs of the Peregrine. When one has been disturbed from prey on which it was feeding, it will, I believe, usually return to complete its meal, but never when the victim has been struck down and totally disregarded at the time. Several keepers and foresters with whom I discussed the subject have given evidence to the same effect; and the scores of dead bodies that I have passed at different times on the hills (minus the head or lacerated on the neck or back) plainly indicate the manner in which they have been destroyed.

It is not on the moors only that I have noticed these destructive habits. While fishing on one of the larger broads in the eastern counties my attention was attracted by the rapid movements of a flock of three or four hundred Starlings which had been wheeling backwards and forwards over the marshes. Suddenly they collected into a compact body at a considerable height from the ground, and in an instant a Peregrine, with the rapidity of a thunderbolt, swooped down from the clouds, scattering the flock in all directions, and leaving three or four dead or disabled birds fluttering helplessly downwards while, without checking his course, he dashed after a Grey Crow, which he pursued within a short distance of my punt, and then, apparently startled, turned off in an opposite direction. On the sea-coast also (and here, perhaps, more frequently than in other situations) the Peregrine exhibits his predilection for slaughter. While lunching one summer among the ruins of the old fortifications on the Bass Rock, two audible shocks were noticed within the space of a few moments, giving the impression that large stones had rolled from the upper part of the rock. On searching the direction from which the sounds proceeded, we discovered a couple of fresh-killed Guillemots lying on the ground among the roofless buildings. The Falcon must have swooped over our heads; but, owing to the constant stream of passing Gannets and other sea-birds, he had not attracted our attention. On other occasions I have frequently met with both Kittiwakes, Razorbills, Guillemots, and Puffins dead upon the Rock; and I have no doubt that the Peregrine was in every case responsible for the slaughter. In my note-books, which I have regularly kept for over twenty years, I can refer back to instances in over a dozen Scotch and English counties, as well as in two or three of the adjacent islands, where I have actually witnessed either this destructive propensity or the unmistakable victims that have been struck down *.

It is of course impossible to convince any one who is thoroughly satisfied that the Peregrine will look for prey but once in twenty-four hours and will never destroy life unnecessarily; I, however, simply state what I believe to be true from my own experience. Those whose opinions differ will deny that the dead Grouse were the victims of the Falcon, suggesting that they owed their death either to disease or wounds, or the attacks of some other vermin. I should not have brought such a sweeping accusation against a species I admire as one of the most interesting of our native birds, had I not carefully examined several of these dead bodies. I have shot the Falcon when in possession of a Grouse, found carcases on the ledges they frequent, and picked up those I have watched struck down. The injuries inflicted by the stroke of the Peregrine, though usually severe, do not necessarily prove fatal; at all events the bird is not on every occasion instantly deprived of life, whatever might be the ultimate result. From the position in which the dead bodies were found, from the character of the injuries, and from the state of the remains, I have come to the conclusion that the Peregrine alone can be responsible. The healthy state of the feathers, the condition of the bodies, as well as the localities in which they were discovered and the manner in which they lay, would preclude the idea that disease was the cause of death. A wounded bird will, as we all well know, occasionally fly a considerable distance and fall in any position; but the majority that escape for the time and eventually perish from effects of gunshots, usually creep into some secure retreat, and there pine away and die. The Sparrow-Hawk and Merlin may, as some falconers assert, be guilty of destroying a few Grouse; I must, however, confess that not a single instance has come under my own observation. With regard to four-footed vermin, the manner in which they seize and kill their prey cannot fail to leave marks that are easily recognized. Even if disturbed and pursued, the fox, as a rule, bears off his prey; but feathers leave a trace more or less visible from the very spot where it was captured to either the earth or the place where it was devoured. The work of a stoat can mislead no one used to study their mode of slaughter; and wild cats were few and far between, if not totally absent from the localities where I have met with the greatest number of remains. In addition to the birds previously mentioned, I have seen one or two cases where Blackgame and Plover were wantonly slaughtered. Ducks, Coots, Rooks, and Snipe appear to be also frequent sufferers.

It would be useless to repeat any of the accounts of the damage inflicted on game by this species that I have heard from keepers or gillies, as I am well aware that both scientific naturalists and falconers are pleased to consider all such men both ignorant and lazy and only too glad to bring unfounded charges against the poor Peregrine in order to account for their own shortcomings and neglect of duty. It is not, however, from keepers and their assistants alone that I have received evidence that corroborates my own experiences. While gunning on the east coast during the present month (December 1881), a Peregrine passed within a short distance of the boat; and, pointing out the bird, I inquired of my puntman if he was acquainted with the species. The local name, I discovered, was the "Game-Hawk;" and the bird was well known to the natives. The man also stated he well remembered, many years ago, picking up a pair of Coots which had been struck down on one of the marshes and left, both being quite dead. He had also more than once noticed this species attacking the large flocks of Coots that frequent these waters, driving the birds into compact bodies and causing the greatest consternation in their ranks, none daring to take wing, but occasionally flapping a

* My observations have been made in the Hebrides, Caithness, Sutherland, Ross-shire, Cromarty, Inverness-shire, Perthshire, East Lothian, the Bass, Northumberland, Cumberland, Yorkshire, Norfolk, Kent, Surrey, and Cornwall.

short distance over the surface. The Falcon had never, while in his sight, either captured or struck any of these birds, being possibly unwilling to make the attempt while they were over the water or until they were well on wing. Pywipes (local name for Peewits) he had seen flown at on two or three occasions, and a single bird struck down and left. Once in his presence the Hawk had driven down a covey of Partridges into a dry ditch under a fence; and from this cover they refused to emerge while their enemy remained close at hand. On making further inquiries of another gunner who was working my second boat, I found his evidence was much the same with regard to the attacks on Coots and Partridges; but the only bird he had seen struck was a Sandy-head Poker (local name for the Pochard), which had risen with a bunch of fourteen or fifteen others in front of his boat and been knocked down. He himself had made an attempt to secure it; but, after diving a short distance, it had fluttered into a reed-bed and escaped. The remarks of these two men concerning the habits of the Peregrine were much what I should have expected from the knowledge I have acquired while watching the bird in their district.

In the matter of food the Falcon accommodates itself to the locality it inhabits, preying on Grouse, Plover, Ducks, and Pigeons in the Highlands, sea-birds (such as the smaller Gulls and Guillemots) on the islands, and Partridges, Pigeons, and even the young of the domestic Fowl in the south. This noble bird, however, I am almost ashamed to state, does not despise an occasional meal off such humble fare as a Rook; and, though the instances have been far from numerous that have come under my own observation, it will at times even condescend to make shift with either a Carrion or Grey Crow. For any one to attempt to give the true bill of fare of a Peregrine is perfectly impossible, as on examining a dozen breeding-places there might be found the remains of different victims on each.

How the existence of such a rapacious species on preserved moors is beneficial to the well-being of the Grouse, I confess I can scarcely understand. From what I have myself seen I cannot believe that a Falcon will, as a rule, prey upon diseased or weakly birds (I could credit it of a Buzzard, or even of the Eagle or Kite); still this is the doctrine that is preached by many who have written on the subject. That his admirers should term him a scavenger is, I consider, a poor compliment to this fine bird: far better to describe him in his true colours as a bold and pitiless marauder, and trust that British sportsmen have too great a respect for the few wild creatures left in our islands to order his total extermination. The plea that some naturalists put forward, viz. that the presence of the wild Falcon causes Grouse to lie to dogs till late in the season, will not hold good in every case. I have seen some few districts where Peregrines and all kinds of vermin were abundant enough to suit the taste of even their most ardent supporters; but, strange to relate, the few Grouse that remained were wilder than even the Hawks themselves. The fact that the artificial Kite has been invented to aid shooters (I was going to say sportsmen, but I consider my second thoughts more appropriate) to make a bag is certainly a strong argument in favour of the presence of Falcons on a moor. This, however, is a subject on which I can state little or nothing (beyond what I have read), as I have never yet seen one of these machines in operation. From what I have heard, this method, if frequently resorted to, is understood to drive birds from the district; I should be of opinion that too many Falcons would have much the same effect.

It must be a rare occurrence for the Peregrine to condescend to make a meal off any prey that he has not procured by his own exertions, as I have never obtained a single specimen in a baited trap, neither have I ever heard of but one being taken by keepers in this manner. The captured bird, I was informed, had received some injury to one of its legs, caused probably by a wound from a large shot or bullet. It was in poor condition; and without doubt its weakness rendered it incapable of obtaining its food in the natural manner. Some writers affirm that this species will never condescend to take prey unless it is seized on wing; this statement, I am afraid, is hardly correct, as on two or three occasions I have noticed unfledged young brought to their brood.

In parts where they are numerous I have known this species taken by traps placed on their favourite resting-places in the faces of cliffs or steep mountain-slopes. Some years ago, I remember a gamekeeper on the west coast of the Highlands destroying seven in the course of a few weeks by these means. Where it is necessary to keep down their numbers on account of their depredations on the game, it is generally found the safest plan to trap or shoot them at their nesting-quarters.

The situations usually chosen for breeding-purposes are either small shelves or inequalities in the face of steep rocks, or ledges more or less broken and difficult of approach among the inland mountains. I have never examined any eyrie to which access could be gained without the assistance of a rope. In several different localities it has been possible to look down upon the young, and even to crawl within a short distance; but the situation (in every eyrie I visited) has been chosen with due regard to safety. When these birds resort to the sea-cliffs, either in the islands or on the coast-line of the mainland, the spot they select is generally even more secure from intrusion, the rocks being of greater altitude and frequently perpendicular, if not overhanging.

The nest of this species has been minutely described by some authors, who apparently have been misled by the fact that now and then it appropriates the old nurseries of Ravens or even Grey Crows. The Peregrine most commonly lays its eggs upon the rubbish and dust or dried strands of grass that have accumulated on the ledges it frequents, without the slightest attempt at building.

Those who have kept these Falcons in confinement could best give information concerning the age at which the mature dress is assumed. My own experience is entirely gained by observing the habits of the birds in a wild state; and it is seldom possible to obtain a view where all the details or varieties in plumage could be accurately judged and studied. From the numbers that I have met with frequenting certain localities, all apparently immature, I should be of opinion that they do not pair till the third or fourth year.

The Plate represents an adult male and the unfledged young. The specimen from which the drawing is taken was a remarkably shy and wary old bird, whose daring forays on the Grouse had been a source of trouble to the keepers for many years. Regularly every season the female had been trapped; and on one occasion a second and then a third that made her appearance shared the same fate as her predecessors. Still the male defied all attempts at capture. The eyrie was on a ledge in the face of a precipice of grey and moss-grown rock about one hundred and fifty feet in height. With but slight assistance from a rope let down from above it was by no means difficult to reach, as a rough sheep-track led within a few yards of a large cavity or fissure beneath overhanging slabs of stone, that stretched, with the exception of a break of only four or five feet in width, to the spot where the young were situated. On my first visit, having carefully watched the arrival of the female, I endeavoured to obtain a shot as she flew off. The work of climbing to the upper portion of the grassy slope immediately below the ledge (and within a distance of fifty feet) was soon accomplished; but, owing to the steepness of the ground, I found the attitude I was forced to assume far too cramped to use a gun with any certainty. The bird, however, totally disregarded all attempts to drive her off; shouts were of no avail; and it was impossible to pitch up stones, owing to our position immediately below the spot. At last, while retracing our steps, she glided from the rock, skimming far down into the valley below before she mounted into the air. Then returning at a considerable height, she remained for at least an hour flying over our heads, uttering constantly the low scream of rage or anxiety that these birds always give vent to when their quarters are invaded. She never approached within one hundred yards of where we were standing; and the male, who shortly after made his appearance, was still more careful. As waiting for the chance of a shot seemed useless, the ropes were produced; and the ledge was speedily reached. The young were four in number, covered with a thick white down, and differing but slightly in size. The three smallest were taken, and the largest and strongest bird removed a few yards from the open ledge on which they had been hatched to a spot below the overhanging rocks, where it was firmly but carefully secured by a string round the leg. Here it would be impossible for the parents when bringing food to avoid the traps which we set all round. The bones and feathers scattered about indicated that Grouse and Golden Plover had furnished the greater part of the prey supplied; there was also the carcase of a Ptarmigan much decomposed. After leaving the neighbourhood for a few hours, we returned just as evening was closing in, and found the female captured by both feet. The traps were then reset; but although they were regularly attended and the place was carefully watched for the two following days, not a sign of the male was observed. The young bird was kept alive on trout fresh caught from the loch at the foot of the hill; and on this it thrived well. On the third day I had resolved to give up the attempt, as I imagined the male had been scared from the spot; however, on visiting the ledge I discovered he was taken. The poor bird had brought an unfledged duckling as food; and with this he had sprung the first trap; then, in his vain endeavours to drag both duckling and trap to the young one, he had been captured in the second.

MERLIN.

FALCO ÆSALON.

Though the true home of this dashing little Falcon is without doubt in the land of the heather and mist, I can safely assert from my own experience that it is widely distributed over the British Islands. I have met with the nests and eggs within a short distance of John o' Groats, and obtained immature specimens both on the Kentish shingle-banks and the cliffs near the Land's End. Not an autumn that I have passed in East Norfolk has gone by without several having been noticed sweeping over the Snipe-marshes in the vicinity of the coast; and on several occasions I have come across their breeding-stations in the Outer Hebrides.

The Merlin seems as much at home on the steepest hillsides of the Central and Western Highlands as it does on the flat moors of the north and east. I have but once seen the adult male further south than the fells of Cumberland; in this instance I was surprised to notice a fine old bird, which dashed past me in front of the beaters while a wood was being driven in East Norfolk; this was in the month of December. In April 1876, while driving along the coast-road between Shoreham and Lancing, my attention was attracted by a small Hawk that skimmed close past the trap and settled on a ridge of beach a few yards distant from the rising tide. The bird was so intently watching the actions of a large flock of Dotterel and Dunlins wheeling over the sands, that it took not the slightest notice of my approach. As it sat so low in the shingle, I could scarcely make out the species; so, waiting until it made a move, I obtained a shot, and then discovered it was an immature male of this species, with only a few blue feathers showing on the back. The Plate is taken from this specimen, and clearly shows the state of plumage. With this single exception, all the Merlins I have observed in the south of England have been either old or young females, or males in too early a stage to be recognized.

On the South Downs these Hawks are not unfrequently captured in the nets of the bird-catchers. At times they dash suddenly down with an impetuous swoop and destroy the brace-birds; occasionally they approach in a more cautious manner. I have noticed them settle first at some short distance, and then draw on towards their intended prey. In one instance a very young Falcon alighted on the pull-line, where it remained for several minutes, regardless of half a dozen persons within a distance of twenty yards, its attention being apparently entirely engrossed by the decoys in the net.

It is stated on good authority that this species will attack birds of considerable size; my own observations, however, would lead me to believe that it will seldom fly at any prey of greater weight than a Snipe; consequently the damage it inflicts on game must be exceedingly slight.

The food they procure in order to supply their young varies according to the district in which they are found. In the Hebrides I observed they preyed principally on Snipe and Thrushes; and a pair nesting within a short distance of the lodge where I was staying in 1877, whose depredations I had a good opportunity of watching, carried off, in addition to their usual victims, a splendid male White Wagtail and a pair of Redwings, greatly to my disgust, as I was intending to search out their nest, being convinced by their presence at this season that they must be nesting somewhere in the neighbourhood. In Perthshire I have seen Titlarks, Wheatears, and large moths brought to their young. I also noticed some feathers apparently belonging to the Ring-Ouzel. On one occasion I stamped down a couple of nestlings just ready to fly; and as they were well supplied by their parents, I had a good opportunity of observing their bill of fare. Though it was in the centre of a well-stocked moor, I detected no indications of damage to game. A brood of young Grouse, with hardly a feather upon them, were running among the heather at the distance of only a few yards when I first discovered the young Falcons. I have never noticed the unfledged young of any species taken by the Merlin. In Sutherland and Caithness, where Dunlins are more common during the nesting-season, they appear to have a partiality for these small Waders. I have also seen the remains of Snipe and Titlarks and the wings of the Egger moth scattered in considerable numbers round their haunts in this county. The Common Sandpiper is occasionally attacked. One summer, while fishing on the Lyon, in Perthshire, I observed a Merlin dash down in pursuit of a bird of this species that was flitting across the river. Barely evading the swoop of the Falcon, it took to the water and dived instantly, making its way below the surface till it reached the shelter of some spreading bushes. The Merlin, apparently sulky at his failure, or puzzled by the disappearance of his intended victim in such an unexpected manner, pitched in a tree close by, where he remained perfectly motionless for over an hour.

The position of their nests varies considerably. I have seen them placed among the heather on the flat moors, and on more than one occasion on small ledges in the face of steep rocks. The construction of their cradle is not particularly elaborate, small heather-stalks, roots, and fine twigs and fibres of grass being utilized in the construction; it, however, as a rule, fits easily into some natural hollow in the ground.

Several years ago, while searching for a male of this species which I had knocked down broken-winged among some large rocks near his nesting-place, I stumbled on the best-concealed whiskey-still I ever came across; the exciseman who makes a discovery in this case without the assistance of previous information will be particularly cute.

Early in July 1868, during a continuance of remarkably hot weather which succeeded several weeks of almost incessant rain, I came across a nest of this species in Sutherland, where all the eggs were bad. One was perfectly empty, while the rest appeared scarcely above half the ordinary weight. The keepers had known of this nest some weeks, and were well aware that the birds ought in the usual course to have hatched off a considerable time earlier. I have seen it stated that eggs are soon deserted if their vitality is destroyed by damp or other causes; in this case, however, both parents continued sitting, as, on passing the spot twice during the day, I disturbed on the first occasion the male and subsequently the female from the nest. Birds of prey, are I believe, as a rule, less suspicious of interference with their nests or eggs than most other species. I have already mentioned the case of the Buzzard; I also tried the same experiment with the Hen-Harrier, and found the female just as easily imposed upon. I have also known Ospreys and Eagles to sit on their nests after the eggs had been carried off. A shepherd in the west assured me that he had watched a Golden Eagle return and pitch on her nest in which he had placed the head of a lamb, having previously removed her two eggs. The bird, he declared, appeared perfectly contented; but on visiting the spot on the following day, he found the head lying at the foot of the rocks, and the nest deserted.

KESTREL.

FALCO TINNUNCULUS.

The Kestrel is without doubt the most numerous as well as the best known of the Hawk tribe that frequent the British Islands. In every county and in the greater part of the islands I have visited, this species appears common, readily adapting its mode of living to the nature of the country it inhabits.

Though not generally so regarded, it is one of our most useful birds, being a decided ally both to the farmer and the game-preserver. I have been so frequently assured that Kestrels have been detected preying upon young game, that I suppose some misguided old bird must, when greatly pressed by the cares of providing for a hungry brood, have snatched some precocious young Pheasant from the neighbourhood of the coops, and, like many another poor bungling thief, been caught at the first attempt, while the greater rogues go free. The rats alone that these birds destroy while procuring food for their young would commit ten times more damage in one year than the poor inoffensive Kestrels could possibly effect in their whole lives. I observe most authors draw attention to the number of mice on which this species preys, and simply mention rats as rather an exception to the general bill of fare. I particularly remarked some years back, when I was engaged in taking notes regarding their food and habits, that rats (none less than three-parts grown and many full-sized) formed a part, and in some instances the whole, of the food that the old birds had provided for their brood at a dozen nests I examined in various districts in Scotland.

During the winter of 1881 I had several opportunities of observing the prey captured by a couple of Kestrels that frequented the rush-marshes in the neighbourhood of one of the larger broads in the east of Norfolk. It was seldom that they strayed far from two or three plantations which formed their head quarters, being usually seen, at almost any hour of the day, hunting over the marshes or perched on either some small bush or the raised bank of a water-dyke. In every instance when I examined the spot where they had devoured their prey, I discovered that they had been feeding on the large brown field-mouse. Occasionally they appeared to have consumed every portion of flesh, bone, and skin, and the only vestige remaining was that portion of the intestine containing the green food on which these animals subsist; at times they had plucked off a considerable quantity of the fur, which was scattered in small clots round the open space where they had made their meal.

I never yet heard of the young of either Partridges or Pheasants being carried off from wild broods; neither have I seen young Grouse among the victims on their nesting-places. Since the habits of birds of prey are gradually becoming better understood by game-preservers, and as keepers (with but very few exceptions) are by no means the ignorant class of men that certain writers have been pleased to describe them, it may be hoped that the Kestrel will long continue as plentiful as it now is. I am convinced that, if only the neighbourhood of the coops were strictly guarded, but little harm could possibly be laid to their charge.

It frequently happens that the blame is laid on those that are by no means the most guilty. There is little doubt that the losses attributed to the Kestrel are in many instances inflicted by Sparrow-Hawks or

Crows; and at times even the unsuspected Moorhen has been proved the aggressor. Rats and stoats, as well as snakes or adders[*], are also now and then tempted by such a tender morsel as a young Pheasant.

The Kestrel in the game-preserves of the southern and midland counties, like the Eagle and Peregrine on the Highland moors, is made responsible for all injury when the real culprit has managed to escape observation. To recount all the instances I have met with where this species has been unreasonably accused would be superfluous, though the following may perhaps afford an insight into the justice of certain charges of theft brought against the larger birds of prey. A few years back I passed part of the spring on an extensive sheep-farm in the west, where Eagles were looked upon as the most desperate robbers, in consequence of the damage they were declared to have inflicted on the flocks and the number of lambs they had carried off. That they were exceedingly destructive I never for a moment doubted; but how the poor birds could possibly be guilty of all the crimes imputed to them I was at a loss to conjecture. Shortly after leaving the islands I returned to the neighbourhood of Inverness; and while crossing a hill overlooking the lochs in the Caledonian Canal I observed a number of boats belonging to the east coast, which had been prosecuting the fishing in the Minch, making their way home. The boats were naturally delayed some time in the lochs; and I was particularly interested as soon as I noticed that one or two lambs were on every craft. A grassy bank stretched close down to the water-side; and it was an amusing sight to watch the gentle manner in which the sturdy fishermen tended their sportive charges while they gambolled on the hill-side, and the care with which they were led back to their respective boats when the passage of the lochs had been effected. I have often wondered how or where these lambs had been procured.

Birds up to the size of Blackbirds or Thrushes are now and then struck down by this species. Last spring I was informed by the gardener that a Kestrel had made several attacks on these birds in my own garden near Brighton. It appeared from his report that the Hawk had not succeeded in making any captures, although one Blackbird had only escaped with the loss of its tail. I was of opinion that the culprit must have been a Sparrow-Hawk; but being hastily summoned shortly after, I had a good view of a large female Kestrel tearing at a Blackbird, on which she was perched on the middle of a bed of Hyacinths. On being disturbed the Hawk at once made off, carrying the Blackbird in her talons.

I should be sorry to venture an opinion as to whether the British Islands are visited by any considerable numbers from the Continent during the autumn. There can be little doubt that a few cross the North Sea; I have met with them on the passage, and have also noticed an accession to the usual numbers on the east coast during the middle of October. I have more than once remarked that they appeared to come about the same time as the Grey Crows. My attention was attracted early in the morning of October 26, 1881, by the commotion created by a pair of Black Crows attempting to drive off some of their Grey brethren who seemed inclined to take up their quarters in a plantation they usually frequented. Later in the day the Crows were busily employed in repelling the advances of three or four Kestrels who had approached their domain. In some instances they followed them a considerable distance across the marshes before they desisted from their pursuit. These, I should imagine, must have been fresh arrivals, as during the summer months the Crows and Kestrels live in perfect amity, both species breeding in close proximity to one another, the Kestrels, as a rule, appropriating the old nests of their black neighbours.

For breeding-purposes this species resorts to various situations. On the downs in the south I have repeatedly observed them to rear their young in chalk-pits; they also make use of the deserted nests of Crows and other birds in the woodland districts, while along the sea-coast and among the islands the crevices and ledges in the cliffs furnish secure and almost inaccessible eyries. At times they are noticed

[*] I have a vivid recollection of killing a large adder, about thirty years ago, in Sussex, near a coop in which some newly-hatched Pheasants were located, and discovering that it had swallowed one of the young birds.

frequenting the towers of churches and other buildings; on the moors in the north the steep rocky faces of the numerous ravines and old ruins are for the most part resorted to. In the summer of 1868 I found a brood of young Kestrels on a perfectly bare spot on an open moor in Sutherland. It was not for the want of a suitable locality that such an unusual spot had been chosen for a cradle (there was not the slightest suspicion of a nest), as a rough and broken precipice was within a few yards distance. The following year I was shown three eggs on a shelf in a shepherds' dwelling on Ben Alisky, in Caithness, which had only been deserted by its rightful owners the previous month, the bird making its escape through a hole in the chimney while we were entering the building. I do not believe that the Kestrel makes any attempt at building a nest for itself. I have frequently noticed that not even a strand of grass or a single twig was on the ledges where their young had been hatched.

The number of rats that one pair will occasionally destroy, and the pertinacity with which the female will return to her nest in spite of frequent interruption, will be seen by the following short extract from my notes of 1867, jotted down while collecting specimens in East Lothian. The nest was in a small hole six or eight feet from the top of the cliffs on the east side of Canty Bay. Being anxious to secure the young as soon as they were perfectly covered with down, I had gone over the rocks with a rope on two or three occasions to learn how they progressed.

"June 1. On examining the Kestrels' nest I found the young in the state I required for preserving. The female was now more reconciled to having her treasures inspected, and simply hissed without making the slightest attempt to use either beak or claws when I lifted her up. As on previous occasions, the remains of rats were the only food. After paying the poor bird so many visits, I did not feel inclined to catch her on her young ones and slaughter her in cold blood; so I left her sitting, and hauled myself to the top of the cliffs with the assistance of the rope. On reaching the summit I determined to let her have the chance of a fly for her life; so picking up my gun I took up a position with firm standing-ground, from which I could shoot as she flew out. It required three or four stones pitched onto the ledge to induce her to move. At last she dashed out, but instantly swept round a projecting slab of rock, and was out of sight before she was twenty yards distant. When once on wing she appeared wild enough; and as she gave no signs of approaching within range, I discovered I should have to use the traps (which I had brought to set for the male) in order to effect her capture. The work of placing the traps (it needed a couple to cover the space at the entrance of the hole) was by no means easy, swinging on the rope with only a small ledge about an inch wide on which to get a foothold. At last the operation was accomplished; and the traps being of considerable weight, I did not think it would be necessary to make them fast. The rope was then drawn up, and we left the spot, making our way down to the inn. An hour and a half later we retraced our steps; and on stretching over the cliff I was surprised to find the traps vanished. On descending to the ledge I discovered the young were also gone. Before regaining the top of the rocks my attention was attracted by a party of three or four small boys diligently engaged in scraping a hole in the sand at the foot of the cliffs, between two and three hundred yards to the west. On examining their movements through the glasses, I discovered them just in the act of placing two traps in the hole and carefully covering them. I also noticed that they carried a couple of covered baskets. As I had strong suspicions that these youngsters had managed to possess themselves of our traps and birds, I directed the two men with me to take the path at the top of the cliffs and cut off their retreat towards North Berwick, while I watched their movements through the glasses. The time they spent in endeavouring to conceal the spot where they had buried the traps enabled the men to get round them. I could only discern, from where I was stationed, that the contents of the baskets were given up and the traps brought out from their place of concealment. On their return the men brought with them the four young Hawks, the old female, and also the traps. They also had the remains of the rats I had noticed on the ledge, in addition to a large one the captured bird must have brought with her when taken. It seems that the boys, who had come on purpose to take the young (for which they had already obtained a market as Peregrine Falcons at North Berwick), had previously paid several visits to the nest. The descent to the ledge had been effected by the aid of a piece of old rotten clothes-line, which, under the threat of prosecution for appropriating the traps, the terrified juveniles confessed they had stolen from a house on the East Links. The tameness of the female was probably due to the number of times she had been inspected while sitting, though it appears strange she had put up with such frequent interruption. With a leg and a wing broken (she had been in both traps) it was necessary to kill the poor bird at once. As I still required the male I returned the young to their nesting-place, reset the traps, and then retired a short distance to keep watch. In less than half an hour he came in with a large rat, and was secured."

Rats were in those days very numerous in the neighbourhood of Canty Bay. If I remember right, the natives attributed their presence to some old vessels that had been wrecked along the coast. The surrounding country for several miles was also remarkably well stocked with these destructive animals. It was no uncommon occurrence for the ratcatcher, when paying his periodical visits to the farm-steadings, to destroy between three and four hundred by means of traps or ferrets. The benefits conferred by Kestrels in such a country could not be overestimated. With the single exception of the above-mentioned family, required as specimens, I have always used my utmost endeavours to protect this useful species from persecution.

I noticed that on every occasion, when visiting the spot, I found the female on the nest. The male was observed carrying prey to the rock; but I did not see him take his part in the labour of incubation.

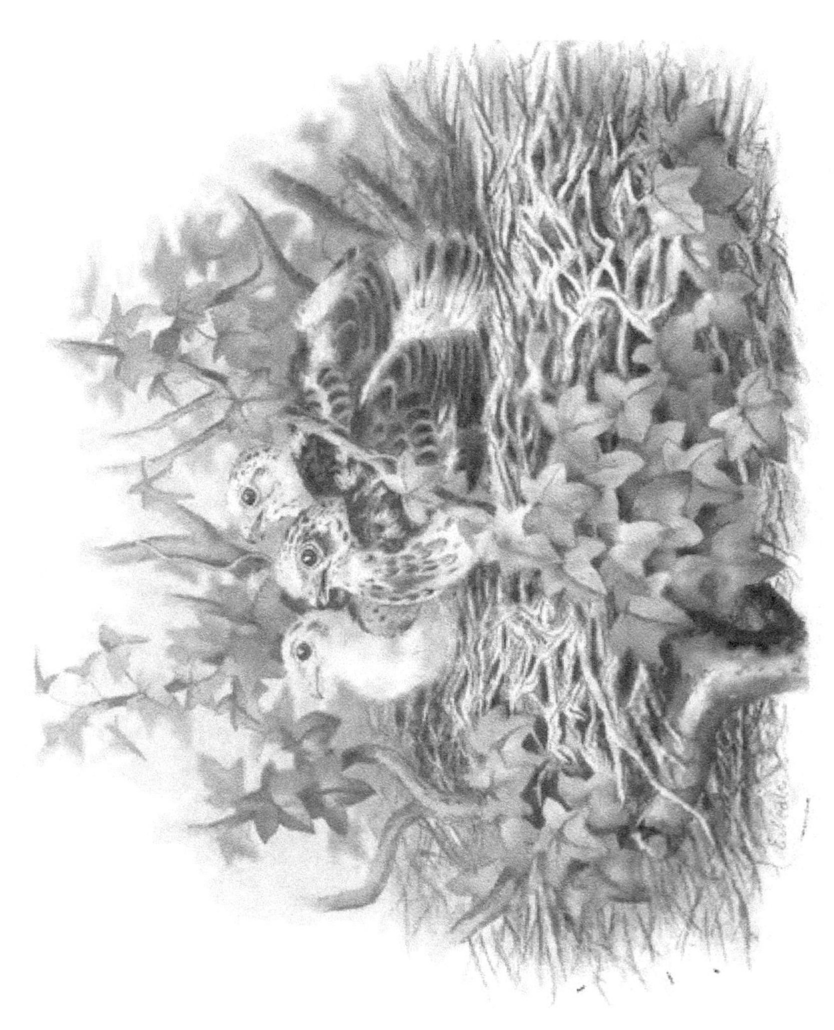

SPARROW-HAWK.

ACCIPITER NISUS.

Notwithstanding the almost universal persecution that the Sparrow-Hawk meets with, it is still tolerably numerous from north to south. I have seen several pairs breeding in the birch-woods of Sutherlandshire, and, to the best of my recollection, have never passed a week in any district between that county and Sussex without having met with a bird or two of this species. Wooded districts are its favourite haunts; but it may be noticed sweeping over the barren and treeless Grouse-moors, dashing past the buildings surrounding the lone farmhouse or shooting lodge, and gliding with rapid flight over the fens and rush-grown marsh-lands.

Falconers and naturalists frequently put in a plea for that still greater robber, the Peregrine; but I never yet remember to have seen a single line written in defence of the Sparrow-Hawk. No one who has had the opportunity of becoming acquainted with its manner of living can possibly doubt that it merits to a certain degree the bad name it has acquired; but that it will kill for the mere pleasure of slaying (which sportive trait in the character of the Falcon can only be denied by those who are ignorant of its true habits) cannot be laid to its charge. The poor bird is simply endowed with a vigorous appetite; and when engaged in providing for the wants of its ravenous brood, the destruction it commits is not unfrequently detected, and the contents of its larder accurately described and commented on. Judging from my own experience, the damage he is able to inflict on wild game is only small compared with the loss caused by his frequent raids on the broods that are reared in an artificial manner and deprived of their natural protectors. Small birds, such as Larks, Pipits, Buntings, and Finches, form the greater part of the food of this species; but at times it will strike and carry off still heavier victims, and it is probable that none below the weight of a half-grown Pheasant are perfectly safe from its attacks.

That this Hawk will fly at and buffet almost any species that approaches its nesting-quarters has, I believe, been recorded by several authors. A few months back I was watching an immature Marsh-Harrier which, after searching over several of the adjacent marshes, was steadily making its way towards its next hunting-grounds, past a plantation where a pair of Sparrow-Hawks were rearing their young. No sooner had it approached within the distance of about one hundred yards of the wood than it was attacked by the male. The difference in size between the two was particularly striking as the little Hawk gradually drove the Harrier higher and higher in the air. Both birds were almost lost to sight (having risen in large circles, the Harrier evidently attempting to get above his diminutive antagonist) before the chase came to an end.

The Sparrow-Hawk is occasionally mobbed by a mixed flock of small birds. I lately noticed one glide down under the shelter of a hedgerow, carrying a bright cock Yellowhammer in his talons, pursued by a chattering swarm, to whose clamour he payed not the slightest attention. I particularly remarked that, although noisy in the extreme, they exhibited their discretion by keeping at a respectful distance, and as soon as the Hawk settled the whole crowd at once dispersed.

At the time of migration these birds are occasionally seen on the North Sea. I have heard of a few from the lightships; and the master of a Yarmouth fishing-lugger told me that he observed a large female Sparrow-Hawk strike at a Peewit, when both came down into the water. This occurred while he was engaged on the home voyage, halfway between the "Newarp" lightship and the "Knoll" buoy, about the middle of October. As the birds appeared unable to rise, the boat was headed towards them and the deedle* got ready so as to effect a capture. When close at hand and just in front of the net, the Hawk fluttered towards the Peewit, and, mounting on its back, spread her wings and succeeded in making her escape. The Plover was secured, and his flight-feathers being cut, he was kept on the deck of the boat, where he speedily became reconciled to confinement.

It is stated that this Hawk occasionally places its nest in rocks where trees are scarce. Not one, however, so located has come under my own observation. In every instance where I have examined their breeding-quarters they appeared to have made use of the deserted nests of some of the various members of the Crow tribe. I noticed both male and female employed in supplying food to their young brood. I mention this fact, as it has been remarked that the female in some instances receives the prey from the male and conveys it to the nest. The young are at first covered with a white or rather a dirty whitish down.

The Plate shows a brood rather more than half-fledged. The nest had been constructed and made use of the previous season by a pair of Grey Crows in the birch-wood overlooking Loch Craggie, in Sutherland.

While engaged in procuring the above-mentioned specimens, I was somewhat surprised to notice the early hour at which the old birds brought food to their young. Both male and female were exceedingly wary; and, having attempted in vain to obtain a shot as they came in to roost, I determined to be on the spot before daylight. Neither bird appeared to be in the vicinity of the nest when I cautiously made my way to the foot of the tree soon after two o'clock; but before many minutes had elapsed I heard their screams in different parts of the wood gradually drawing closer, and before it was fairly light I had shot both birds, though not before one of them had managed to pay one visit to the nest and make its escape, owing to the darkness, beneath the trees. I discovered that two Pipits had been brought as food, though how they had been secured at that early hour does not seem clear. The small birds could hardly, I should imagine, have been astir before daylight; and it would almost appear that they must have been captured the day before and stored up for future use. Possibly owing to our presence in the neighbourhood of the wood during the previous afternoon and evening, the old birds had been hindered from bringing in what food they had procured. The Meadow-Pipit was remarkably plentiful in the district; but I cannot call to mind having ever noticed them on the move till after sunrise. The Hawk tribe are particularly restless; I have frequently heard their warning cry at all hours of the night when passing near their quarters.

* The landing net.

MARSH-HARRIER.

CIRCUS ÆRUGINOSUS.

Considering the time I have spent at all seasons of the year in the neighbourhood of the fens and broads of the eastern counties, as well as in other quarters that are frequented by this species, the observations I have been enabled to record concerning its habits are scanty in the extreme.

The Marsh-Harrier is stated on good authority to occur in Scotland. Here, to the best of my knowledge, I have seen but a single specimen, an immature bird which I noticed in East Lothian. The only adults I could ever positively identify were a pair I observed sailing over the reed-beds on Wicken fen, near Ely. Occasionally one or two were seen beating about the fen-lands of Quy, Waterbeach, and Swaffham, in the neighbourhood of Cambridge; these, I believe, were all immature. In Norfolk the species is still far from uncommon, although I never discovered the nest. I have watched them at all seasons of the year; but none I met with appeared to have arrived at maturity. Fifteen or twenty years ago a stray bird was now and then observed in the vicinity of the reedy pools on Romney Marsh, in Kent; and in Sussex the flat country round Winchelsea and Pevensey Marsh were occasionally visited by these Harriers, though none, I believe, were ever reported to have bred in either county. In Cornwall a single specimen came under my notice hunting over the furze-covered hill-side that slopes down to the pool on Marazion marsh, near Penzance.

During a residence of a couple of years within a mile or two of Gullane links, in East Lothian (a favourite locality for this species according to some writers), I had the opportunity of observing the habits of many birds of prey. The rabbits on these sandy hills, which are here and there interspersed with pools of water and beds of rushes, are, I imagine, the chief attraction to the larger species, while the numbers of small Waders that haunt the marshy portions of the ground afford an almost endless supply of food to those less powerful. At different times, between the two extremities of the links (which stretch for several miles along the coast from the fir-woods of Archerfield on the east to the shores of Aberlady burn on the west), I have watched two or three young White-tailed Eagles, several Peregrines, Kestrels, Sparrow-Hawks, and Merlins, as well as an occasional Buzzard. Harriers, however, with the single exception mentioned above, were only conspicuous by their absence. Early in the autumn of 1868 this specimen was noticed flapping backwards and forwards over the low-laying marshes towards the west end of the links. A Snipe, which I had partially crippled by a long shot, took refuge among the sedges and water-plants near the shores of the firth; the bird was almost incapacitated from flying, and while falling attracted the attention of the Harrier. In order to obtain a shot at the latter I withdrew behind the shelter of one of the sandbanks, hoping that he might settle to his prey. The Snipe, however, had sufficient strength left to rise when closely threatened; and this performance was repeated so often, the Hawk working as if desirous of wearing down rather than striking his victim, that I came to the conclusion he would make no attempt to take any prey while it was able to get on wing.

In Norfolk, although I seldom passed a day while shooting in the eastern part of the county without one or more coming under observation, I have never been able to record an instance even of wounded birds being attacked. The Buzzard, as this species is always styled by the natives, appears to be perpetually sailing over the rush-marshes and reed-beds in the neighbourhood of the broads. I have noticed one pitch, as if on prey, at least half a dozen times while hunting over a single marsh; but on subsequently examining each spot, the bearings of which were carefully marked, I could discover no signs of any bird or small animal having been destroyed; the prey, if any was captured, must in every case have been entirely consumed. I have frequently seen the greatest excitement displayed by Peewits and Redshanks while the Harrier was beating over the marshes in which their young were concealed. At times, after hovering for a second or two, the robber would descend into the cover; and I have little doubt that the unfledged young would prove an acceptable and easily procured meal. Snakes, frogs, and mice, and even such small game as dragonflies, are, I conclude from the remains I have come across, included in their bill of fare. Dead or disabled birds, if incapable of flight, form most probably the chief portion of their diet. I discovered the toe of a Hawk I believe to have belonged to this species in a trap I set baited with a Coot; the teeth had unfortunately proved too sharp, but a feather or two adhering to the mud left little doubt as to the identity of the escaped bird.

I can state nothing on my own authority with reference to the nesting of this species. Those I observed on Wicken fen were evidently, from their actions, breeding somewhere close at hand. Among the broads in Norfolk I have been informed that nests have been found during the last few years; but the descriptions of the birds given by my various informants were so conflicting that it was impossible to place any reliance on their reports.

The eastern counties during the months of September and October 1881 were visited by several wanderers of this species, as well as numbers of Buzzards. One or two young birds that I examined fresh-killed by the gunners of the district were particularly rich in their colouring, the feathers on the head being remarkably tawny. I have noticed a few at times, during summer and the early months of autumn, so worn and ragged in their plumage as to give the impression that some of the stuffed monstrosities one observes in the windows of second-rate taxidermists or on the shelves of museums had suddenly been restored to life and allowed to return to their former haunts.

HEN-HARRIER.

CIRCUS CYANEUS.

Though by no means an exceedingly rare species, the Hen-Harrier can scarcely be termed common at the present date in any part of the British Islands I have visited. A few pairs may still be found scattered over the flat moors of Sutherland and Ross-shire; I have also met with several nests in different parts of Caithness. In Inverness it seems less common; and in Perthshire not more than half a dozen specimens have come under my observation. Among the Hebrides it appears, from the information I gathered from keepers and shepherds, to be found in considerable numbers, though I failed to notice more than two or three single birds in the Long Island. I have seen one or two beating over the Yorkshire moors in the neighbourhood of Whitby, also in Cumberland near Penrith. The broad-district of Norfolk, the fens of Cambridge, and the marshes and furze-covered downs of Sussex are also at times frequented by this species: females, however, and immature specimens are most commonly met with. I have never observed a full-plumaged male further south than Norfolk.

Several writers assert that this Harrier has been distinctly observed to make an attack upon Grouse and Partridges. Unless the bird had been seen in the act of capturing its prey, I should be inclined to believe that it must have picked up some of the victims struck down by the Peregrine. Small birds, such as Larks and Pipits, together with mice, and even frogs appear to be its most natural food; it will also, I imagine, carry off the unfledged young of Partridges and Land-Rails. I never detected the remains of such prey at their resting-quarters, though I frequently watched a pair hunting over a marshy hay-field in the Highlands which was the resort of a brood or two of Partridges and at least a dozen pairs of Land-Rails. I was never close enough to determine exactly, even by the aid of powerful glasses, the nature of the prey they captured; but on one or two occasions it appeared to be either a dark-coloured field-mouse or, what is far more probable, the downy young of the Corn-Crake.

The adults of this species, I believe, with but few exceptions, remain as residents in the district they inhabit, the majority of the wanderers being the young while in the immature stages. I have heard it stated that these birds disappear entirely from the north on the approach of winter: this, I am inclined to consider, is incorrect. I was informed by a keeper well acquainted with the species, that he had noticed two fine old males in perfect plumage during very severe weather in Glen Afferic, closely searching the riverside for prey. Their usual haunts on the moors were deeply covered with snow; and they were probably driven to the low ground in order to procure food. When punt-gunning early in the year on Loch Shin, in Sutherland, I observed a male, apparently in change of plumage, hunting over the moors near the waterside on two consecutive days. The females I have seldom recognized at this season.

The Hen-Harrier invariably rears its young on the ground. All the nests I examined in the north were constructed of small heather-stalks, and lined with fine twigs and a few strands of coarse grass. As a rule they were placed in heather of moderate growth or rough tussocks of grass, at times much exposed to the weather; but one or two nests were most cosily situated in sheltered corries, screened from almost every wind. In the eastern counties they frequent the rush-marshes, breeding among the sedges and other coarse herbage. I generally noticed that they selected some spot where the cover was from two to three feet high.

In the summer of 186[illegible], while walking over a moor in the east of Sutherland, I disturbed a Ringtail (the female of the Hen-Harrier is known by this name) from her nest, which contained one young one just out of the shell and five eggs on the point of hatching. As both the old birds were flying round in a state of great consternation, I sat down to watch their actions for a few minutes. On rising to leave the spot, I discovered I had laid my gun on the back of an old Grey Hen, who now got up from her nest, in which were three fresh-laid eggs, evidently showing that she herself had chosen this apparently dangerous locality for her nursery, as the Harriers' nest was within six or seven paces. This is not the only instance I have met with of game and birds of prey being found in close proximity.

Within the distance of half a dozen miles of the above-mentioned nest I came upon another female sitting on eggs. In this instance I approached close enough to obtain a good view of her before she rose. Whether fear or anger at my intrusion had caused her to puff herself out to the fullest extent, I am unable to state; anyhow her appearance was most remarkable. Her tail was spread and standing almost upright, while the plumage on her back was elevated, and every feather on her neck and head on end, the ring round the face being particularly conspicuous. After watching her closely for a minute or two, I drew cautiously back to obtain my drawing-book, which was in one of the gamebags, in order to make a sketch of her position. On endeavouring to approach the second time, she rose at once in the air; and a subsequent attempt to take her portrait met with no better success. Whether this is the usual manner in which the females of this species comport themselves while engaged in the work of incubation, I am unable to state from personal experience, as I never obtained another chance of judging.

The Plate, showing the male and nestling, is taken from specimens obtained in Caithness. When first discovered, this nest contained five eggs; but on visiting it a fortnight later I found a single young bird was the only occupant, the eggs having most probably been carried off by some Grey Crows which were breeding in a steep rock at no great distance.

The young, when newly hatched, are covered by a dirty whitish down. The soft parts of the beak and the cere, as well as the iris, are also of much the same dull tint.

MONTAGU'S HARRIER.

CIRCUS CINERACEUS.

THE numbers of Hen-Harriers that formerly resorted to the neighbourhood of Bonar Bridge and the moors stretching from the north of Loch Shin towards Ben Armine and the adjacent lofty mountains probably led to the statement that this species frequented the district. During the years spent in the north I traversed this locality on several occasions, meeting with many pairs of Harriers and inspecting their nests and young *; though every bird that came in view was examined with the utmost care, not a single specimen of *Circus cineraceus* could be detected. I have only observed this species in the southern and eastern counties of England; according to my own experience it evinces a partiality for either furze-clad downs or rough and uncut rush-marshes, the nature of the country in which it is found differing considerably from the stretches of wild moorland that form the favourite haunts of the Hen-Harrier.

On many of the unreclaimed marshes in the east of Norfolk, rushes and other rank herbage are grown for litter, frequently remaining uncut for one or more seasons, by which means a heavy crop (termed "double whole" in the district) is obtained; the docks and lofty thistles, with the endless varieties of tangled marsh-plants and coarse grasses that flourish on the moist portions of the ground, render these flats almost impenetrable. Where the soil is occasionally flooded, or swamps and sludes are still undrained, the common reed (*Phragmites communis*) springs up in profusion, rearing its feathery heads above the dense undergrowth. To such spots these birds usually resort in this locality; though occasionally straying while on their rounds in search of prey to the drier marshes as well as the hills round the broads, it is only under the shelter of reeds or rushes that they attempt to rear their young. When breeding where the rush (*Juncus glaucus*) grows thick and strong, I remarked at times that the bare patch on which the nest is placed was exceedingly small, the surrounding cover leaving barely sufficient space for the bird to spread its wings. Within a short distance other similar spots were occasionally found; these, the marshmen declared, were the roosting-places of the male: one such station, evidently frequently used, was pointed out below an old furze bush on a marsh-wall about one hundred yards from where the female was sitting; here the grass was trampled down, and many feathers, doubtless plucked out while the bird was dressing its plumage, were scattered around.

Though many opportunities for watching these Harriers have fallen to my share, I am enabled to state little or nothing from personal observation concerning the nature of their prey. Vipers, lizards †, mice, insects, and large moths ‡ are supposed by the marshmen to constitute a considerable portion of their food. I

* During my last visit to these parts I ascertained that Hen-Harriers had greatly decreased in numbers.

† "Vipers" and "Swifts" were the names given by the natives to these reptiles.

‡ Moths are commonly known in the district as "flies." I well remember on one occasion, after permission had been granted to go round the buildings of a farm at night to search for a certain species of moth, that while engaged in examining the sugar with a lamp, the door of the farm-house opened, and a voice was heard exclaiming "Is it the flies you're after?"

frequently remarked that their presence caused far less uneasiness to the Redlegs and Peewits than that of the Moor-Buzzard: this fact might lead to the belief that they were not destructive to the offspring of these birds; it is, however, possible that their flight while skimming over the marshes, being more rapid, does not attract the same amount of attention. A Marsh-Harrier often remains for a quarter of an hour or twenty minutes hunting backwards and forwards over an acre of rushes and sedge, swooping down repeatedly to the surface, while the present species, as a rule, passes onward without turning to the right or left, only pausing for a few moments when the capture of prey appears inevitable.

The drainage and cultivation of swamps and fens have much restricted the distribution of these Harriers; their numbers also have been thinned down by gamekeepers, and their eggs removed to supply the demands of collectors; as yet, however, they are by no means exterminated, and a few pairs still succeed, at not unfrequent intervals, in rearing their young in some of the most inaccessible of their old haunts. Some fourteen or fifteen years ago, when in quest of this species, I fell in with several pairs in the eastern counties; having been misled, however, by a statement (from a well-known sportsman whose chances for observation, one would suppose, ought to have rendered his remarks reliable) that this Harrier exhibited no white over the rump, I allowed the females on two occasions to rise unmolested from their nests without attempting to obtain specimens. The males resolutely refusing to permit a sufficiently close inspection to identify their plumage with certainty, I was led to believe that all observed in the district were Hen-Harriers; not needing specimens of that species, little attention was paid to either birds or nests. If the females of the two species are closely examined it will be seen that though the white band at the base of the tail of *C. cyaneus* is decidedly broader, a distinct white line is apparent at the roots of the feathers on *C. cineraceus*; this marking is especially conspicuous as the bird spreads its wings to rise from the ground. The warm brown streaks and the general tint of the flanks, which come well into view as the bird mounts in the air, ought to have proved a sufficient guide, had I been better acquainted with the general colouring of the females.

Various means of distinguishing Montagu's Harrier from its relative have been pointed out by writers on natural history; the plates, however, in several works indicate plainly that little attention could have been paid to the specimens from which the sketches were taken. The ruff or frill round the head is by no means so perfect as in the Hen-Harrier; still it is represented in the drawings given by several authors as continued prominently below the beak. Macgillivray tells us that "the ruff is obscure," and again remarks that "the ruff is obsolete;" though somewhat singularly worded, these remarks are evidently intended to convey the impression that the ruff or frill is imperfect. The head of the male represented in the small woodcut in Yarrell differs from all others that I have seen figured, but agrees precisely in the extent of the ruff with specimens I have examined in the flesh, the frill being entirely wanting on the throat below the beak. The same author also informs us that "the third quill feather of the wing is much more pointed" than in the Hen-Harrier; this also accords in every instance with the measurements I have taken from freshkilled birds. I am enabled also to add that this feather in Montagu's Harrier is considerably longer than the second and fourth. The third and fourth were found to be almost equal in length in several specimens of the Hen-Harrier that came under my observation when taking notes on the two species; the fourth, however, is usually allowed to be slightly the longest. My attention has also lately been drawn by a friend to another method for distinguishing the species. In Montagu's Harrier the second, third, and fourth primaries only are emarginated on the outer web, whereas in the Hen-Harrier the emargination * is carried on from the second to the fifth primary inclusive.

* I take the term "emarginate" to mean the cutting away of the edge of a feather. Macgillivray, however, in his Introduction, when explaining the terms used in the structure of birds, states as follows:—"Emarginate, having a notch in the end." A woodcut is then given, representing a feather notched at the point.

While still in the down the youngsters of this species differ greatly from those of the Hen-Harrier; shortly after hatching they exhibit a dull white down, which, as the bird increases in size, assumes a warm red tint. This colour fades considerably after death, but never approaches the dirty white or dull leaden hue which pervades the down on the nestlings of *C. cyaneus*.

The colouring of the soft parts of a female and brood obtained on the 3rd of July, 1883, may be described as follows:—Female: iris pale warm hazel, with bright yellow ring round the pupil, pale yellow ring round eyelids; tips of upper and lower mandibles black, merging gradually into a pale blue slate towards the cere, which was bright chrome-yellow; legs and feet deep chrome, claws black. Young: beaks black at the tips, continuing a dark horn up to the cere; cere yellow, inside of mouth a pale flesh-tint; the skin between the base of the beak and the eye showing up through the bristles a livid slate-tint; iris dark hazel, a pale yellow ring round eyelid; legs and feet Naples yellow, claws horn.

This brood consisted of three young birds and one egg, two of the youngsters being much alike in size, though one was rather more advanced and stronger; these both exhibited a warm red blush on the down. The third juvenile was much smaller and weaker, its naked skin being barely covered by a scanty white down. The manner in which this tiny mite sought repose was most singular, the head, with its scraggy neck fully extended, being curled up under the body. At times, when rolling about uneasily, it would elevate its legs above the bare wing-joints, and scratch violently with the claws at the back of its head. The two larger birds now and then fought viciously, but speedily became reconciled and settled down together. When awaiting their food, one would occasionally seize the distended crop of its companion, and endeavour to tear away a portion with its sharp hooked beak; the flesh showing red through the down and bearing a certain resemblance to raw meat, in all probability led to this mistake. After remaining in captivity for about a fortnight, the whole family, though taking their food with avidity in the first instance, gradually became weaker, in spite of the most careful attention, and dropped off one by one. Doubtless the brood were taken far too young to be successfully reared; the food also (the flesh of small birds sliced up raw) with which they were supplied was probably unsuitable.

I carefully measured the eggs taken from a couple of nests of Montagu's Harrier during the summer of 1883, and discovered they were considerably smaller than those figured on the plates in a recently published work on British birds; one clutch were especially round and small, and proved to be three sixteenths of an inch less in length.

It is many years since I had an opportunity of examining a nest of this species placed among furze, and the composition of those that came under my notice has entirely slipped my memory. For a couple of seasons, about five and twenty years ago, I procured eggs which must have belonged to this species on an extensive stretch of furze, known in the district as the "heathy field," near Catsfield, in the east of Sussex. One or two of the birds were shot by the keeper, who termed them Marsh-Buzzards: the size of the eggs, however, which remained in my possession for some time, plainly indicated the species when compared with those of the Hen-Harrier taken in the Highlands; the nature of the country in which the nests were placed would also leave little doubt on the subject. In the fen- and broad-districts the cradle is very simply constructed, consisting merely of a scanty collection of the dead and dried stems of the surrounding rushes and grasses scratched together without the slightest attempt at neatness.

It is mentioned in several works that this species occasionally exhibits a darker tint on the colouring of the plumage. During the summer of 1883, I carefully examined a fresh-killed male, shot in one of the eastern counties in the vicinity of his nest, that showed a dark tint on the back and wings; there were also several feathers of an ash-brown, intermixed with the slate-grey of the remainder of the plumage. Whether this bird was one of the dark variety, or only too young to have assumed the perfectly mature dress, I had no means of ascertaining: I remarked that he contrasted greatly with a fine adult male frequently seen beating over the marshes and breeding near at hand. Not having, however, obtained the specimen myself, the rules stated in the Introduction preclude the insertion of a plate to better illustrate his peculiar colouring. The female with which this singularly tinted bird paired was of the ordinary type, possibly young, if we may trust to the statements of certain authors, who describe the eyes of young females as hazel and those of older birds as yellow.

The female previously referred to, and the two largest of her brood, are figured on the Plates; the woodcut gives a correct representation of one of the favourite attitudes of the smallest and most helpless of the same family.

SHORT-EARED OWL.

OTUS BRACHYOTUS.

THE old name of Woodcock-Owl was probably given to this species on account of its arrival having been supposed by our ancestors to denote the fact that Woodcocks would shortly make their appearance on our coasts. Without doubt, large flights at times reach our eastern shores during the autumn and early winter; these, I conclude from reports I have received from the light-ships, are birds that have crossed the North Sea. We are also visited in the spring by a few stragglers that have passed the winter months on the continent. On several occasions, usually soon after daylight, I have met with single birds in advanced breeding-plumage within a short distance of the English Channel, both in Kent and Sussex, the date of their appearance being from the middle to the latter end of April. I particularly noticed that these birds seemed lighter in plumage than those that passed the winter on our shores.

During summer the Short-eared Owl may be found nesting in many parts of the British Islands. I have met with them in the Hebrides and Inverness-shire, and in one instance on the west coast of Ross-shire. In the north-west of Perthshire they are particularly numerous; I have come across their nests on many occasions on the Grouse-moors. I found one pair, which I believe to have been breeding, on the hills near Whitby in Yorkshire, though I was unable to detect either eggs or young. Many years ago I captured an unfledged nestling on the outskirts of Wicken fen, near Ely; and at the present date this species still breeds in considerable numbers in the east of Norfolk.

Small birds about the size of Larks and Pipits, together with two or three different members of the mouse family, appear to be the usual food of this Owl. The pellets, which may be found in immense numbers in the neighbourhood of their haunts, clearly indicate the description of prey on which they subsist. I have heard it stated that they are at times destructive to young game; this I should much doubt, unless a partly-fledged Snipe has happened to come under their observation.

During the winter months these Owls may usually be seen hunting for prey as early as 3 P.M., occasionally in dull weather even earlier. In summer they may be noticed soaring at all hours of the day over the marshes or moors where their young are located. When disturbed by the intrusion of visitors to their haunts, they remain circling over the intruders, uttering a sharp barking cry, swooping down at times as if with the intention of making an attack in defence of their progeny, then sailing slowly away to a distance, and ever and anon returning again, till their quarters are left in peace. I repeatedly watched them while the sun was shining brightly; and they appeared not in the slightest incommoded by the strong light.

I have found their nests in the north in heather and rough grass. On the east coast, where I met with many opportunities of studying their habits, they seem to prefer the roughest and wildest situations they are able to select. In some localities the rush-marshes are left for several years uncut; here a luxuriant crop of thistles, docks, and other rank-growing plants soon becomes established: these wastes are the favourite quarters of the Marsh-Owl, as this species is termed by the natives.

The young, I imagine, leave the nest some time before they are able to get on wing. I have frequently come across a single young one seated by itself in some snug corner among the dense cover; and after hunting further, a second and then a third might eventually be discovered. Even after they are capable of flight the family keep within a short distance of one another, appearing to resort to a certain spot for resting and digesting their food. I have disturbed several broods in the *marshes* of East Norfolk, where for a space of twenty or thirty yards the greater part of the rushes and herbage were broken down by regular runs or tracks; the surface of the grass also was mottled by their droppings, and thickly strewn with pellets as well as quantities of their feathers.

At times I have noticed one perched on a gate or post; but more frequently they may be observed steadying themselves on the small stunted willow bushes or the old stumps that are found along the marsh-dykes.

Their nest, if they construct any, is simply a few strands of grass placed in a depression that is either scratched out or formed by the bird while sitting.

The first Plate shows a male in the summer plumage and two young ones unable to fly. It will be readily seen that the breeding-plumage of the adult is much lighter than the winter dress, in which we are accustomed to meet with the bird. I find in my note-book the following remarks referring to young ones taken in Norfolk on June 23, 1881. "Eyes king's yellow; beak dark horn or almost black; inside of mouth pale flesh; feet yellow-ochre; soles of feet king's yellow; claws dark horn."

The second Plate gives the regular winter plumage, which is usually assumed by both old and young by the middle of autumn. The bird was shot in Norfolk in December.

LONG-EARED OWL.

OTUS VULGARIS.

This species is by no means uncommon in most parts of Great Britain. I never yet observed a Long-eared Owl on the barren moors or treeless deer-forests of Sutherland and Caithness, or on the Outer Islands; but with these exceptions I have found it generally distributed over almost every county I have visited. It appears most numerous in those localities where fir-plantations of moderate size are to be met with. I particularly remarked in several districts in the Highlands, where the hill-sides for miles are covered by dense forests of Scotch fir or larch, that not a single specimen was either seen or heard.

The Long-eared Owl is strictly nocturnal in its habits, seldom venturing far from its haunts till twilight has set in. During the day it rests in some thick fir in the densest part of the wood it frequents. I noticed that, when these birds have young to provide for, they commence to move about from tree to tree some time before the sun has disappeared. An excited mob of Blackbirds and Thrushes occasionally collects, and, with angry screams, persistently follows the hated intruder every time it shifts its position.

Small birds and mice are the usual prey of this species. When living in East Lothian, I used to observe these Owls during the summer coming regularly at dusk to the stack-yard for rats or mice, though the woods where they nested were at a distance of nearly two miles. I have repeatedly seen them perched on the stacks or farm-implements, intently watching for the slightest rustle among the straw, when they would instantly glide to the spot. Unfledged nestlings are also taken. I noticed a Long-eared Owl making several visits one evening to a boat-shed on one of the broads in Norfolk; and on examining the place the next morning I discovered that a brood of young Swallows had disappeared during the night. I do not think that the most ardent game-preserver could make the slightest complaint against this species.

The young birds have a peculiarly sad and plaintive whistle (something resembling a deep-drawn sigh) when calling for their food. When there are several broods in the same plantation, the effect of their wailing cries is any thing but lively when listened to on a still night in the gloomy depths of the pine-woods, their mournful notes breaking out first on one side, then on another, and finally being answered from all quarters at once.

The Long-eared Owl is by no means fastidious when choosing a cradle in which to rear its family. A mass of dead leaves and twigs that have lodged in a cleft among the branches, the old drey of a squirrel, or the deserted nest of a Crow appears equally suited to its requirements. I have never met with an instance where there was evidence that the bird had been its own architect; indeed, I believe this Owl will not make even the slightest additions or repairs to the collection of rubbish or the antiquated structure it selects.

The Plate shows the adult male and a young one shortly after leaving the nest.

The plates in some of the older works represent Owls as sitting with three toes in front of their perch and one behind; all, however, I believe, place two toes in front and two behind. This error is very excusable, as of course the habits of the bird in this respect could only be ascertained by studying its actions in confinement.

A young bird of this species that I took from the nest in Norfolk lived for a couple of years about the house, and, although allowed the use of his wings, never made the slightest attempt to escape. During the day he appeared to prefer the darkest corner of a room, and if carried into the open air seemed confused by the light, refusing to move if placed on the ground or on a tree. Once or twice after dark he started from the window on a voyage of discovery, but never remained absent more than a few minutes, appearing particularly pleased to return to his accustomed quarters. He showed the greatest antipathy to dogs, puffing out his feathers and spreading his wings as soon as he caught sight of one; on a near approach he became greatly excited, bowing his head and intently following with his eyes every movement of the animal, and occasionally giving vent to loud screams.

Although he would, when hungry, feed readily on raw meat or birds, his especial fancy was for mice. Up to three-parts grown he bolted them whole, taking down the head first, the tip of the tail remaining in sight for some time from a corner of his mouth. If full-grown, he occasionally held them in his claws, and tore off the head and other portions before swallowing.

I imagined that his death, which occurred when he was rather more than two years old, might possibly have been caused by the greater portion of his diet having consisted of shot birds.

TAWNY OWL.

STRIX STRIDULA.

The Tawny or Wood-Owl (as this species is often termed) may be met with in most parts of England, with the exception of those moorland districts that are utterly devoid of trees. Its favourite haunts appear to be dense woods of oak or elm; I have also now and then found a stray bird or two resting by day in a thicket of Scotch firs. It is described by several writers as being of not unfrequent occurrence in many localities in the Highlands. As I have not observed above two or three specimens farther north than East Lothian, I can state but little on my own authority as to its distribution in Scotland.

I have seldom noticed this Owl venture beyond the darkest recesses of the wood it frequents during daylight, even if driven from its place of concealment. It does not usually start forth in pursuit of prey till some time after sundown.

On several occasions I have heard this species accused of preying on young game; but never having seen it abroad by daylight, I fancy the charges brought against it are without foundation. Mice, rats, and moles are most probably the chief items in its humble bill of fare, though the sharp and powerful claws with which it is furnished (and by means of which a wounded bird defends itself most desperately) would make short work of young rabbits or even leverets. That it may now and then be guilty of an attack on these quadrupeds cannot, I am of opinion, be denied by even its greatest admirers. I am aware that several instances have been recorded where these birds were ascertained to have provided their young with fish; but I have never met with a chance of observing this habit; indeed, according to my own experience, they appear less addicted to hunting for prey in the neighbourhood of water than any other species of our common British Owls.

For breeding-purposes the Tawny Owl makes use of hollow trees, old nests of Crows or squirrels, or even the cavities formed by the decay of some large limb; the litter and old dead leaves that have collected in the aperture appearing to satisfy all its requirements in the way of a nest. Not unfrequently this species resorts to rabbit-holes. This curious habit is not the result of the scarcity of large timber, as I saw one captured in a trap placed in a burrow in Stanmer Park, in Sussex. The large woods in the park invariably harbour one or two pairs of these Owls; and I always imagined they bred in the thickest part of the cover till I discovered in this manner that they preferred an underground domicile. I have subsequently met with a similar instance in Norfolk.

In addition to the names Tawny and Wood-Owl, this species is also known as the Brown and the Hooting Owl—the latter title being given on account of its note. The wild "hoo! hoo! hoo!" this bird gives utterance to has startled many a benighted traveller while passing through the woods it frequents.

BARN OWL.

YOUNG ON FIRST LEAVING THE NEST

BARN-OWL.

STRIX FLAMMEA.

The Barn-Owl is generally distributed over the southern portions of Great Britain. It occurs less frequently towards the north, while in the Highlands not more than a dozen specimens have come under my observation.

Large numbers of this quaint-looking bird are killed down without the slightest cause or reason. A visit to the shops of the local stuffers in any country town will plainly show the senseless slaughter to which this useful species is exposed. An inspection of the immense quantities of pellets thrown up by these Owls in their resting-places would speedily convince those who might be inclined to doubt the fact that the benefits they confer on farmers by the destruction of small vermin are by no means imaginary. The apertures left in many old-fashioned barns for the accommodation of the Owl indicates that our ancestors were better acquainted with the habits of the bird and anxious to encourage it to take up its quarters on their premises. I have now and then heard farmers, even at the present day, insisting that these inoffensive birds regularly destroyed their Pigeons, and also bringing other impossible charges against them. From my own experience, I have no hesitation in stating that this is one of the most harmless as well as the most useful of all our British birds.

This Owl is decidedly nocturnal in its habits, seldom making its appearance abroad during daylight, unless disturbed from its resting-place. If driven beyond the outskirts of the wood it frequents, or the shelter of its haunt in the barn or church, it soon collects a mob of excited small birds to follow in its track. Shortly before dusk one afternoon during the winter of 1881, my attention was attracted to a commotion created by four or five Grey Crows which were flying over a fir-plantation in the east of Norfolk, screaming loudly, and occasionally darting down among the trees. I soon discovered the cause of their anger when a White Owl, which had left his quarters in a neighbouring church-tower rather before the accustomed hour, flapped out from the cover. He, however, appeared to pay but little heed to the noisy demonstration of the Crows, as, after continuing his uncertain flight for some distance over the adjacent marshes, he again entered the wood, where he continued searching for prey, utterly regardless of the mobbing of the Crows. I noticed that these birds took not the slightest notice of a Short-eared Owl which was beating over the rushes close at hand. Possibly they were used to the sight of their constant companion the Marsh-Owl (as this species is termed in the district), and considered his white relative an unwelcome stranger.

For building-purposes this Owl resorts to hollow trees, church-towers, old barns, and ruined buildings. The same situation is made use of year after year, unless the tenants are forcibly evicted or destroyed.

In different localities I have heard various names given to this species. Its most common title, perhaps, is the Barn-Owl; but it is also known as the White, Screech, and Church-Owl.

The Plate shows a young bird partly feathered, with the slightly reduced figure of an old male in the background. The sketch is taken from a family group I disturbed in the bell-tower of Chiltington church, near Plumpton, in Sussex.

At times I have found the young birds composing a brood to vary considerably in size; in this instance, however, there was but little difference between the whole of the juvenile members of the family.

RED-BACKED SHRIKE.

LANIUS COLLURIO.

The Red-backed Shrike (known in most country districts as the Butcher bird) is one of the latest of the migratory birds to arrive on our shores in the spring. It is stated by some authors that it makes its appearance in the end of April: this, according to my own experience, is an early date; I have frequently noticed in cold seasons that the first week in May is passed before all the usual stations are occupied each by its pair of Shrikes, who during summer seldom stray far from their accustomed haunt.

This handsome bird may be observed in most parts of Sussex and other southern counties. I have also met with it particularly abundant in the grass country round Harrow-on-the-Hill, ten or a dozen miles north of London, the dense thorn-hedges in that locality being well suited to its requirements for breeding-purposes. In Norfolk, a few scattered pairs have come under my observation in the eastern division of the county; but I have not recognized even a single specimen further north.

The food of this species consists for the most part of beetles, bees of various kinds, dragonflies, and other large insects; these, at times, it impales on the thorn-hedges along its beat; field-mice are also occasionally taken. I cannot at the present moment recall to mind a single instance where I have seen more than two or three victims transfixed on one bush, and seldom, if ever, above half a dozen along a whole hedgerow: according to several published accounts, however, their larders are at times well stocked. The most elaborately garnished twigs I ever had an opportunity of inspecting were a couple of small shoots of whitethorn in the possession of an enterprising naturalist. A scientific gentleman, being anxious to become acquainted with the manners and customs of the Butcher bird, had expressed a wish to examine their larder; and this obliging individual had obtained these two splendid specimens for his edification. Like the marvellous tales in children's story-books which we are told are founded on fact, these interesting collections were fixed on the very twigs which had been made use of by the birds, and contained *among others* the original victims they had themselves impaled*. The reason for this curious habit appears to be extremely doubtful. I once noticed a male flying with what seemed to be an old male Yellowhammer in his beak: though it is stated that the Shrike occasionally destroys young birds, I should hardly have imagined one capable of slaying a full-grown Yellow Bunting.

The nest is a somewhat bulky structure for the size of the bird, consisting of small twigs, green moss, wool, coarse grass, and hair, loosely though neatly put together. In almost every instance that has come under my observation it has been placed in a thick thorn-bush at no great height from the ground.

It is a singular fact that this species lays three distinct varieties of eggs,—a pale pink ground, with red-brown spots; a pale yellow ground, with dark cream-coloured spots; and a still paler yellow or almost a dirty-white ground, with brown or bluish-grey markings. There seems no rule to account for these varieties. Each

* I mention this fact as I have carefully studied one or two published accounts concerning the larder of this species, which so greatly exceeded any thing of the kind I have ever met with, that I am of opinion the writers must have been [illegible]

clutch, however, consists of similar eggs; but the next nest, perhaps within the distance of half a mile or less, may be of one of the other varieties and totally different. I am of opinion I have come across most of the pink shade of egg in Sussex, while the yellow varieties were more commonly met with in Middlesex. In Norfolk the only nest I ever examined contained pink eggs thickly spotted with red-brown.

A young bird that I captured shortly after leaving the nest soon became remarkably tame in confinement. It fed readily on raw meat, but greatly preferred live insects, such as bluebottle flies, beetles, caterpillars, and butterflies or moths. On one occasion I captured an immense dragonfly; this was partially crippled, and then placed on the table in front of his cage. "Bitters" (on account of his habit of jerking his tail, he had been christened "Cock-tail Bitters") was out in a moment, and, after setting at the fly like a miniature gamecock for a few seconds, he commenced the attack. Striking it several blows with his beak, he next seized it at the back of the head with one claw and bit off the head, which he consumed at once with evident relish. The disposal of the body and wings was a somewhat laborious undertaking; but he resolutely refused to quit the spot till he had bolted every vestige of his vanquished foe. The description of beetle known to country people as the "devil's coach-horse" always gave him a severe tussle before it succumbed. At times the insect would pin his assailant with his formidable nippers by the head, when the two would roll over one another in a desperate rough-and-tumble fight, poor Bitters shrieking with rage or pain. These contests seldom lasted more than a minute or two, and Bitters was always good for two or three beetles at a meal. His untimely end was brought about by overfeeding, not sufficient time having been allowed him to throw up the pellets* of a couple of peacock butterflies before offering him some caterpillars of the cabbage-butterfly. Unable to resist these luscious morsels, the unfortunate bird swallowed them and expired from the effects.

As I had so far trained him that he would sit on my finger, and dart at and capture flies and other insects, returning at once to his perch, he would, I imagine, in time have become a most amusing pet.

* These birds throw up the indigestible portions of their food in pellets, after the manner of Owls.

GREAT TIT.

PARUS MAJOR.

In England this bold and lively bird is plentifully dispersed over most of the wooded portions of the country. It becomes less numerous after crossing the Scotch border; and I can call to mind but few instances where I have met with it further north than Perth. On the Outer Islands, according to my own experience, it seems to be unknown.

I have never noticed in this species the habit, so common with most other Titmice, of assembling in flocks during the winter, two, three, or four being, as a rule, the greatest numbers seen together. They appear particularly hardy and regardless of cold. I observed a pair during the severe weather in January 1881, which joined for a few moments the large party of pensioners busily engaged with the food provided for them in front of the windows. After flying down and hurriedly inspecting the bones and scraps of meat, they were up and off at once, the rest of the party being almost helpless from the effects of the continued frost.

I do not know whether we are regularly visited by these birds from across the North Sea; I, however, noticed a single specimen among the feathered passengers that had come on board for rest and shelter, one stormy evening about the middle of October, a few miles east of the 'Newarp' light-ship. The wind was north at the time, blowing fresh after a still morning. When I was making inquiries among the light-ships off the east coast concerning the birds that came on board the vessels during the autumn migration, I could gain no information concerning this species; so I imagine that few, if any, visit us from across the North Sea. The masters or others of the crew kindly undertook to cut off the right wings of all the birds that fell on board; these were forwarded to me from time to time, together with a few remarks as to wind and weather at the time large numbers were obtained; and by these means I was able to form some idea of the seasons at which the flights were passing across the North Sea. During the autumn and winter of 1872, and the spring and summer of the following year, I received thousands of wings from the 'Newarp,' 'Cockle,' 'Lynn Well,' and 'Leman and Ower' floating light-ships.

Several writers mention the interior of old pumps as favourite nesting-quarters for this species. The young birds in my own collection were taken from a nest so placed at Portslade, near Brighton. They also resort to holes in walls, decayed trees, and other similar situations.

In confinement the Great Tit is a sprightly and amusing bird. As I have, however, heard grave charges brought against it, such as a propensity to pick holes in the skulls of its fellow prisoners, it can hardly be considered a desirable acquisition to an aviary of small birds.

COAL TIT.

PARUS ATER.

THE Coal Titmouse is plentiful from north to south, being probably more numerous in some of the fir-plantations of the Highlands than in any other districts. They appear to prefer Scotch firs of moderate size to those of larger growth. Inverness and Ross-shire furnish extensive tracts of recently-planted ground, where this species, in company with Blue Tits and Golden-crested Wrens, may be observed at almost any time of year. During autumn and winter they may frequently be found in small parties making their way across the country.

Those who are not well acquainted with the difference between the Marsh and Coal Titmice may easily distinguish the species while climbing among the trees, if they will only bear in mind the following short description of the two birds:—*Parus palustris* is dull and sober-coloured, while *Parus ater* is somewhat similar, but the wings are slightly relieved by a couple of small white bars near the shoulder, and the back of the head plainly shows a white patch. This small strip of colour is particularly conspicuous while the birds are moving from limb to limb. I am of opinion that this prominent mark has now and then led to the bird being mistaken for the Crested Titmouse. I well remember one instance where a short-sighted naturalist was greatly delighted by watching a small party of Coal Tits that were working their way through a straggling plantation of fir trees in the west of Perthshire, under the impression that he was gaining an insight into the manners and customs of the Crested Titmouse. I humbly ventured to suggest that he was wrong in his supposition as to the identity of the species; but I received at once such a decisive rebuke for my interference that I refrained from any further remarks.

As I perceive by a perusal of some of the recently published works that scientific naturalists are inclined to separate our native Coal Tit from the *Parus ater* of the continent, it may not be out of place for me to state (though I venture no opinion as to the decision of these learned professors) that I have never observed this species at sea while in the act of migration, neither have I ever received a wing* from any of the light-ships off the eastern coasts.

The food of this species is mainly composed of various minute kinds of insects, as well as caterpillars; probably it will also at times partially subsist on seeds. I have repeatedly noticed these birds paying short visits of inspection to the bones and scraps of meat thrown out to the eager companies of pensioners that gather in front of the windows during a protracted frost.

Like the majority of the family, the Coal Tit nests in holes, choosing frequently situations at a low elevation, and at times even underground. It is by no means easy to distinguish their eggs from those of the Marsh-Titmouse; and, indeed, they much resemble in their markings those of others of the family.

* Vide note on the Great Tit.

CRESTED TIT.

PARUS CRISTATUS.

I have only met with this species among the forests in the neighbourhood of the Spey. As a rule they frequent the pine-woods; but I have occasionally noticed a few in the plantations of birch that are found on the low grounds or straggling some distance up the mountain-sides. There is little in their habits or actions, or, indeed, in their appearance at a certain distance, to distinguish them from their relatives the Coal Tits. Both frequent the same forests, and gain their living in much the same manner.

In their native woods they are by no means uncommon; but, owing to the presence of other small birds, such as Coal and Blue Tits, as well as Gold-crests and Willow-Wrens, whose movements among the branches while constantly changing their positions are somewhat similar, they are not easy to identify. If one is anxious to gain a sight of this species, and continues wandering from place to place through the woods, it is possible that a considerable amount of ground may be traversed before the wish is gratified. When keeping quiet for any length of time, either resting, lunching, or more particularly while lying in wait for birds of prey, I have repeatedly observed that it was seldom many minutes elapsed before one or two made their appearance. They seem of a fearless or even an inquisitive disposition, and will now and then approach within a few feet in order to make a close inspection.

The Plate shows the female and the young birds a day or two after quitting the nest. I watched the brood for some hours, and consequently had a good opportunity of ascertaining the manner in which they procured their food. I first discovered the family party in the topmost branches of some large Scotch firs. The female was busily employed in hunting for food among the old stems of the juniper bushes which grew in profusion all round. As soon as a mouthful was procured she flew up to the young ones, who continued calling and hopping from branch to branch, but made no attempt to follow her while searching for their food. As well as I could judge, she collected small insects, such as moths and flies or minute caterpillars, that were abundant among the cover. The male was absent for some hours; and the whole care of providing for the family of six young appeared to devolve on the female.

There is little or no difference between the male and female in this species.

BLUE TIT.

PARUS CÆRULEUS.

This active member of the Tit family appears common in most parts of Great Britain. I have no record among my notes of having observed this species in the Hebrides; so I conclude that, if found at all, it is far from numerous in those barren islands. As far north as Ross-shire it is plentiful in most wooded districts, the specimens in my collection having been obtained in a plantation on the east coast, near Nigg.

The Blue Tit is a most courageous little bird, the female generally resenting an approach to her nest to the utmost of her ability, and occasionally attacking the intruder with the greatest ferocity. The pair that I required as specimens, together with their brood (who were just in the act of leaving the old stump in which they had been hatched), were all captured by means of a butterfly-net, the parents refusing to desert their young.

It is an open question whether this species is so injurious to the buds of fruit-trees as some gardeners would have us believe. At all events, the damage they inflict at one time is amply compensated for by the immense number of insects they destroy when providing for the requirements of their brood.

Like most others of their family, this species, in order to rear its young, resorts to holes in trees, walls, old buildings, and other similar localities. Numerous quaint situations have come under my observation, perhaps the strangest (owing to constant traffic) being a hole in one of the iron lamp-posts in the Montpellier Road, in Brighton. If I remember right, the bird made use of this massive cradle for several years, and safely brought out its brood.

In winter these birds collect in flocks numbering from three or four to a dozen or more. They may commonly be met with frequenting the reed-beds in the eastern counties. I have on several occasions noticed a party join company with Bearded Tits, the two species intermingling while climbing among the stems of the reeds. The partnership, however, would not last long; on being disturbed the Bearded Tits would take a short flight and then drop into the thickest cover, while their visitors, mounting in the air, would betake themselves to fresh quarters. An immense quantity of insect life is to be found among the stems of the reeds during winter; and this abundance of food accounts for the presence of these birds in such localities at this season. Early in November 1881, while sheltering from a storm of wind and rain in a boat-shed which was newly thatched with fresh-cut reed, I noticed that large numbers of caterpillars dropped down from the roof soon after we entered. The smoke from a couple of pipes appeared to disagree with the insects, and they fell down in hundreds. The extensive reed-beds that surround some of the larger broads must contain an endless supply of food for insect-eating birds; and it is strange that some other members of the Titmouse family have not discovered the fact.

MARSH-TIT.

PARUS PALUSTRIS.

It is, in my opinion, extremely doubtful why the scientific name of *Parus palustris* was bestowed on this species. Possibly those who gave it in the first instance were but little acquainted with the true habits of the bird. Small parties of these Tits, it is true, may at times be found frequenting plantations in the neighbourhood of water, or busily engaged in searching for food among the bushes in marshy localities; but the majority of the race are by no means residents in such situations. I have never come across them in the rush-grown dykes of the fen-country or among the reed-beds of the broad-districts of the eastern counties, where, during autumn and winter, numbers of Blue Tits may constantly be observed. To mention the localities they mostly affect is almost impossible; it is hard to describe a spot where a small party might not be met with. I have watched them working their way through the fir-woods in wild and uncultivated tracts of country, and equally at home while pecking about among the grimy litter and stunted bushes of gardens in close proximity to smoky towns. I noticed in the east of Sussex that these birds appear to prefer plantations of moderate-sized undergrowth, where the larger timber consists of oak.

During autumn and winter Marsh-Tits may usually be found in small flocks of six or eight individuals, these parties probably being composed of a pair of old birds with their brood of the previous summer.

Insects furnish the greater part of their diet. At times they may be driven to subsist on seeds; but flies of various kinds, spiders, and other minute insects, together with small caterpillars, are without doubt their favourite food.

The nest is occasionally found in holes in trees or banks. One was pointed out to me some years ago in a small cavity in a grass-park, that must originally have been either a mouse-hole or a bees' nest. The eggs, like those of the rest of the Titmouse family, are, when first laid, of a beautiful pale-pink tinge, with red-brown spots. As soon as incubation commences the beauty of the shell disappears, the general colour becoming a dirty white, and eventually a livid hue.

I have observed this species more numerous in Sussex than in any other county; they are, however, to be noticed in most parts of England that I have visited. In Scotland they are decidedly less plentiful. A few may occasionally be met with in the Lothians; but, with the exception of a few stragglers in the neighbourhood of Dunkeld and near Perth, I have observed none that could be positively identified in the Highlands. In Strathspey and in the east of Ross-shire I have carefully examined the flocks of Coal Tits that frequent the large fir-woods in those districts, but could never with certainty pick out a single specimen of *Parus palustris*.

LONG-TAILED TIT.

PARUS CAUDATUS.

The Long-tailed Titmouse may be observed in greater or smaller numbers in most English counties. In Scotland it also occurs, though I have seldom noticed it in the Northern Highlands.

The elaborately-constructed nest of this species is well known to even the most juvenile of egg-collectors. In its position it varies considerably, being occasionally discovered within a yard of the ground in some prickly furze bush or thorn-hedge, or at a height of twenty or even thirty feet in the branches of some lofty tree. If I remember right, I have never noticed it at any considerable elevation, unless in an oak.

There are some curious descriptions given of the nest in various publications. It has been stated that a couple of apertures are left, by which means the parent birds are able to dispose comfortably of their long tails, their heads being reported to look out from one hole while their caudal appendages protrude from the other. This, I fancy, is simply imagination; if two or more openings have been found in one nest, their presence can only be accounted for by the injury the structure has suffered by removal from its original site. Branches or twigs are built into the outer covering; and when taken, however carefully, some part of the exterior is certain to be torn; and these openings have been considered natural. I have examined nests removed from oak-branches, which might easily be supposed to have been furnished by the builders with a couple of entrances.

These birds are seldom noticed singly during autumn or winter, the families of the preceding summer keeping company till the approach of the following spring. They also occasionally join in considerable flocks.

Strange names are often bestowed on the various members of the Titmouse family by the natives of country districts. The Long-tailed Tit is commonly known as the "Bottle-Tit," and also as the "Feather-poke," both these titles being apparently given on account of the manner in which this species constructs its nest. In the east of Norfolk the Blue Tit is invariably called the "Pickcheese," while the Great Tit is known as the "Saw-sharper," the latter bird in Sussex being not unfrequently styled the "Tinker"—these three names, without doubt, being derived from the call-notes of the birds. In many parts I have found the whole family of the Paridæ known solely as Tom Tits; this, however, does not refer to the east of Norfolk, where that name is given to the Common Wren. I was surprised to find that many of the country people in that district, who earn a considerable amount of money by egg-collecting and are unusually well up in the knowledge of birds, were quite unacquainted with either the Coal or Marsh Tits.

BEARDED TIT.

PARUS BIARMICUS.

The drainage of marshes and reclaiming of waste lands all over the country are banishing numbers of our native birds from the strongholds they have held for ages. This handsome little bird, unlike some of the larger species, is at present in no danger of being entirely driven from our islands, as the more extensive broads and meres in the eastern counties offer them a safe retreat. The districts, however, that are suited to their habits are fast becoming much reduced; several spots where they were formerly common have been completely changed by the new style of farming and other innovations.

In the east of Norfolk this interesting species is still to be found in considerable numbers, though the never-failing persecution they suffer from dealers and collectors tends to greatly restrict their numbers. The price of four shillings a dozen, which is offered for their eggs, induces the natives of those dreary wastes to search diligently; and but few of the first nests ever escape their sharp eyes. After the reeds get up to a certain height it is more difficult to make out the whereabouts of the birds, and consequently the later broods escape. No one but a practised hand would ever discover the nest of this species. There are, however, in the fen and broad districts generally a class of men who make a living by egging, gunning, and fishing. This occupation seems to have been handed down from father to son; but I am afraid that, like many of the rarer denizens of the swamps, they will before long be either driven from their quarters or forced to adopt a new style of life.

Over twenty years ago I observed a small flock in Romney Marsh, in Kent, my attention being attracted to the reed-bed by their clear bell-like notes. Since that time I have occasionally visited the district, but have never met with a single specimen.

The Bearded Titmouse commences its nesting-operations as early as the latter end of March, and would in all probability rear two or three broods in a season if unmolested. The demand for their eggs, however, is, as previously stated, so great that but few of the earlier nests escape. I have on several occasions seen young birds able to leave the nest by the 4th or 5th of May, and so late as the middle of August have known the female sitting on eggs: the nest was accidentally discovered on August 10th. Some years back I noticed early in the summer a couple of pairs on a small island in Heigham Sounds, in Norfolk; and being then in want of a specimen, I shot one of the male birds. On again visiting the spot a week or so later, I discovered that the lone female had joined the other pair (whose nest with six fresh eggs I had previously seen), and had laid five eggs in their nest. The two sets of eggs, the one fresh-laid and the other hard-set, were easily distinguished by their colour, both females being equally demonstrative and excited while we remained in the vicinity of their joint establishment. A day or two later the first eggs were hatched; but I never ascertained how the second clutch progressed.

In winter the Reed-Pheasants (as the marshmen style these birds) join in flocks varying from three or four to ten or fifteen, and keep together till early in the spring. Though such delicate-looking little birds, they are remarkably hardy, and seem able to contend against severe weather with greater success than many much larger and apparently stronger birds. The fact that they can at all times obtain a supply of food from the seeds of the reed and the insects that are found adhering to their stems, as well as shelter in the thick beds of rushes, probably accounts for their lively and active condition during the heaviest storms of snow, when many other species appear numbed by cold and weak and helpless from want.

The nest is generally placed among the stems of the reeds on some boggy spot that is difficult of access, though now and then I have discovered that the birds have selected firmer ground; and in the neighbourhood of Somerton Broad, near Winterton, I found a nest, containing eggs, that was built into the roots of a tussock of rushes in a field of marsh-hay. The leaves and other portions of the reed (*Phragmites communis*) are the principal materials that are used in the construction of their cradle by the Bearded Titmice; and it is wonderful how neat a structure is produced by the means employed. The nests are not unfrequently situated but a few inches above the level of the water, and consequently are extremely liable to be submerged if the tides rise suddenly, either from a heavy fall of rain or a flow of salt water up the rivers. In such cases the birds at once commence a second nest on the top of their first edifice. This habit is so well known to some of the egg-seekers of the district that in wet seasons they invariably scrape up the rubbish below the nests they find, in hopes of discovering another set of eggs.

The first Plate represents the adult male and female with their brood just after leaving the nest. At this early stage it is quite possible to distinguish the males from the females, as the beaks of the former show a yellow tint, while those of the latter are not so brightly coloured.

The second Plate gives the immature birds in the plumage of the first autumn.

PIED FLYCATCHER.

MUSCICAPA ATRICAPILLA.

Though not a particularly scarce species, the Pied Flycatcher is extremely local. My own observations would tend to show that it may be found in considerable numbers in Yorkshire and Cumberland. In Norfolk and Sussex I have now and then met with stragglers at the time of migration, but have noticed no instance of their nesting in any of the southern counties. In Scotland I have seen but two specimens—a female on the Bass rock about the middle of May 1867, and a male in Strathspey a few days earlier the following year. The cracks and crevices among the old ruins on the Bass would afford suitable breeding-quarters for this species; but I could see no signs of a second bird, nor any evidence of a nest. A bitter cold east wind was blowing at the time; and, either to escape its effects or to procure food, the bird appeared unwilling to quit the shelter of the buildings, its favourite resort when disturbed being a dilapidated chimney-stack in a roofless house among the fortifications. At times it made its appearance at the summit, or dashed out from the lower end or the holes in the crumbling stonework. The male that I observed in Strathspey seemed also to be only a visitor to the district. I watched him for some hours frequenting a patch of old timber near the waterside, and concluded his nest must have been near at hand. He was absent, however, on the following day; and no traces of him could be found on searching the wood on several subsequent occasions. Though I have often passed a week or two in the spring in this locality during the last ten years, I have never again met with the species.

In the neighbourhood of Penrith, in Cumberland, I have had many opportunities of studying the habits of these birds. They appear to prefer situations more densely wooded than their relative the Spotted Flycatcher. I observed two or three pairs among the fine old timber in the large woods in the park at Edenhall; and they also frequented the plantations on the banks of the Eden. On two separate occasions in this locality I have come across instances where the nests of this species have been destroyed by other small birds. There was not the slightest doubt that Starlings were the culprits in one case; and I strongly suspect they were also guilty in the second. But a number of the feathers of the Greater Spotted Woodpecker were scattered around; so it is possible that these birds may have dragged out a portion of the nest after a commencement had been made by the Starlings. The hole from which the nest was extracted was eventually deserted by all parties; but the other was made use of by a pair of Starlings, who might have reared their young in peace had they not been shot in order that the Flycatchers might return to their rightful quarters.

Insects of all descriptions, as well as flies, form, I believe, the usual diet of this species. I have more than once known them captured in a Nightingale-trap baited with a mealworm.

What course these birds usually take at the time of their annual migration is, I imagine, influenced by the winds and weather at the time of their flitting. I have seen a single specimen on the North Sea during the autumn, but have never received wings from any of the light-ships off the east coast. Twice I have met with single birds, much fatigued by their journey, within a short distance of the sea-coast between Hastings and Rye. On both occasions the date was within a few days of the first of May.

SPOTTED FLYCATCHER.

MUSCICAPA GRISOLA.

This is one of the latest of our migratory birds to make its appearance in the spring, the middle of May (or even a week later) having usually arrived before its accustomed haunt is taken possession of. The date of its departure is early, the nature of its food probably necessitating a move across the Channel before the appearance of cold weather. It is seldom that one is observed after the beginning of October.

In the south and over most parts of England this quiet and unpretending, though somewhat conspicuous, little bird may be found very generally distributed, though more or less plentiful in certain localities. In Scotland it is to be met with in many districts, its numbers growing scarcer towards the north. I have now and then come across a pair or two in some of the extensive pine-forests of Inverness, and on a few occasions in Ross-shire.

In some parts of the eastern counties I have found this species known to the natives by its familiar title of "Wall-bird;" in most districts in the south it also goes by the same name. It is frequently a matter of no slight difficulty to make out the derivation of some local names; in this instance, however, the reason is obvious. For nesting-purposes in these localities the Spotted Flycatcher generally resorts to a garden-wall, a situation being chosen either where a cavity is formed by the loss of a portion of a brick, or where sufficient space is afforded on the limb of some trained fruit-tree. It also occasionally places its nest on the arm of a fir or some other forest tree.

Although in most parts of England this species frequents gardens and pleasure-grounds, and appears to prefer the vicinity of dwellings, in some of the northern counties it may be met with in the remotest districts.

As its name implies, it gains its living by preying on insect life. According to some writers it is accused of occasionally making inroads on the produce of the fruit-trees; I can, however, state nothing on this subject from my own experience.

KINGFISHER.

ALCEDO ISPIDA.

There is unfortunately a certain class of prowling gunners who never can resist a shot at this beautiful and harmless little bird. Beautiful it certainly is, though its beauty departs with its life, as the effigies one sees in the windows of the ordinary taxidermist are only a caricature of the living bird.

I have met with this species in suitable localities in most parts of England that I have visited. It becomes scarcer, according to my own experience, when the border is crossed; and not above one or two specimens have come under my observation in the Highlands. I have no desire to affirm that the bird is exceedingly rare in the north, as I believe some writers declare it may be commonly seen in several different counties; I only state that it has escaped my notice.

In Sussex the Kingfisher is, or rather was, especially numerous. During autumn I have, in days gone by, often observed as many as forty or fifty of these birds fishing in the channels among the mudbanks in the Nook at Rye. They used to commence working down the creeks soon after the turn of the tide; and, closely following the falling water, they found abundant food in the numerous shallow pools. About half-flood they would generally make a move, flying up the creeks, and so on, to the small drains that led through the marshes, and then dispersing themselves over the levels. I have occasionally observed a score or two fly past in small parties of threes and fours within a quarter of an hour while watching them from the shingle-banks close at hand, one or two now and then steadying themselves for a moment and then making a dash after a shrimp or small sea-fish. Twenty years makes a difference in most things: the mudbanks and creeks are certainly gone; and I expect the numerous parties of Kingfishers that frequented them remain only in the memory of those who have had the pleasure of watching them. The last time I visited the spot some fine specimens of South-Down mutton were grazing stolidly and complacently on the luxuriant turf that had formed where previously hundreds of acres of mudbanks were covered by every flowing tide.

I perceive this habit of coming down to the salt water, and even into the harbours, is common at several ports of the south coast during autumn. If unmolested these birds are remarkably unsuspicious of danger. I have on several occasions, when the tide was low, watched a bird or two early in the morning, before the day's work had commenced, perched on the chain cables of the colliers lying alongside the wharfs in the harbours both of Rye and Shoreham, their bright colours, lit up by the rising sun, being peculiarly attractive against the grimy background. Intent on watching for their prey, they would pay not the slightest heed to a boat dropping past with the tide within ten or a dozen yards of their station.

In the broad-districts of the east of Norfolk the birds are not nearly so common as might be expected. A few stragglers may be met with during autumn and winter; but, owing to the flat nature of the country, they are forced to seek other localities for breeding-purposes. While Snipe-shooting one winter round Hickling Broad, I noticed some small object splashing in the water at the side of a dyke; and on proceeding to the spot, I discovered an unfortunate Kingfisher that had come to grief in a rather singular manner. The bird had evidently at some former time been struck by a shot, which had passed through the upper mandible. This wound was quite healed up; but a small piece of the horny substance of the beak had been splintered, and into the crack produced by the fracture two or three of the small fibres which form part of the flowers or seeds of the reed were so firmly fixed, that the bird was held fast. While flying up the dyke it must have brushed too closely to the reeds that grew on the banks and been caught in the manner described. The struggles of the captive had broken down the reed, which was lying flat on the water, except when lifted up by the victim in his vain attempts to escape. When released from his unpleasant position he flew off, apparently none the worse for the mishap.

I have come across a few quiet spots in the southern counties where this species is in the habit of breeding regularly. In every instance the bank resorted to was either directly overhanging the stream or in its immediate vicinity. It has been stated that rats' holes are occasionally made use of; but those I examined were, I am confident, excavated by the birds themselves. The layer of small fish-bones on which the young or eggs are found are frequently described as the nest; these bones, however, in my opinion, are simply the castings thrown up by the birds.

Many who are well acquainted with the appearance of the Kingfisher as it darts like a flash of light from its perch on the penstock or a branch overhanging some small stream during the bright days of summer, would fail to recognize the dingy-looking bird that would be presented to their view on a dull and gloomy day in winter, when the stream looks black against the surrounding snow. Under these circumstances a Kingfisher has more the appearance of a Dipper or Water-Ouzel. I have repeatedly noticed this fact.

CHOUGH.

CORVUS GRACULUS.

Up to the present date I have met with few opportunities for closely studying the habits of this species. I was never enabled positively to identify the bird on the south-east coast of Scotland, though they were said to be occasionally met with when I first visited that district, now over twenty years ago. A pair or two were now and then sighted at a safe distance on the wildest part of the south-west coast, where they were, I believe, far from uncommon; but I remained an almost total stranger to the Chough till I explored the rocky portions of the Cornish coast.

The Daw, as this bird is called by the natives (Jackdaws are known as Chaws), is now far from plentiful in the county from which it takes its name; and miles of rocky ground along the summits of the cliffs may be passed over without more than a stray bird or two being noticed. During autumn Choughs appear to keep away from their roosting-quarters for the whole of the day, seldom showing themselves in the vicinity of the place in which they intend to pass the night till the afternoon is well advanced. Owing to their scarcity, and the rocky and impracticable nature of the ground they frequent, I met with considerable difficulties while endeavouring to gain an insight into the movements of these birds. As far as I was able to ascertain, the few pairs that came under my observation seldom strayed far from the sea-coast, apparently following a regular and well-known course along the shore or over the cliffs, and only making a halt on any likely spot where food might present itself. Though I repeatedly examined, with the greatest care, the numerous parties of Rooks and Jackdaws scattered over the fields within a few miles of the shore, I never detected a single Red-legged Crow among them. If met with at a certain hour along the coast, there was but little doubt that, within a few minutes of the same time, they would make their appearance on the following day. When once well known, Choughs are readily distinguished at a considerable distance. Their actions on the ground are more active, and their walk more sprightly, than those of either the Rook or Jackdaw.

Worms and grubs appear to furnish a considerable portion of their diet; and it is seldom one will pass a lump of cow- or horse-dung without thoroughly investigating it. Rapidly sweeping the bill from side to side, the fragments are scattered in all directions. During the whole operation the bird will be bowing and scraping in the most amusing manner, and occasionally rising a short distance in the air, at times uttering its well-known cry. The flight of the Chough is also slightly different from that of his sable relatives. Though a pair may be noticed winging their way along the coast in a straight course, they will frequently pause, wheel round, and then proceed in an undulating manner, rising and falling to a considerable height; and, both in the air and on the land, the Cornish Daw may be said to conduct himself with a more jaunty bearing than the rest of the family.

I remarked that a pair which frequented the coast near Porthleven paid invariably (unless disturbed) a short visit during the afternoon to a sandy bay, where they remained stalking round the pools of water left by the tide. What food they secured I am unable to discover. They also alighted, on more than one occasion, on a field from which potatoes were being lifted; and here they diligently explored the fresh-turned soil; but whether worms or the smaller roots were the object of their search, it was impossible to decide. At times the pair would settle down in the roadway that ran through a small village consisting of a few scattered hovels; and here they seemed to have but little respect for the youngsters who now and then rushed from the dwellings and pelted them with stones, as they moved but a short distance when assailed. They were, however, as cunning as the Rook (who is declared to smell powder), as the sight of a doubtful-looking individual with a gun was sufficient to put them immediately on guard; and when once their suspicions are aroused there are few birds more wary.

Though my visit to the parts of the coast where these birds may still be met with was in the autumn, I examined several situations in which their nests had been placed and, I believe I may add, in nearly every instance, robbed. Ledges in almost perpendicular rock were at times resorted to; occasionally, however, their quarters are by no means dangerous to reach. I closely inspected two or three cavities among the slabs of stone in the rough and broken face of the cliffs, from which young birds had been removed during the past season, and where the nests were still remaining. To these a very moderate climber might have made his way with but little difficulty or risk. The crumbling sides of the funnel-hole, the well known "Tol pedn penwith," in the neighbourhood of the Land's End, are still used as a nesting-place; and here a few pairs resort at roosting-time during the autumn. It is, however, hopeless for them to rear their young, as the natives of the fishing-villages in the vicinity make a regular business of taking them, as soon as they can with safety be removed. In one or two other localities that are not so well known, it is possible that a brood or two may still escape, though I fear, from all I could learn, these favoured spots are few and far between. As I have only to plead guilty to causing the death of a pair of Choughs, I can hardly be accused of having accelerated their extermination in any very alarming degree.

The cause of their scarcity on the Cornish coast is not hard to find. There is a great demand for young birds; all that are taken command a ready sale. Consequently, as the nests are not, as a rule, in situations very difficult to be reached by those accustomed to the use of ropes, at the end of the breeding-season there are few beside old birds left. If such wholesale robbery is continued, the result is not difficult to anticipate, and its accomplishment can hardly be long delayed.

In several districts the Chough seems to have become extinct without having suffered any very great amount of persecution, unless perhaps the Jackdaws may be responsible for intruding on their haunts. Some authors state that these birds, in days gone by, frequented the inland rocks in several of the wildest Highland glens; and local tradition tells the same story, though neither, as far as I am aware, can give reasons for their disappearance, or the date at which it is supposed to have occurred. It is a strange fact that now and then a wanderer returns to the identical spot that was formerly the home of his race. A few years back a curious bird was noticed by a stalking-party in the upper part of Glen Cannich; and as there was at the moment no fear of disturbing the deer, the stranger was cautiously approached and brought down by a rifle-bullet, when it proved to be a Chough. Though they were said formerly to have frequented the glen, the time of their departure was a mystery even to the oldest inhabitant.

There are, I expect, few parts of the British Islands, with the exception of the Cornish coast, where the whole of the Crow family might be in view at the same time. One afternoon, early in November 1880, while waiting near the old mine at Trewavas for a shot at a pair of Choughs, which were working their way along the coast towards their roosting-quarters in the rocky cliffs at Rinsey, I was enabled, by turning from east to west, plainly to distinguish, by the help of the glasses, no less than two or three representatives of each branch of the family. The Choughs previously mentioned were searching for food on a grassy bank that sloped down towards the shore; a pair of Ravens, croaking loudly, hovered round the rocks immediately below where I was concealed; numbers of Jackdaws clustered on the chimney and buildings of the ruined mine; while at a lower elevation two or three of a small party of Grey Crows, who frequented the shore, were busily engaged with some shell-fish. Further inland a pair of Black Crows kept watch on all sides from the stone dyke that separated the pasture above the cliffs from the cultivated ground; and a large flock of Rooks were scattered over the hill-side towards the north. In addition to these, a couple of Magpies had occupied themselves for a considerable time in investigating some carrion lying at the edge of a pool of water in the nearest hollow towards the west.

During my wanderings in that district, while attempting to pick up a knowledge of the habits of this species, I made the acquaintance of an antiquated native of a small village in the neighbourhood of the coast, who well remembered the time when these birds had been plentiful along the cliffs in most parts of the county. The poor old fellow evidently looked back with regret on the days when he had been enabled to shoot them in such numbers that a Daw-pie was by no means an uncommon addition to his usual humble fare; but he remarked, with a sigh, that he had not tasted one for the last sixteen years. As he occasionally made himself useful by the information concerning the locality he was able and willing to supply, and volunteered one day to drive up and signal the approach of a pair of Choughs, which were visible on a grassy slope at a short distance to the west, I asked him, when he had successfully performed his work, if he would not join us at lunch-time. It is needless to state that he was soon hard at work at an enormous hunch of bread and meat, and, what was far more to his liking, an unlimited supply of bottled Bass. As the beer disappeared, the old man gradually became more communicative as to his personal affairs, and eventually disclosed the fact that he was no stranger to the various hardships and adventures of a smuggler's life. After dilating in a somewhat rambling fashion on several of what I suppose he considered the most stirring and exciting episodes of his chequered career, he concluded by remarking, with a quiet chuckle and evidently intense satisfaction, "buried my ole 'oman last Friday."

RAVEN.

CORVUS CORAX.

This quaint bird is very generally distributed over the country, being found in larger or smaller numbers from north to south. The wild and deserted ranges of moor and the steep hillsides of the Highlands, as well as the broken and precipitous cliffs of the adjacent islands, are most suited to its habits; and here it may be met with at all seasons of the year.

I believe that a partial migration takes place in some parts of the north, as I have noticed, during several years, a large increase to the numbers of these birds on the hill-sides of the north-west of Perthshire as soon as autumn commenced, the first comers usually making their appearance early in September. As but few pairs nested in the district, it was easy to notice the time of their arrival, parties of ten or a dozen, and now and then a score, being observed hunting over the moors. I have no evidence that our shores are visited by migrants from the north of Europe; so I consider it most probable these birds had strayed from some part of the Northern Highlands or the desolate islands off the west coast. The immense numbers of blue hares that infest the hills in this part of the country are without doubt the main attraction to the locality. As winter advanced I have on several occasions seen large flocks collected together on ground where an extensive hare-drive has been held. It was no uncommon sight to have from fifty to sixty Ravens in view at once while going over the hills on the day following the shooting. For several seasons I made a practice of closely observing these gatherings, in order to become thoroughly acquainted with the numbers and variety of the vermin frequenting the district. As the Ravens were collected to feed on the wounded hares that escaped from the guns, they were simply acting the part of scavengers on the ground, and their visits were beneficial rather than otherwise.

In the vicinity of their nesting-quarters I have good evidence that they will destroy both young birds and eggs. The few pairs that breed in the west of Perthshire usually have their nests at a considerable elevation among the hills; and I noticed them on several occasions carrying off the eggs of the Ptarmigan. In some of the wilder islands off the west coast these birds, together with the Grey Crows, wage a constant war against the eggs or young of the few Grouse that manage to subsist in their neighbourhood.

There is nothing in the way of carrion that will come amiss to these keen-sighted birds. I have observed them preying on every kind of animal refuse cast up by the waves, disputing, both on the shores of the salt-water lochs and on the hill-sides, with Gulls, Crows, and Buzzards for the carcasses of defunct seals, sheep, horses, or hares, and barely giving place when the Sea-Eagle made his appearance and claimed his share. It is also well known among shepherds in the north that weakly sheep or lambs are now and then attacked while living, the ravenous birds snatching their favourite portions from the quivering victim before life is extinct. Several times during September and October 1876, while passing over the South Downs near Saddlescombe in Sussex, I noticed a pair of Ravens flying from the Dyke Hill. A year or so later a dead body or, rather, a skeleton was discovered in a patch of furze near the top of the hill. The remains and the clothing had been so much destroyed by the attacks of vermin and exposure to weather that it was almost impossible to judge to whom they might have belonged. A few scraps, probably from an old fustian jacket, the toe-cap and sole of a boot, and the texture of the small remaining pieces of rag, indicated that their owner had belonged to the labouring class or might have been a tramp. As the Ravens were always noticed near the same spot, I have not the slightest doubt that they had discovered the body, and returned there regularly to feed as long as they could find any thing to prey upon. Though I have passed the same hill repeatedly of late years, I have never seen one of these birds within miles of the spot since the autumn previous to the discovery of the remains.

Game-preservers are so accustomed to look upon the Raven as an enemy, that they commonly forget his black feathers may possibly conceal a few redeeming qualities. There is, however, little doubt that in some districts he will consume a number of rats in the course of the year. I watched one on the shores of the Firth of Forth, near Tantallon, busily engaged in making a meal off a large rat he had surprised below high-water mark. Quantities of these destructive brutes resort during the summer to this part of the coast, betaking themselves in winter to the farmsteadings. Other instances of an almost similar nature have come under my notice.

The Raven, like most of the Crow tribe, is remarkably easy to capture by means of traps. Though generally considered a cunning and sagacious bird, he appears to be unable to resist a bait, even if he has witnessed one of his kind struggling at the identical spot a short time previously. While laying out traps a few years back in Perthshire, early in September, for some Buzzards which had been seen frequenting the high moors (one or two of which I was anxious to secure as specimens), I noticed that large flocks of Ravens were busy searching the hills for food. We had only set one trap, and moved about a quarter of a mile to prepare a spot for another, when I became aware by the commotion among the black party that one of their number must have been taken. Between a dozen and a score were flying in circles over the place, darting down and croaking in the greatest excitement. When we had completed the second trap, we returned to the first, and, after removing the victim and resetting the trap, proceeded uphill to set a third. Before the work was again finished it was evident that two more were taken; and during the whole day we could set no more than four traps, as I did not like to leave the poor brutes when I knew they were struggling in the traps. Every bird caught after the first one (and there were over a dozen captured) must have seen the fate of those that approached the bait; but it had no effect as a warning. As I stated previously, these Ravens were perfectly harmless on the moors at this season; and though I have known as many as two or three hundred captured before the winter set in, it would, I am now convinced, have been no detriment to the ground had they remained unmolested. It was, however, impossible to set a trap in the open with any conspicuous bait without it being sooner or later discovered by these birds.

Early in September 1866 I captured, in the north-west of Perthshire, a Raven whose tongue protruded through a small hole in the loose membrane under the lower mandible. The skin was perfectly healed round the wound, though the bifurcation at the base of the tongue prevented the bird retracting it into the mouth. It is difficult to imagine how such a mishap could possibly have been brought about, unless it was caused by a sharp-pointed bone belonging to some prey that the bird had been tearing, which passed through the skin, and was followed by the tongue in the efforts of the sufferer to clear the wound. This Raven was in perfect health and plumage, and weighed as much as (if not more than) two or three others taken at the same time. During the following year I trapped another in precisely the same plight. As in the former case, its misfortune appeared to have had not the slightest effect on its health or condition.

In order to become thoroughly acquainted with the manner in which the Raven gains its living, and also to study its habits when in company with other birds of prey, I have at different times put up bothies or shelters on the mountain-side, from which I was enabled to watch some dead carcase—either a sheep that had succumbed to disease, or a worn-out horse we had driven uphill and slaughtered for the purpose. Several writers have described so exactly how these foul-feeding birds revel in the midst of the decomposing remains and contend with loud and angry screams over their putrid banquet, that it is useless for me to enter into the details of such an unsavoury subject.

In the north this species nests on ledges and in crevices among the rugged and broken slabs of stone in the most inaccessible parts of the inland mountains, and also in wild rocky precipices overhanging the sea. On various parts of the coast a few stragglers may still be met with all round our islands. One or two pairs resort to the chalk cliffs near Beachy Head in Sussex; and I have several times observed the birds in the neighbourhood of the Lizard and the eastern portion of Mount's Bay, and also along the wild and moss-grown headlands between the Logan Rock and the Land's End. I am afraid the greater number of those that frequented the large woods in the interior of the country are now driven from their quarters by the felling of the timber or constant persecution. The nest itself is a large coarse structure, heather-stalks being freely used in its composition in the barren districts of the north, and the architects making use of whatever branches and twigs come nearest in other localities. The interior is a mixture of sheep's wool, moss, hair, fine grass, and other soft materials.

The Plate shows an adult bird with a dead white hare—a common sight on the hill-tops on the day following a big drive in many counties in the Highlands.

The tricks and eccentricities of Ravens in confinement have frequently been described and commented upon by various writers; and numbers of these birds whose habits were more or less peculiar and amusing have come under my own observation. I cannot, however, pass over, without a few remarks, one that I became acquainted with while at the University. In the centre of the town of Cambridge there was in those days (now over twenty years ago) an establishment well known to most undergraduates whose tastes inclined towards sporting matters. Any one who remembers the graphic sketch of the dog-dealer's yard in 'Tommiebeg Shootings' can form an idea of the place, as the surroundings were almost identical. Rifle-shooting, practised after an original method at live pigeons, drew sundry embryo marksmen; but the main attraction was the spacious pit, in which all sorts of battles between birds and beasts used to be fought, in addition to the legitimate sport of ratting. The encounter between the tame Raven and a rat could hardly be termed a fight, as it invariably ended in the discomfiture of the quadruped. A large strong rat would, however, occasionally prove a tough customer. After having flown several times at the head of the bird, it would discover it could not face the terrible raps it received from the powerful bill of its adversary, and, partly crippled, would attempt to seek safety by flight. The aspect of the Raven would now have been a fine study for an artist; with every feather on end, hopping and croaking, and occasionally almost screaming with rage, he would relentlessly pursue his retreating victim round and round the pit. When at length a lucky blow had put an end to the contest and "Old Nick" (the Raven) had been lifted out of the pit, he would shuffle off across the yard to his cage, bearing in his beak the body of his fallen foe, on which to regale himself at his leisure. His roguish glance of distrust at the company, evidently fearing to be robbed of his prey, while he sidled back to his den was comical in the extreme.

The domestic arrangements of the happy family that were inmates of the same enclosure with "Old Nick" were at feeding time exceedingly amusing. The group, as near as I can remember, consisted of a Goose (a pink-footed, winged on Midsummer Common), some Owls, a few small Hawks, a couple of Magpies, a single Jay, and two or three Jackdaws. If it happened that his sable Majesty had been performing in the pit and his appetite was appeased, he would content himself with simply examining every piece of food that was provided, and then retiring to his favourite perch he would quietly regard the contentions of his subjects, apparently thoroughly disgusted by their gluttony. When, however, he was "sharp" like the rest, his excitement increased as the hour drew near, till at last, when the basket containing his toothsome repast appeared in sight, he positively danced with delight; and small indeed were the portions that would have fallen to the share of his companions in captivity had their interests not been looked after by the attendant. There never was a better illustration of the old Scotch saying, "He needs a lang spune that sups wi' the De'il."

BLACK CROW.

CORVUS CORONE.

From north to south the Black Crow is scattered over the country. I never identified a specimen in the Outer Hebrides; but with this exception I have met with it in almost every part of England and Scotland. Though by no means abundant in any district I am acquainted with, I found the most frequent opportunities of studying the habits of this species in the west of Perthshire and in the east of Norfolk.

These crafty birds do not appear to flock together like Grey Crows. The brood of the previous summer, however, usually keeps with the parents during the whole of the autumn and winter, the family (in many instances that have come under my observation) only breaking up on the approach of spring or the death of some of their number. I am aware it has been stated by more than one author that Black Crows take their departure southward on the approach of winter. This I have never remarked. In every district where I have been able constantly to keep a watch on the species they remained stationary during the whole year.

The bad character borne by these Crows, and the persecution they suffer in consequence at the hands of gamekeepers, easily accounts for their number being kept within bounds. In any locality where preserving is neglected Black Crows increase rapidly, and levy a heavy tax on eggs and young birds. I have never witnessed them in the act of destroying lambs; but I see no cause for discrediting the stories I have heard to that effect from shepherds and keepers. It is well known to all who have studied their habits in a wild state that no flesh comes amiss to them; and as I have found them, in company with Grey Crows, making a meal on sheep before they were cold, I think it highly probable they only require to find one in a weakly or disabled condition to commence operations at once. These birds cause far greater destruction to game in England than the Grey Crow, as the latter, for the most part, take their departure early in the spring for their breeding-haunts in the northern counties or across the North Sea. I have had many opportunities of witnessing the havoc they will commit among the eggs and young broods of the various species of Waders that nest on the marshes in the neighbourhood of some of the large broads in the east of Norfolk. Every small plantation within a mile or so of the water-side contains a pair at least of these inveterate thieves. During spring and summer they may be noticed frequently hunting over the swamps and rush-grown marshes, the shrill cries of the Peewit and Redshank being constantly heard while they are hovering over the vicinity of their nesting-quarters. On searching the ground I have discovered plenty of proof of their evil deeds, in the shape of empty egg-shells scattered about in all directions. The Snipe-shooting in this locality would be greatly benefited if these birds were restricted in number; keepers, however, are few and far between, and the game is mostly left to the tender mercies of poachers. I have repeatedly watched Black Crows feeding on the maize or Indian corn supplied to some decoy-ducks I kept on Hickling Broad, and carrying off any bread or meat that had been thrown to them. In the same neighbourhood a farmer, who cultivated a few acres of ground, assured me these birds totally destroyed a small field of beans. Whether these plunderers ever make any reparation (after the manner of the Rook) for the robberies they have committed is, I am of opinion, an open question. It is probable a certain quantity of destructive grubs and insects form part of their diet; and I have no doubt, from what I have observed, that they clear off large numbers of mice, if not young rats and voles, during the course of the year.

Many years ago I frequently observed this species pairing with the Grey Crow in the Highlands; and for some time I believed, when this was the case, that the young took after one or the other of the parents. In the summer of 1866, when living in the north-west of Perthshire, I trapped one young bird and shot another near the same spot, both of which exhibited signs of being a cross between the two species. In each case the plumage of the whole of the body was black, with the exception of a small patch of grey on the neck and back. On first examining them I was in doubt whether they might be young Jackdaws, being uncertain whether that species had a white eye in the immature state. A glance at a Jackdaw's nest, however, disclosed the fact that the iris is of the same colour in the mature and immature stages. A few days later two more young birds, in almost similar plumage, were killed in the same glen by the keeper, who reported that he saw them flying after a pair of old Crows, one of which was black and the other grey. During the remainder of my residence in Perthshire I met with no further opportunities of observing this curious intermediate plumage. We kept down so effectually the whole race of Crows, whether Grey or Black, that I do not remember a single young one being hatched out in the neighbourhood. There were usually several Black Crows to be seen early in the spring; these in every instance paired with Grey Crows. I never met with a pair of Black Crows in that part of the Highlands. I often remarked that, however closely any species of this description of vermin might be killed down, the places of those destroyed were filled up the following season. As but little attention was paid to preserving on many of the adjoining shootings, there was always a reserve of Crows close at hand to fill up all vacancies.

A few years later I again fell in with the Black and Grey Crows interbreeding in the more northern counties. The result of my observations only confirmed the opinion I had previously formed, viz. that the offspring most frequently resembled either one or the other of the parents, though occasionally they showed a half-and-half state of plumage. The information I received from foresters and keepers in the various districts I passed through plainly indicated that those who had paid any attention to these birds were all aware of the same facts; and in almost every case their experience was identical with my own. It appears that certain scientific naturalists have at length arrived at the conclusion that the Grey and the Carrion or Black Crow are simply varieties of one and the same species. According to the experience of several careful observers and sportsmen, the progeny of a pair of birds, where one is black and the other grey, may be either perfectly Black or Grey Crows, or even young ones exhibiting a curious mixture of colour, black, as a rule, predominating. This agrees with what I have myself witnessed and the reports I have received from keepers in various parts of the Northern Highlands. Some writers also assert they met with Crows showing "every stage of plumage, from pure black to the perfectly marked Hooded Crow, and this without reference *to age or sex*" (the italics are my own). As I have never come across these hybrids paired and breeding, I conclude the writers must have been more successful in their observations than myself. Unless the birds had been clearly distinguished engaged in nesting-operations, I should be of opinion it was scarcely justifiable to state that they had been recognized *at all ages*. It is, however, quite possible that such observations may have been made and recorded in some work to which I have not had access. I should not have noticed these statements, had I not called to mind that they somewhat differed from the ideas of a very close observer of nature (a resident in Inverness) with whom I had, some years ago, several discussions on the above subject. This old Highlander was perfectly convinced in his own mind that whatever colours the offspring of the Grey and Black Crows might take in their first plumage they would eventually turn into either the perfect Black or Grey Crow. The facts he related would certainly lead to the belief that such changes must (occasionally at least) take place.

As I have never yet had an opportunity of rearing any of these hybrids and keeping them in confinement for any length of time, I am unable to give an opinion on the subject.

Though I have frequently observed the Grey or Hoodie Crow, at the time of migration, in the act of making the passage of the North Sea, I was never able positively to identify the Black Crow. From the crews of the light-ships off the east coast I could gather but little information concerning them. It is probable that a few, at all events, reach this country during the autumn, as I recognized a bird of this species on board a fishing-boat a short distance off Yarmouth, and the skipper informed me it had flown on board that morning.

The Black Crow is to be met with in many parts of the British Islands; and I have spent a considerable amount of time in studying their habits; but in no single instance have I ever noticed them nesting (even where one was mated with a Grey Crow) except on trees or bushes. I mention this fact, as I believe it is reported by some writers that their manner of breeding corresponds with that of Grey Crows, whose nests, as often as not, are placed on a cliff or an inland precipice. I have of course not the slightest wish to question these statements; I merely describe the habits of the birds as I have witnessed them. The nest is a large and coarse structure. The outside materials vary according to the locality, the birds making use of whatever sticks and twigs they find easiest to collect. Heather-stalks and roots, together with branches of birch or fir, are largely used in the Highlands. Nests that I have examined in the southern and eastern counties were composed of dead twigs of the trees that grew nearest at hand. The remains of an old nest that has been occupied in former years is often resorted to and patched up. The interior is warm and comfortable, being lined with sheep's wool, hair, dried strands of fine grass, or any soft material.

I was particularly struck by the depth and warmth of the interior of the cradle that a pair of Crows (one Black, the other Grey) had prepared for their anticipated brood. The nest was placed on the topmost branches of a lofty tree overhanging a hill-burn that dashed down the mountain-side through a rift or chasm in the solid rock. Both parents having been shot within an hour of one another, the nest was now untenanted; and I was anxious to remove it, so that it might no longer attract any wandering Crow to the spot. To reach it by climbing was decidedly risky, even if practicable. The branches of the tree on which it was built stretched over the gorge, at an angle that looked excessively dangerous; and it appeared that, to take the nest, the whole limb would need to be sawn off. Before commencing this somewhat arduous undertaking, I resolved to attempt to cut it down by means of a rifle-bullet. The main branch, that sustained the nest, was not less than from two to three inches in diameter immediately below the structure; but having found a convenient rest for the rifle, the operation was completed far more rapidly than I had anticipated. The first shot cut away a considerable portion of the supporting limb; and the second having smashed the remainder, the nest and the surrounding twigs dropped at once. Being caught, however, by a lower arm of the tree, it needed a third shot to bring it to the ground. The eggs, which were partly incubated, had fallen out and smashed among the rocks. While examining the materials with which the nest was composed, I discovered the remains of the shell of the egg of a Ring-Ouzel still adhering to some of the sticks. This had probably been brought as food to the female while sitting. The situation chosen by this pair of Crows was particularly suitable to the requirements of these ever-watchful and rapacious birds. From the upper branches of the tree an uninterrupted view could be obtained of the wild and rocky glen, rendering an undetected approach to their quarters almost impossible; while the steep and rugged banks of the burn (concealed in several parts by long and rank heather) inveigled many an unfortunate sheep to its doom, affording, consequently, an almost inexhaustible supply of food. It was seldom, if ever, that I passed the spot without noticing a carcass or two of highly scented mutton slowly decomposing in some quiet pool, or firmly wedged between the stones that formed the rocky bed of the torrent. I was greatly amused one spring at the horror expressed by a stranger to the district (more used to paved footways than mountain-sides), who persisted in indulging in a copious draught of the sparkling waters of this identical stream. Weary and utterly fagged out by the unusual exertion, he made his way to the side of the burn, a few yards below the spot where it emerged from the steepest part of the gorge, and, accepting as a hoax my repeated warnings that within the next hundred yards he might find the remains of at least half a dozen defunct sheep, he totally disregarded the advice that a wee drop of the cratur might help to qualify the possible impurities, and, hastily snatching a cuach* from the hands of one of the gillies, he emptied it again and again. I shall never forget his look of hopeless dismay (or the doses of whiskey needed to bring about his recovery) when, mounting a few steps farther up the hill-side, he looked down and became aware of the revolting spectacle in the pool, immediately above the spot where he had quenched his thirst. A dead ewe almost blocked up the course of the water (now low from continued drought); and the tiny streamlet that bubbled slowly along meandered peacefully through the decaying carcass, and found a vent near the chest, where the bones were split asunder from the force of the fall or the effects of decomposition.

* A wooden drinking-cup; pronounced "quay."

GREY CROW.

CORVUS CORNIX.

The Grey Crow is a permanent resident in almost every part of the Highlands that I am acquainted with. It is allowed to nest occasionally in some of the southern counties of Scotland; but I have not (with certainty) observed it breeding further south than Perthshire. In England it is likewise reported to remain at times during summer in certain districts on the north-east coast. Some years ago I watched a pair or two that frequented the moors and rocky glens in the neighbourhood of Whitby; but this is all the information I am able to give on my own authority.

This species usually arrives on the east coast of England about the middle of October, the 7th, 8th, 12th, and 14th being dates on which I have met with large numbers either just landed or on the passage. It is probable that they continue to cross for some weeks later, as I have fallen in with several stragglers in the North Sea well on in November.

In some parts of the Highlands these birds occasionally desert their quarters on the hill-sides during winter, and betake themselves to the vicinity of the farm-yards and the low grounds. On the shores of the firths and the lochs in the neighbourhood of the coast, they may at this season be found in great numbers; but I am ignorant whether these birds are migrants from the North Sea, or only visitors from inland glens attracted to the shore by the prospect of more abundant prey.

In the south Grey Crows generally frequent the sea-coast, living on the dead fish or any decomposing remains that may be cast up by the tide. When more substantial food is scarce, they also manage at times to subsist by extracting the contents of mussels, cockles, and other small shells they are able to pick up along the shore. I have often noticed them, on the large broads in the east of Norfolk, flying one after another over the litter washed up on the lee shore, hunting for any dead or wounded birds that might have escaped from the gunners. As soon as a prize was discovered, the croaking and screaming of those near at hand would bring the whole of the black fraternity together with frantic haste; and, living or dead, the unfortunate victim would speedily have its flesh torn from its bones.

These troublesome pests have frequently destroyed fowl I knocked down before there was a chance to bring them to bag. This has occurred repeatedly in all parts of the country; but the most wholesale robbery of this description was perpetrated in the east of Ross-shire. While gunning on Loch Slyn one stormy day during the winter of 1868, I succeeded in making (more by good luck than management) a heavy shot at a large flock of Mallard as they rose from a bank on which they had been resting. Owing to the long heather that grew round the shores of the loch, we experienced considerable difficulty in collecting the cripples, many of the wounded crawling into the thick cover before we were able to gather up those nearest at hand. Not expecting any use for a dog (it was blowing a gale of wind), I had left my retriever at a farm by the loch-side, and consequently failed to secure several disabled birds that could never have escaped the nose of that infallible quadruped. An hour or so later I remarked a large party of Grey Crows, numbering in all at least forty or fifty birds, screaming and quarrelling near the spot where I had fired the shot. On returning and again searching the ground, we discovered they had succeeded in dragging from their hiding-places seven more Ducks. Four were cleanly picked, though the remaining three had only been sufficiently torn to render them useless. The following morning we detected two more skeletons, which had previously escaped our notice. A dozen fowl at least had fallen to the share of the Crows at this single discharge. In addition to the remains we found, they had evidently got possession of three or four which dropped in a swamp, where we had not attempted to reach them.

With good cause game-preservers look upon the whole of the Crow tribe with distrust; and the present species may be considered the worst of a bad lot. On the moors in the north they are without exception the most destructive vermin a keeper has to contend with. They may be seen in the spring quartering the ground like setters; and the nest of a Grouse or other game-bird, once discovered, is soon robbed of its contents. These thieves usually have some elevated spot to which they carry the eggs before sucking them, leaving the empty shells lying about in dozens, as if to draw attention to their bad deeds. I have occasionally found eggs consumed close by the nests from which they were stolen; but I believe their most common custom is to remove them to one of their favourite feeding-places. A pair of Crows will have several of these stations; and the number of eggs they destroy would appear incredible to any one who had not carefully watched their proceedings. At times they will resort to trees to consume their plunder. One spring, while in the west of Perthshire, I noticed a pair of Crows very busily engaged in the topmost branches of some trees, in the upper part of a birch-wood that covered a sloping hill-side. On examining the spot a day or two later, I discovered, under some of the highest trees, the shells of between twenty and thirty eggs. In almost every instance it was evident black game had been the sufferers from their depredations. When Grey Crows attack eggs too large or heavy for them to carry off conveniently, they break holes in the shells, and extract the contents without removing them. In the nests of the White-tailed Eagle and the Osprey I have seen their work; and I have also known them to destroy and subsequently devour the young of the Golden Eagle after one of the parent birds had been shot. From observations I have made in the Highlands, I believe that this species is in the habit of visiting the nests of some of the larger birds of prey in hopes of carrying off some portion of the food from the larder that had been stored up for the use of the young.

Though many keepers commence to trap both these birds and Ravens in the autumn, I have come to the conclusion that the time to effectually destroy all the various members of the Crow family is in early spring, as soon as they have laid. During autumn they are simply acting the part of scavengers on the moors; and it is only when the eggs of the game-birds appear that they are enabled to cause the slightest damage. To expect to clear the ground before severe weather sets in is useless as well as hopeless; the traps must shortly cease working on account of frost; and the places of those that have been killed will be filled up by fresh arrivals before the breeding-season. I have never been able to detect the slightest harm that these birds inflicted on Grouse, except during the time of nesting, or when the young birds were in the down. As soon as the migrants from the far north or from the outer islands have taken their departure, and the residents have commenced their preparations for breeding, then every bird that is killed down makes one less in the number of the robbers. To watch and shoot them at their nests I have found by far the most effective plan. By leaving the Crows alone till they have hatched off, and then securing the old birds with traps when they come to bring food to their young (which plan is advocated by some experienced game-preservers), I should be of opinion that a considerable number of eggs must be lost, which might be saved by commencing operations at an earlier date.

In spring these birds are especially keen, and consequently easy to trap. On a moor in the west of Perthshire I once put up two or three from a bait, while one poor victim was struggling in the trap. A keeper in Inverness-shire, whose veracity I can thoroughly depend on, showed me a trap where, only a day or two previously, he had discovered a party of eight or ten gathered round the hare that had been used as a bait. As they were so intent on the food, with which the whole number were busily engaged, he was enabled to crawl within range, and succeeded in stopping three or four with his two barrels. On examining the trap he was surprised to find that one of the Crows had been held a prisoner; his misfortune, however, had not the slightest effect in deterring the others or impairing his appetite.

Of late years I have always made a practice of setting two or more traps to every bait, the two nearest the quarry being placed side by side. By these means I have often secured vermin that were but slightly held by one of the traps, as during their struggles they have blundered into the second. Early in December 1881, when visiting the traps I had set at the carcass of a domestic cat, on a marsh in the neighbourhood of one of the large broads in the east of Norfolk, I found a couple of these Crows, one being held by each of the traps. Having been placed as close as possible, it is strange how the two had been taken. Each of the poor wretches evidently imagined that his misfortune was due to his companion in adversity, as they were fighting desperately when first seen. Only the previous day a Black Crow had been secured at the same spot; and this malefactor had managed to spring both traps, and was discovered with one leg in each.

During the autumnal migration I have often met with Grey Crows on the North Sea, apparently tired out by their long flight, and glad of a rest on any boat or vessel they might meet in their course. These birds, according to my observations, seldom fly in very large flocks. Ten or a dozen may now and then be seen together; but for the most part they make their passage in small straggling parties. I have frequently noticed as many as fifty or sixty in view at the same time from the deck of the steamboat, though perhaps not more than three or four would be keeping company. Two Grey Crows and a Jackdaw, which had followed us one day in a thick fog for a considerable distance, at last settled on one of the paddle-boxes. A shot or two which I fired at some Gannets at first greatly alarmed them, and one of the Crows beat a speedy retreat; it soon, however, returned; and after a time they got used to the noise of the shooting and the shouts of the men who were fishing, and stalked gravely about on the bridge, evidently taking particular notice of what was going on. Towards dusk the wind freshened, and the pitching and rolling of the steamboat appeared to disagree with them, as, after looking very miserable for some time in their vain attempts to keep their footing in spite of the combined effects of wind and sleet, together with the constant breaking of the spray, they at last took a reluctant farewell, flying slowly against a head wind towards the land.

From what I have observed in the North Sea, I should be of opinion that some of the larger migratory birds (such as Rooks, Crows, and Jackdaws) are by no means so weatherwise as their smaller feathered relatives. I find the following entry in my notes for 1872, under date of October 10, at which time I was cruising in the North Sea for the express purpose of watching the migration :—

"1872, Oct. 10. I did not observe any small birds crossing, though I kept a constant look-out; and we met with only a few straggling parties of Grey Crows and three or four small flocks of Rooks during the early part of the day. While steaming out, we passed several drowned Rooks and one or two Grey Crows floating on the water, about fifteen miles from the land. Soon after midday the weather came on thick and squally from the south-west; and towards night it blew strong, with drifting rain. The small birds had probably been aware of the rough weather approaching, and had not attempted to make their passage in face of it. Next day several of the more venturesome Rooks were washing about a few miles off the land. In the afternoon, while on the beach at Yarmouth, I noticed a small black-coloured bird swimming in the Roads; and having no glasses with me, I took it to be a Little Auk. Shortly after, the bird was picked up by a shore-boat, when my Little Auk turned out to be an unfortunate Jackdaw. A couple more (both dead) were floating at a short distance."

The note of the Grey Crow is usually allowed to be a harsh and most unmelodious croak. The extraordinary sounds, however, that the species is capable of producing when excited ought to be heard in order to be thoroughly appreciated, as any description must fall short of the reality. Towards the latter end of December 1881, I observed a party of eight or ten of these birds "mobbing" a Rough-legged Buzzard, which was beating about over some rush-marshes in Norfolk. One or two would fly round, croaking as they went, and, after two or three turns, settle at some short distance. Others would then take up the attack, repeatedly dashing down, as if with the intention of striking, but taking evidently especial care to keep at a respectful distance. This style of warfare was carried on for some twenty minutes or half an hour, when the Buzzard (who paid little or no attention to the noisy demonstrations of his assailants), having searched over the marshes without success, flapped slowly off to a large oak, and took up his position on one of the topmost branches. After wheeling round, screaming and croaking loudly for several minutes, the dingy rabble broke up, and departed in various directions; three of their number, however, shortly returned and settled in the outside branches of the same tree, at a distance of eight or ten feet from the Buzzard. It was difficult to account for their animosity, as Hawks (the Common and Rough-legged Buzzards, the various Harriers, and an occasional wandering Peregrine) are by no means uncommon in the locality, and I have seldom noticed the Crows to exhibit any excessive signs of displeasure at their presence. This particular bird, for some inexplicable cause, appeared to be regarded as a special object of hatred. For an hour at least they continued to give vent to a succession of the most discordant and unpleasant sounds I ever heard proceed from the throats of any living creatures: to describe them I am utterly unable. While so engaged, they occasionally stretched out their necks, and assumed what I suppose was intended for a threatening attitude; they, however, confined themselves to this noisy manner of expressing their anger, and, having at length apparently exhausted themselves by their efforts, first one and then the remaining two flew slowly back to the marshes, leaving the Buzzard in undisputed possession of the situation. During the whole of the time he had been exposed to this abusive outcry, he had remained without changing for a moment his position on the tree, or exhibiting the slightest signs of annoyance, treating their clamour, indeed, with utter contempt. For another hour or so after their departure he retained his perch, utterly regardless, as before, of an occasional visit, one or two of his former assailants returning from time to time and after circling once or twice round the tree, again beating a retreat.

On the sea-shore I have noticed these birds harassing and attacking any stranger that made his appearance, weary and worn out by the force of the autumnal gales. In the latter end of October 1879, I observed several Pomarine Skuas drifting before a strong north-easterly breeze along the coast. Occasionally they would settle on the sandbanks a few yards distant from the breakers, but in not a single instance were they permitted to rest above a moment or two, as a party of Crows would swoop down on them at once, and, with threatening screams, compel them to move on. The squalls of rain and mist obscured the view beyond the distance of a few hundred yards, or, I conclude, I must have seen some of the poor wanderers (who were evidently exhausted by the buffeting of the storm) struck down and killed by their numerous assailants.

I have frequently come across Grey Crows feeding on the refuse, dead fish and other garbage, that is carried from the mouths of harbours or rivers by the ebb-tide. They will occasionally follow the floating filth a considerable distance at sea, hovering over the water, and stooping down and seizing in their beaks any tempting morsel as it bobs up and down in the current. At such times they are often seen in company of Gulls—Lesser Blackbacks and Herring-Gulls in immature plumage, and numbers of Common Gulls in all stages. The Crows are by no means backward in plundering these unfortunate birds when they may have secured any particularly inviting fragment. I have watched as many as forty or fifty of these robbers engaged in this manner at once. While seeking their food in this somewhat unusual fashion, I have but little doubt that they may have been at times mistaken for Skua Gulls. Early in November 1879, a week or so after the disastrous October gales had driven large flights of Skuas to our shores, I met with a couple of gentlemen on the beach near Yarmouth, evidently greatly interested by witnessing a score or two of Crows feeding in the tideway in the sands. Under the impression that the birds attracting their attention were a party of Skuas, they were closely studying their manner of procuring prey; and the voracity with which the whole rabble rout contended with the hungry sea-fowl afforded them every opportunity of gratifying their curiosity. The ferocity with which one or two Crows just then attacked a Gull that had picked up a heavy mouthful of offal, which it vainly attempted to make off with, was certainly misleading to any one who had never had a chance of observing the habits of the various species of Skua Gulls in a wild state.

For breeding-purposes this species resorts to trees, ledges, and cavities in the face of precipitous rocks, and cliffs in the vicinity of the sea-coast. In some exposed districts on the north-west of Scotland, and also on several of the islands on inland lochs, I have come across their nests in bushes of birch and stunted fir, at the height of only a few feet from the ground; at times, however, they will make use of almost the highest tree in some dense forest. The composition of the nest varies according to the materials within reach of the architects—twigs and branches of trees in woodland districts, and roots and stalks of heather in the more open localities. The lining consists of wool, moss, and grass.

The Plate shows an adult male and a nest. It is taken from a rough sketch made on one of the barren and uninhabited islands off the west coast of Scotland. This nest was entirely constructed of bleached and weatherbeaten stalks of heather, finer twigs being used for the formation of the interior and the binding down of the upper portion. The lining was composed of sheep's-wool, white lichens, and strips or strands of bark. Whether this latter material had been torn from large coarse heather-stalks or stunted birch bushes, I was unable to decide. The interior was a most elaborately worked-up cup-shaped cradle, six and a half inches deep by seven inches in diameter at the upper rim of the nest.

This species is known in various localities by several different titles. Throughout the Highlands it is commonly styled the "Hoodie;" in the Midland counties and on the south coast I have heard it spoken of as the "Grey," "Saddleback," "Royston," or "Norwegian Crow;" while by many of the Norfolk punt-gunners it is named the "Kentish Crow:" the more familiar term, however, for the bird (when conversing among themselves) would be an "Old Kentish man." Over a somewhat limited district within a few miles of Huntingdon this species is known among the natives as "Potter Brown's Crow."

ROOK.

CORVUS FRUGILEGUS.

THE Rook adapts itself to circumstances with the greatest equanimity, appearing as much at home among the grimy trees of the metropolis as in the lofty woods of some extensive park. To give a list of the localities in which this familiar bird may be met with is unnecessary. Though less frequent in the north, there are scattered colonies to be found in every county I have visited, from Caithness to Cornwall.

Opinions differ as to the useful or destructive habits of many of our native birds, and the present species comes in occasionally for much abuse and also well-merited approbation. I fully believe that, for about three fourths of their time, Rooks, owing to the nature of their food, act the part of benefactors to the farmer. There is, however, no denying the fact that they now and then exact toll for the service previously rendered. Few of our feathered friends are more omnivorous; it would be difficult to find any substance, animal or vegetable, containing the least particle of nutriment that they would not make a meal off when pressed by want.

A newly sown field of corn, wheat in particular, will suffer considerably from their visits, while potatoes, peas, and beans are also patronized. Their attacks on the grain when stacked also occasion no little annoyance to the owners, as wet and wind find an entrance where a commencement has been made, and in the end considerable loss is entailed. When food is scarce in dry seasons, Rooks are exceedingly destructive to the eggs or young of game: they hunt the ground continually, and do as much damage as Grey or Carrion Crows; in many counties in the Highlands I have watched them while so employed—Grouse, Blackgame, Wildfowl, and Waders being all plundered alike. I am afraid that they can scarcely ever be held perfectly blameless, and, however abundant their natural food may be, an exposed nest would never be safe if once detected by their sharp eyes. Some years ago I was assured by the keepers of Stanmer Park, near Brighton, that these robbers carried off at least thirty young Pheasants from the coops before they were able to put a stop to their depredations; the Rooks were distinctly seen to seize them, and fly off with their plunder at once to the high trees where their nests were situated. On the South Downs they now and then so persistently search out the nests of the Norfolk Plovers that not an egg is left to be hatched in the district. The nests of these Plovers are much exposed, being usually placed either on the bare hillside or concealed only by the scanty shelter of the young corn. While passing over the downs near Falmer in May 1872, I noticed, at the distance of less than a couple of hundred yards, a Rook fly down and attack the eggs of a Plover which had accidentally been driven from her nest. The newly fledged young of many species of small birds are also carried off. I have repeatedly seen them flying away with the nestlings of Larks, Pipits, and Ring-Dotterel. On one occasion I learned that a most impudent robbery had been perpetrated by a pair of these birds. The sufferers were a brood of young Larks placed in a cage, in order to be reared by their parents, the offence being committed but a few yards from a cottage. On their first visit they managed to drag one of the young Larks from between the bars of the cage, but being detected at the next attempt they departed with the heads only of their victims. The surviving young one was then removed to a safer spot, and the dead bodies thrown out. The Rooks, however, were not to be balked of their prey, as they shortly returned and were distinctly seen to carry off the headless carcasses from the ditch into which they had been flung.

At all seasons of the year Rooks may be met with along the sea-shore; in some districts they resort regularly to the mudflats at low water, in quest of marine worms, diminutive crabs, shrimps, or any small fish. On Breydon mudflats I repeatedly watched large bodies collecting all through the summer, and on the Sussex shingle-banks small parties are constantly to be seen. They are especially busy in the latter locality during the mackerel season, large quantities of fish being captured by means of seines shot by boats and then drawn ashore. After a haul, numbers of small fish and shrimps are scattered about on the shingle, mixed up in the weeds dragged in by the net. For these the Rooks keep a sharp look out, eagerly darting down and claiming their share as soon as the men have left in search of a fresh shoal. Though intent at the time on sea fish, these cunning birds are by no means so unobservant as to let a chance of a good substantial meal escape them. While on the beach between Shoreham and Lancing on June 30, 1880, I remarked from twenty to thirty Rooks closely searching over the heaps of refuse lying on the shingle. The men who effected the capture had withdrawn some distance to the top of the ridge of beach, and having sent for a liberal supply of bread and cheese, proceeded to enjoy their well-earned repast. A commencement had scarcely been made when another shoal of fish broke up on the surface, within a few hundred yards. As there appeared a good chance, the food was at once relinquished, and the crew started in pursuit of the mackerel. On returning an hour later, it was evident that the Rooks, who had been observed on the spot, had discovered and cleared off the whole of the bread and cheese, a few crumbs being all that remained.

In severe winters, when the ground is covered deep with snow, or hard with frost, these birds are frequently put to cruel straits to procure food. At such times they will attack any weakly bird, or one that is partly disabled by wounds. I have also seen them rising from dead and decomposing carcasses, and large flocks, considerably in excess of those usually observed, betake themselves to the sea-shore, where a scanty living on shellfish and other offal is picked up. When scraps and crumbs have been thrown out to the starving swarms of diminutive feathered pensioners that congregate below the windows during protracted storms, I have frequently noticed the Rooks so emboldened by want, that they would dash down at once and carry off all the smaller portions; and it was only by providing a quantity of pieces too heavy for them to lift, that those for whom the feast was intended could enjoy their share.

I had previously been of opinion that flesh was only consumed by this species when their regular food was scarce, either in the depth of winter or during the prevalence of dry winds. A couple of Rooks, however, attracted my attention while driving between Brighton and Shoreham, on March 20, 1882, the weather at the time being exceedingly mild. The birds were busily engaged with some object by the side of a heap of mould, within a short distance of the roadside; and on proceeding to the spot and investigating the nature of their prey, I discovered that they were tearing the meat from some bones, dragged from under the covering of the soil. Their repulsive banquet (suspicious certainly, but possibly the remains of some ewe that had died) appeared particularly suited to their tastes, as they refused to move above twenty yards on my approach, and returned immediately and commenced again as soon as my back was turned.

It is probable that Rooks occasionally convey a supply of dry materials to their young, in order to assist digestion. On May 17, 1882, I carefully examined an old bird, shot on purpose to ascertain the food it was carrying, and discovered it had six small land-snails, each about the size of a sixpenny piece, as well a mouth, or, rather, a pouch, full of dead and perfectly dried worms. The snail-shells were all untenanted and empty, with the exception of one, which was full of mould, while the dead worms were so brittle that they had broken up into scraps of about an inch in length. The entire mouthful contained but little of a nourishing character, with the exception of the lower portion of the supply of worms, which the moisture in the bird's throat had reduced to a consistency somewhat resembling potted beef or ham. It certainly was not scarcity of food that caused such an apparently unpalatable mouthful to be collected, as on examining the field from which the bird had risen when shot, I discovered several lively worms still struggling in a furrow in which they had recently been disturbed by the plough. With but few exceptions, the large number of Rooks and Jackdaws frequenting the ground were then engaged in searching over a portion of the land which, being newly sown with tares, had undergone both harrowing and rolling. It is probable that the dead worms had been collected in this part; after having been cut and disabled by the number of teams passing over the ground, the heat of the sun would soon dry them. I could find no signs that the tares had suffered in the slightest degree.

Grubs of various kinds and many noxious insects also form a large portion of the food of this species, the crops necessarily being freed by their attentions from a great source of danger. In parts of the eastern counties I discovered that farmers brought grave charges against the Rooks for the destruction of turnips, one of my informants stating that to his knowledge nearly one third of a field of seven acres had been destroyed by these birds during a single morning. The attack is declared to be made soon after the rows are cleaned and thinned out, the crop being supposed to suffer most in dry weather. When, however, it is generally allowed that the birds only drag up the young plants in order to get at the wireworm, it is a question whether any really healthy roots are affected by their depredations. I have often observed large parties of Rooks busily engaged on the South Downs tearing up the short turf, and on examining the spot have ascertained that the roots were loosened or removed in patches over a considerable extent of ground. Though apparently destroying the grass, they were simply seeking out the grubs at work below the surface and effectually ruining the pasture. The birds are doubtless guided in their search by the want of vigour in the herbage that is attacked by the insects. During the winter of 1882-83, and throughout the following spring, a few birds occasionally settled on a marshy spot near the sea-coast between Shoreham and Lancing, and in a most energetic manner dragged up large patches of long coarse grass by the roots. For several months I remarked their work on an acre or two of ground, but was unable to procure a specimen so as to ascertain the peculiar grub or worm attracting them to this spot. The benefits conferred on agriculturists by Rooks are now generally well known, and there is little fear that such unfounded charges as were formerly brought against this useful species will again be put forward.

I find the following in my notes, under date May 6, 1874:—"Wind south-west, weather fine and still: numbers of Rooks tumbling in the air. This performance is in some parts considered a sign of rain. Whether there is the slightest truth or not in this old saying, the rain certainly fell within a few hours after a dry period of several weeks."

Numbers of Rooks arrive on our eastern coast during autumn; I have often met with large flights in the North Sea, evidently making their way straight for land. It was seldom that they flew in straggling parties after the manner of Grey Crows; those seen singly appeared to have fallen out of the ranks from fatigue. After a gale of wind from the south-west, it was no uncommon occurrence to pass several floating dead on the water between twenty and thirty miles from land. I also received a few wings from the light-ships off the east coast during the winter months, the birds having fallen disabled on deck after striking the lamps. Having failed to observe them on their return journey in the spring, or obtained any wings from the light-ships at that period, I am ignorant whether they take up their residence in this country, or again return to the north of Europe; it is possible that a few, at least, of our visitors remain with us and assist in founding those new colonies from time to time recorded.

In the opinion of certain authors a partial migration of our native birds takes place towards the south on the approach of winter. If such is the case, the number of those that leave our shores must, I imagine, be small and composed for the most part of the migrants from across the North Sea or of young birds of the year. I have never met with any unusually large bodies of Rooks on the south coast during autumn or winter, or an increase to the regular fraternities that inhabit the rookeries in the neighbourhood of the coast. In severe weather it frequently happens that a general movement of mixed multitudes of small birds takes place along the south coast from east to west; and among the countless swarms of fugitives, I have on several occasions noticed a few scattered parties of Rooks. They were not, however, in sufficient numbers to represent anything approaching to even a partial migration.

Every observer who takes an interest in our native birds must be thoroughly conversant with the breeding-habits of this species. Elm, oak, and beech are perhaps the trees to which they mostly resort for nesting-purposes in the south; though in the outskirts of Brighton a few broods are annually reared in both Scotch and silver firs. In the exposed glens of the north and west I have found them making use of stunted bushes of alder, and also firs bent and twisted by the constant gales. On one occasion in Caithness, after being banished from the rookery they inhabited, in consequence of their depredations on the Grouse eggs, the poor birds nested out on the open moors, trees being scarce in the neighbourhood. The cradle of the Rook is too well known to need minute description; it is, however, occasionally most amusing to watch the architects collecting the materials. Though the greater portion of the sticks they make use of are picked up from the ground or stolen from their neighbours, many twigs are broken off the trees in the vicinity of the rookery. If small or dead, the birds meet with little difficulty in detaching them, though a tough and unmanageable bough is now and then seized hold of. The first attempt to snap off the coveted portion having failed, the bird after hovering round, usually selects a fresh perch, and resolutely gripping the twig between his mandibles again flaps off, endeavouring by the sudden strain to effect his purpose. Frequently, owing to his exertions, the small pieces he may already have collected are dropped; but he almost invariably returns to the attack, each succeeding attempt being characterized by still greater impetuosity.

A severe gale of wind, while the young are in the nests, is often attended with disastrous consequences to the juvenile occupants of the rookeries. The terrible hurricane of April 29, 1882, must have destroyed many thousands of young birds in the southern counties of England.

Young Rooks are looked upon as by no means despicable articles of food, and find a ready market in most parts of England. I am unable to answer for the truth of the report that they furnish the component parts of the majority of the Pigeon-pies that are manufactured in town during the season they are procurable; but can vouch for the fact that large consignments are frequently forwarded to London from certain quarters as soon as the annual slaughter has taken place.

The familiar caw of the Rook is heard alike in town and country; there is, however, another call-note which the bird occasionally utters when on wing, and this bears a strong resemblance to the cry of one of the larger Gulls. It is usually in the early spring that I have detected this wild note. The extraordinary noises that this curious bird produces, while attempting to exercise its vocal powers by singing, appear to have escaped the notice of most writers. It is probable that I might have remained in ignorance of this accomplishment, had not a certain old male perched himself regularly for several successive days on the chimney of my sanctum, in order to go through his matutinal performance. Happening early one fine bright morning to be seated near the fireplace, a most peculiar grating sound, evidently the note of a bird, caught my ear. This strange melody somewhat resembled the well-known chattering note of the Starling (often to be heard on the same spot), though more varied and far louder. On obtaining an out-of-door view of the songster, I discovered a Rook on the chimney-pot indulging in the most eccentric antics, and at the same time giving utterance to the marvellous combination of notes that had first attracted my attention*.

* Those who have kept Hawfinches in confinement will readily be able to form an idea of the performance, the singular attitudes assumed, as well as the contortions gone through, by these birds while singing being almost identical with what I witnessed. Though somewhat similar, the sounds produced were, of course, more powerful.

This species appears not unfrequently to exhibit curious malformations of the beak. I have on two occasions seen birds flying past with elongated or twisted mandibles; and on shooting one in Glenlyon, in Perthshire, I discovered that the beak was curved downwards, and much resembled that of a Chough, only far thicker and at least an inch longer. It was apparently a bird of the year, still retaining the feathers over the bill.

The adult Rook (as all observers must be well aware) exhibits a patch of scurfy skin over and round the sides of the bill; this bare space appears at a short distance of a dirty white tint. In the young bird, immediately after leaving the nest, this space is covered with black feathers or bristles. It is usually allowed that this sign of immaturity disappears after the first moult, when the young bird is supposed to become similar in appearance to the adult. I am of opinion that still further attention will have to be given to this subject before the truth is arrived at. The eye of the young bird on leaving the nest is of a dull slate tint, and differs considerably from that of the adult, which is a dark hazel. After a few weeks the iris changes and assumes the same colour as in the mature bird. I mention this fact, as it appears to have escaped the notice of all writers.

The old-fashioned idea that the absence of feathers was caused by the bird thrusting its bill into the ground, while digging for worms and grubs, has, I believe, long been proved a fallacy. The bare scurfy skin round the base of the mandibles is evidently the natural state, though the date at which it is assumed may possibly be doubtful, should there be any foundation for the theory of those writers who assert that observations made on birds in captivity are not to be relied upon *.

In the adult the colour of the interior of the mouth and tongue is a dull slate, while in the young immediately after leaving the nest it is of a deepened flesh tint. I have repeatedly reared Rooks from the nest to ascertain at what age the bristles were thrown off and the slate tint of the mouth assumed. Little or no difference was detected in any case that was carefully watched. The following is the result of observations on a young bird taken from the nest in May 1882. The colour of the interior of the mouth commenced to change about the end of the first year, when the bird was probably nine months old. The tongue and the interior of the mandibles first showed the slate tint, which gradually spread over the roof of the mouth (detached spots appearing in the first instance) and finally reached the throat. The gullet, at all ages, is of a dark flesh tint. This change in colour was accomplished in about three months, the mouth being thoroughly slate-tinted by the time the bird was a year old. Towards the end of April 1883, a few of the bristles under the beak were lost; none of those on the upper mandible had, however, as yet disappeared. During the first and second weeks in May, small bare patches showed on the upper mandible, though the whole surface did not exhibit the usual white scurfy appearance of the adult till well on in July. It was not till the middle of August that the last signs of the bristles had completely vanished.

The statement that young birds lose the feathers over the base of the beak at the first moult can scarcely be correct, or there must be not unfrequent exceptions to the rule. Not a single specimen that I have had the opportunity of examining in captivity has changed at that age; and during the earlier months of the year I have at various times met with specimens exhibiting the black feathers over the bill.

Being anxious to gain information concerning the number of Rooks showing black beaks in Sussex during spring, I closely examined every party met with on the downs in April 1882. Though some thousands of birds were carefully inspected, I could only positively identify three specimens in this stage. On April 2nd a bird on wing skimmed past so close that the feathers and bristles were visible to the naked eye. On the 6th I remarked another in the same state. This bird repeatedly flew after an adult searching for food on the downs; and although it did not flutter its wings in the manner of the young when first taking after their parents, it gave the impression it was following the old bird for what it could get. Nothing,

* According to my own experience, the changes undergone by birds reared in captivity corresponded, in every instance where I have been able to verify the fact, with those in a natural state.

however, being forthcoming, it at length left the adult and proceeded to hunt for itself. Again, on the 22nd, I watched another keeping company with an adult in much the same manner; and on the latter taking wing, it was followed at once by the younger bird. As in the former case, the adult took not the slightest notice of the immature bird when it approached. In every case I was sufficiently close to see that the plumage was as bright and glossy as that of the adults; this, of course, would not have been the case had they been young birds of the year, hatched at an earlier date than usual. That Rooks with black bristles over the bills were to be met with in the broad-district of Norfolk during May 1871 is well impressed on my memory. While watching for two Black Crows breeding in a small plantation, I shot a couple of black-beaked Rooks as they crossed over my hiding-place beneath the nest, and under the impression that I had obtained the rightful owners, sent off the pair at once for preservation. It was not till receiving word from the taxidermist to whom my specimens had been forwarded that I became aware of the ridiculous error.

Though Rooks, at times, if not invariably, retain the bristles over the beak till the second year, it is quite possible to distinguish them from Crows by a few moments' examination. The interior of the mouth of the Black Crow is at all times a *pale* flesh; the mouth of the Rook, though a *deep* flesh in the juvenile stage, has assumed the slate-colour of the adult before the bird is a twelvemonth old. If examined in the sunlight, the plumage of the Rook is considerably more glossy, a brilliant blue pervading the feathers on the head, neck, and back. Though the Crow will be found to exhibit far less lustre, a dark purple bloom at times is visible. There is in addition a faint and indescribable odour that hangs about the latter bird, which, though by no means so strong as the scent of the Fulmar or Gannet, leaves no doubt in the mind of one who has once "felt" it as to the identity of the specimen. The claws and talons of the Crow are more powerful than those of the Rook; this difference, however, is scarcely discernible without comparison.

From information lately gathered from the skipper of a trading-vessel (an old puntsman well acquainted with birds), I consider it is possible that young Rooks may leave the British Islands and take up their residence for a time on the continent in greater numbers than we generally suppose. I also learned from a couple of gunners who had passed some considerable time shooting on the opposite coast, that during autumn and early winter flocks of Rooks were met with, composed, as far as they were able to judge, almost, if not entirely, of young birds. For these statements, of course, I am not able to vouch; I simply record the facts as they were told me while conversing on sporting matters.

I am ignorant whether scientific naturalists can inform us with certainty as to the age at which the Rook commences to breed; no remarks on this subject can be found in any works I have examined. As far as I am to judge from personal observations, it appears probable that this species does not arrive at maturity before the third year—*i. e.* does not pair and nest till it has arrived at the age of two years.

JACKDAW.

CORVUS MONEDULA.

In almost every town I have passed through, between Inverness and Penzance, I recognized this species as a resident. The wildest districts are also resorted to. Like his constant companion the Rook, this lively bird adapts himself to circumstances, and seems as much at his ease in the midst of the noise and bustle of a city as in the lonely retirement of some lofty precipice among the inland mountains or on the rocks in the neighbourhood of the sea-coast.

Jack is generally supposed to be a mischievous rogue; but I had always believed his character, like that of another black party, was not so bad as it was depicted. One summer, however, when living in Perthshire, I required a young bird of this species, in order to compare with the young of the Grey Crow; and on examining some nests I discovered the shells of dozens of Grouse-eggs which had been destroyed. The remains of the eggs were scattered over the ledges, and also in the cracks and crevices of the rocks among the nests, plainly showing that the robbers had, in some instances at least, conveyed their plunder to their quarters. It was too late that season to do much good by exterminating the colony, as the mischief was already accomplished. Early the next spring I took forcible measures to prevent them from breeding in their old haunts; and the following season the Grouse on the adjoining beat were nearly doubled. The whole of the ground within about a mile of the rocks where the Jackdaws nested had till now been perfectly worthless, never more than a few pair of barren birds being found there. In order to prevent these mischievous brutes returning to the corrie they frequented, it was necessary to be continually on the watch; and numbers were killed before they took the hint that their presence was not required. At last the survivors moved to a fresh station further up the glen; but I believe that in a few years they gradually reappeared at their old quarters.

I never detected Jackdaws doing much harm to game in England, though I have been assured by shepherds and keepers that they occasionally managed to search out the early Partridges' nests on the downs in the south. This charge is probably correct; but, like their cousins the Rooks, they effect an immense amount of good; and, if weighed in the balance, I have not the slightest doubt that the benefits they confer would more than compensate for the taxes they levy on the game-preserver and farmer.

The greatest injury and annoyance that is caused by these birds may, I think, be ascribed to their pertinacity in choosing as breeding-places situations where their nests are particularly undesirable. Chimneys are frequently blocked up by the immense collections of sticks they bring together; and the quantity of litter they carry into the towers of churches and other buildings at times seems almost incredible. Great numbers resorted many years ago to the ruins of the disused portion of Battle Abbey, near Hastings; and here they caused considerable damage to the conservatories and forcing-houses in the gardens. On some of the glass they managed to throw down old pieces of stone, mortar, and other refuse that they scratched out when cleaning their quarters on commencing operations in the spring. On other parts they continually dropped sticks and twigs that they were bringing to form their nests. To drive them away in any manner except by constant shooting was found impracticable; and this plan was disapproved of by the owner. The loss of an enormous quantity of glass was consequently entailed every spring. In chalk-pits these birds are looked upon as an especial nuisance when they take up their quarters above the spot where the workmen are employed. Some years ago, while I was shooting a pair or two which I required as specimens, at Offham, near Lewes, I remarked that the men kept loudly expressing their pleasure as each poor Jack came to grief. One old fellow was particularly eager to render assistance by driving the birds, though his overanxiety caused two or three chances to be lost. I was on the point of inquiring the cause of his animosity, when he removed his hat and exhibited a plate on his head. This he stated was the result of a fractured skull, caused by the fall of a piece of chalk dislodged by a Jackdaw from the upper part of the pit.

We are visited in the autumn by large numbers of these birds that cross the North Sea. I have met with them frequently on the passage many miles from land, and have also received a few wings from the light-ships on which they have fallen disabled. Several times after a gale at that period I have seen them floating either dead or dying on the water, not having had strength sufficient to complete their journey. I am ignorant whether any return in the spring to the north of Europe, as I have never observed them at that season or heard of their capture on the light-ships while crossing. In severe weather, when the mixed flights of small birds migrate along the south coast towards the west, I have occasionally noticed a few Jackdaws following the same course, generally in company with Rooks.

This species is easily accommodated with a nesting-place; a hole in a tree or a cavity in cliffs (either chalk or rock) suits him as well as the comfortable quarters he occasionally secures in a lofty steeple or the battlements of some antiquated tower. In the Highlands I have frequently found large colonies breeding in rabbit-burrows. The holes they selected were generally in rough and broken ground on the face of some steep hill-side. These birds, I believe, do not commence their nesting-operations so early as Rooks. I noticed two or three pairs on the 28th of March, 1880, attempting to force their way into some holes near the roof of a large building in a town in Norfolk, where they had previously been in the habit of breeding. During the winter iron bars had been placed in front of the apertures; and the noisy and fruitless efforts of the birds to effect an entrance were most amusing, and were continued at intervals for several days.

On the Bass Rock Jackdaws were formerly common, breeding in holes in the turf near the summit. At last their depredations on the eggs of the sea-fowl induced the person who hired the rock to take steps to kill them down. For this purpose he unfortunately made use of poison laid out on bread and butter, which certainly had the desired effect on the Jackdaws; but it also cleared off nearly the whole of the larger Sea-Gulls that resorted to the rock. Whether the Daws have returned again I am unable to state. On the last occasion I carefully examined the various birds during the summer, I did not observe a single specimen.

I met with a curious breeding-station of this species within a short distance of the rocks known as the "Sutors," on the coast of Cromarty, overlooking the Moray Firth. The greater number of the nests were placed among the stalks of the coarse ivy that climbed up the face of the cliffs, in several instances in close proximity and even joined to those of the Herons, who also breed in the same range of rocks. I did not observe that they molested their neighbours, though I should imagine an exposed egg must at times have been a temptation almost too strong to be resisted.

Jackdaws are in some districts asserted to relieve sheep of a number of the ticks with which they are infested. As they are, however, declared occasionally to steal a quantity of the wool, it must be doubtful whether their visits are conducive to the interests of the farmer, or even beneficial to the sheep themselves.

MAGPIE.

PICA CAUDATA

In the more northern counties of Scotland the Magpie appears decidedly scarce. A few pairs came under my observation in the south-east of Sutherlandshire; and I have also watched a bird or two crossing the waters of the Kyle from the woods above Bonar Bridge to the opposite shores of Ross-shire. In the latter county it is not uncommon; in the neighbourhood of Tain several pairs are to be seen, nesting in some instances in gardens close to the highroad. In Inverness-shire and Perthshire, the greater part of the country (with the exception of those portions that are let as "forests") is too well looked after to suit the species; still the Magpie is to be met with in certain localities. In the south of Scotland it appears by no means abundant; during a residence of a couple of years in East Lothian I had but few opportunities of studying its habits. Over England it is generally distributed; some twenty years ago it was common in the east of Sussex, but its numbers have now decreased. In Yorkshire I have observed large flocks during winter, having counted at times between thirty and forty keeping company in the neighbourhood of Doncaster. In Cornwall I met with several pairs frequenting the vicinity of the coast-line in the western division of the county during the autumn of 1880.

A male of this species, which I observed flying along the Cornish coast while a fresh breeze from the east was blowing, exhibited a most singular method of progression. This Magpie (the only one I ever noticed venturing any distance off the land) was making for the rocks to the west of Lamorna Cove, and was evidently somewhat incommoded by the length of his tail, which was carried by the wind right underneath the body. The length of the caudal feathers, and the upright manner in which he was forced to proceed, rendered his appearance exceedingly strange. Of course it is possible that the bird might have been slightly wounded, causing the hind quarters to droop; still I imagine (seldom, if ever, having seen one far from shelter during a strong breeze) that the Magpie must find his long and handsome tail-feathers difficult to manage if he is ever in the habit of migrating across the stormy ocean.

There is, I am afraid, but little that can be said in favour of this showy bird. At certain seasons he is forced to seek a living by honest means; but plunder, such as eggs or young birds, is always preferred when available. To carrion, I am of opinion, he has not the slightest objection. Having on more than one occasion closely watched the tactics of an old Magpie busily engaged in foraging for its newly-hatched brood, I conclude that, after the manner of all the Crow tribe, any small quadrupeds, such as mice or young rats, if caught in the open, would at once be pounced upon and seized as prey. Doubtless a considerable number of injurious grubs and insects are also consumed in the course of a year.

Though the Magpie exhibits the greatest caution when aware that his actions are watched, and commonly affords an immense amount of labour to those who endeavour to encompass his destruction by means of powder and shot, yet he speedily falls a victim to a well-laid trap baited with an egg. Early in the spring I have captured numbers by this bait in both the northern and southern counties. In localities where game-preserving is neglected, this usually wary species is by no means shy; it is probable that constant persecution alone accounts for its almost habitual distrust.

I was much amused by the cunning displayed by a female Magpie, who for some time had successfully defied all attempts of a keeper who was bent on her destruction. I happened one day to meet the man while on his way to watch the nest; and hearing shortly after a couple of shots in the direction he had taken, I made my way towards the spot. At length I found him beneath a high tree, to the topmost branches of which he pointed exultingly, declaring the bird was dead in the nest. He stated that almost immediately he had taken up his position, the female Magpie came in sight, and after dodging about for a few minutes she made a straight dash for the nest, and disappeared from sight before he could take aim. Finding it impossible to start the bird by means of sticks or stones or striking the stem of the tree, he fired one barrel at the nest, hoping to stop her by the second as she came out. Nothing beyond a slight fluttering in the nest (which I suspect was only imaginary) resulting from the shot, he came to the conclusion he had at last accomplished his task. In order, however, to make doubly sure, he fired the second barrel; and no signs of the bird being visible, he was now perfectly convinced of his success. I eventually learned that his suppositions had proved erroneous. On meeting the man again a week or so later, he informed me that he had been forced to devote another half day to lying in wait for this troublesome egg-stealer before he finally got rid of her. It appears that the bird must have escaped both of the shots fired at the nest, and had simply refused to stir. Probably her past experiences had enabled her to become acquainted with her assailant, and she had formed a pretty correct estimate as to the shooting-powers of both man and gun.

The pertinacity with which this species will at times continue to return to some favourite breeding-station after constant interruption would scarcely be credited by those who have not witnessed the fact. In a small clump of three or four beech trees, standing in a valley among steep hills in one of the southern counties, there is every spring a Magpie's nest. Invariably one or other of the old birds is shot by the keepers; and although a second may be killed, it not unfrequently happens that a brood succeeds in escaping. Whatever may have been the slaughter effected during the preceding season, the old clump has hitherto been regularly tenanted by a pair of Magpies each succeeding spring.

While crossing the downs near Lewes, in company with a keeper, about the middle of May 1872, my attention was attracted by the curious actions of a Magpie. The bird (a fine male) was flying past at a great height, when he suddenly wheeled round and pitched straight down into a stunted thorn bush standing in a small patch of furze. As we were not above the distance of seventy or eighty yards, and plainly in view on the bare hill-side, I imagined the bird must have detected some particularly inviting prey concealed in the cover. In hopes of discovering the cause of this strange performance I approached as quietly as possible, at the same time sending the man round to the opposite side in order that the bird should not escape unobserved. The bush was not above eight or ten feet high, and the furze but a small patch, perhaps half a dozen yards across; still for some time we were unable to catch sight of the bird, which was eventually discovered skulking in the bottom of the thorn bush. For some unaccountable reason he resolutely refused for several minutes to make an attempt to escape, crouching down among the branches and creeping behind the stems of furze to avoid the stones aimed at him by the keeper. At last he was forced from the scanty cover, and took wing within a yard or two of where I was standing. As I was in want of a good specimen, I shot the bird, which proved to be in most perfect plumage. For at least an hour we closely searched the patch of furze and all the surrounding grass without discovering the slightest signs of a nest or any unfledged young. There was not a vestige of any prey that could possibly have been an attraction and caused him to check his flight so suddenly. Though it never occurred to me at the moment, I have little doubt that a Peregrine was the cause of this strange behaviour. The sun was shining brightly at the time, and it was almost impossible to look upwards. We had only just caught sight of the Magpie, when he instantly dashed down and was hidden from view in the bush. The Falcon might have been within a short distance without attracting our notice*.

The nest is a large and conspicuous structure, placed at times in some lofty tree, and occasionally in a low bush or hedge-row. In country districts I have now and then heard it affirmed that the Hedge-Magpie is a distinct race. The supporters of this view assert that the bird is smaller than the Magpie that resorts to high woods. My own opinion, of course, agrees with the usual judgment, viz. that the British Islands contain but one species.

I have never heard of the Magpie attempting to cross the North Sea; and it seems by nature unfitted for long journeys. I was, however, somewhat astonished, when living in the east of Ross-shire, to notice the confiding habits of a few pairs that nested in close proximity to the town of Tain. I particularly remarked that their manners and customs most closely resembled those of their Scandinavian cousins; indeed in no part of Great Britain have I met with Magpies so regardless of the presence of human beings. It is true that they did not, like their kinsmen on the opposite coast of Norway, place their nests on the dwelling-houses themselves; but they built in small trees in the gardens, and showed little more respect for passers-by than this species exhibits in the outskirts of Christiania and in several of the neighbouring towns and villages.

* While the above paragraph was passing through the press, I happened to alight upon an account of an unquestionably degenerate sport termed "Magpie-hawking." The description given of the actions of the hunted bird so closely resemble those of the specimen I obtained that I am convinced a Peregrine must have been the cause of the sudden descent of this Magpie into the thick cover, and also of its subsequent disinclination to seek safety by flight.

JAY.

GARRULUS GLANDARIUS.

In none of my notes can I find any record of having observed the Jay further north than Perthshire; and in that county I met with it on but few occasions. In the south of Scotland it is less scarce, but, according to my own experience, its numbers are kept well within bounds. Throughout England it is to be found in most wooded districts, more plentiful perhaps in the southern than in other portions of the country. In Middlesex several pairs of Jays used to frequent some thick coverts about halfway between London and Harrow-on-the-Hill. These woods must have been a happy resort for vermin in those days (now about thirty years ago), as, in addition to the Jays (which were abundant), both Magpies and Crows nested in the district, while polecats and stoats were by no means scarce.

The well-known destructive habits of this species render it a particularly hateful object in the eyes of most game-keepers; and as the bird is easily attracted by means of eggs as bait, its numbers are now year by year rapidly diminishing. I have trapped hundreds early in the spring, in Sussex, before the woods had broken out in leaf. A small platform or staging, constructed by broken branches, was formed, at the height of about three feet from the ground, on some bush in an open part of the covert. On this a trap was concealed by means of litter or dead grass; and a Thrush's nest placed at one end completed the very simple but certain method of capture. Eggs of the Thrush were always preferable to those of the Blackbird, owing to their more conspicuous colouring; but I have used the latter with almost equal success. Magpies were also frequently taken; and at times an unfortunate squirrel was made prisoner. When placing the traps on the ground, at the side of a hedgerow or round the outskirts of a wood, I usually baited with the eggs of the tame Pigeon or domestic Fowl; and the Carrion-Crow (and, in one instance, the Raven) was now and then secured, in addition to the usual list of victims.

An old keeper in my father's service used to declare he shot numbers of Jays by drawing them to the spot where he was concealed by means of a hedgehog. His plan was to tickle the animal's legs by scraping them with the teeth of a comb; and the shrill yells the unfortunate brute uttered during the operation were supposed to attract the Jays. I distinctly remember being present at some of these performances; but as it is now nearly five-and-thirty years ago, I am uncertain what amount of success was met with. I, however, still retain a vivid recollection of the large paper bags full of blue feathers from the wings of his victims, which the poor old fellow stored up with jealous care, regarding them as a sure source of unlimited wealth.

The Jay, I conclude, is stationary all the year in the districts it inhabits; and it is probable that our native birds receive no additions to their numbers from the continent.

The nest is a small collection of rough sticks, neatly lined with fibrous roots. It is generally placed near the stem of some small tree, at a height of from five to ten feet.

NUTHATCH.

SITTA EUROPÆA.

According to my own observations the range of the Nuthatch is by no means extended in the British Islands. I have never been able to identify a single specimen, with certainty, further north than Yorkshire. In two different localities in the southern part of that county (large parks containing scattered timber as well as dense woods) I have met with a few pairs. Though stragglers have from time to time come under my notice in the east of Norfolk, the nature of that side of the county is hardly suited to their requirements, and the species appears in greater numbers to the west of Norwich. In the neighbourhood of Harrow-on-the-Hill, in Middlesex, I have seen the nest on two or three occasions; and the birds themselves are tolerably common during the autumn and winter. It is, however, in the woods of Kent and Sussex that I have had the best opportunities for studying the habits of the Nuthatch. I am not acquainted with the east of Kent; but the bird is common in the well-timbered portion of the county near the Sussex border, and may be found in almost every wood in the eastern division of the latter county; it is also abundant (on the north side of the Downs) in the neighbourhood of Brighton.

To the best of my knowledge, this species is a resident, and seldom strays far from the district it inhabits. I have met with no evidence of its crossing the North Sea; neither have I observed it on the English Channel or in the immediate vicinity of the coast.

The Nuthatch is usually noticed solitary or in pairs. On two or three occasions, when cover-shooting late in the season, I have remarked as many as half a dozen, or even more, showing themselves in rapid succession, if disturbed by the advance of the beaters. They are, however, by no means shy, and usually afford abundant opportunities to any one desirous of watching their movements. Their actions while searching the trunks of trees for food are most interesting, if carefully observed through powerful glasses. Unlike the Woodpecker tribe, this species does not make use of its tail as a support while climbing; it will also descend the stem or limb of a tree head downwards as readily as it ascends. Though feeding occasionally on nuts, from which habit I conclude its name is derived, the bird mainly supports itself on insects and larvæ, which it procures from the cracks and crannies in the rough bark of the trees it frequents. I have now and then seen one rise from the ground (usually an open space in a cover); but I never had an opportunity of watching their actions while in that position.

For breeding-purposes this species resorts most commonly to holes in trees, the entrance to its nursery, if not according to its taste, being plastered up with mud. In some instances this substance is made use of in large quantities.

WRYNECK.

YUNX TORQUILLA.

THE Wryneck is only a summer visitor to the British Islands, arriving early in April, and, after rearing its young, leaving our shores about the end of August or early in September. The latest date on which I have noticed one was on the 5th of September; this was within a few hundred yards of the sea-coast. In most of the southern and eastern counties a few pairs are to be met with scattered over the wooded portions of the country, though in no locality I am acquainted with can it be termed abundant. On a fine spring morning during the second week in April, I have on one or two occasions in Sussex met with as many as half a dozen specimens within a short distance of one another, along a hedgerow, on a rough grassy bank. These, however, were birds that had just landed, and were taking their first rest after making the passage of the Channel. On visiting the spot a few hours later it would be found that the whole of them had shifted their quarters further inland. I can find no entry in my note-books concerning observations on this species farther north than Norfolk; and I am unable to call to mind a single instance where I have recognized it in either the more northern counties of England or the south of Scotland.

Owing to the sober tints of its beautifully marked and variegated plumage, this is by no means an attractive species, and, except on its first arrival (when its subdued though somewhat striking note is heard), it might easily escape the observation of those who are not accustomed to its habits or actions. The cry somewhat resembles the words "peu, peu, peu," repeated six, eight, ten, or even a dozen times in rapid succession.

The Wryneck, when unmolested, is most unsuspicious of danger, and is an exceedingly amusing visitor to watch while taking up its residence for the summer months in an orchard or shrubbery. Occasionally the young are reared in close proximity to dwelling-houses. A brood were pointed out to me some years back, near the small village of Plumpton, in Sussex, in a hole in an apple-tree standing at the distance of only three or four feet from the door of a cottage. The woman who lived there was particularly anxious I should make away with the family, as she declared they one and all "hissed" at her every time the door was opened; and she had a notion they were "unlucky birds." This was the first and only time I have heard such an idea expressed with regard to this species.

The remarkably elongated tongue of the Wryneck clearly indicates that it is intended by nature to procure its living in somewhat the same manner as the Woodpecker tribe. Ants and their eggs, together with insects of various kinds, form probably the chief or the whole of its diet.

Wryneck, and Cuckoo's mate, appear to be the commonest titles for this species. Any one who has quietly watched one of these birds sunning itself on the limb of a tree, and carefully noted all the contortions it will go through (elongating its neck and twisting it in the most extraordinary manner, while adding to the strangeness of its attitudes by occasionally raising and dropping its feathers so as to admit the warmth of the sun), will easily recognize the derivation of the name. The date of its arrival, usually within a few days of the Cuckoo, accounts for its being termed, in certain districts, the Cuckoo's mate.

For breeding-purposes these birds resort to holes in trees, making use of those that are formed by accident or decay; at times they take up their quarters in the deserted domicile of the Woodpecker. I have never detected any materials brought in to form a cradle for the young, though I notice some writers mention the nest of this species.

CREEPER.

CERTHIA FAMILIARIS.

I cannot call to mind noticing the Creeper in Caithness or among the Hebrides. With these exceptions, I have found this active species scattered over the wooded portions of most of the English and Scotch counties from Sussex to Sutherland.

These birds, I believe, seldom stray far from the district they frequent; I have on but few occasions seen them, unless in the vicinity of trees of considerable size or age. During autumn and winter they now and then join in company for a time with the flocks of various kinds of Tits that are to be seen busily engaged in searching for insect food through the woods and coverts. Their habit of commencing to hunt the lower portion of the trunk of a tree, gradually working upwards, and rapidly disappearing round the stem if alarmed, readily indicates the species if intermixed with other small birds. When the upper branches are reached they flit downwards towards the next tree they intend to search, and in this manner work their way through the woods. Their association with the Paridæ is usually of but short duration should their companions be inclined to shift their quarters to any distance. I have noticed this in the Highlands when a river was crossed by the main flock, and also in Sussex, where the change was but from one plantation to another.

Since the above lines were written, I remarked a Creeper in company with Coal Tits as early in the season as the 9th of August. My attention was first attracted by the lively party of eight or ten Tits flitting through the branches of a beech-grove in the interior of Sussex. I was somewhat astonished when, a few moments later, a single Creeper made his appearance, steadily working his way from tree to tree, and keeping pace with the Tits as they advanced. Owing to the dense foliage, it was by no means easy to retain the birds in view; but I managed to watch the Tits to the end of a ride that led through the wood, when they turned back and disappeared in the thick cover. As far as I could judge, the Creeper parted from the rest of the company at this point, and struck out a line for himself.

Insects appear to be the principal support of the old birds; and I could detect that they brought no other food to their young when I have watched them engaged in supplying their wants.

For nesting-purposes this species resorts to a variety of situations. Holes in old timber, or the gaps between the slabs in a dry stone dyke*, are frequently made use of in the Highlands. I have also seen the nest in the cavities among the roots of an old dead stump. In this instance the birds had chosen a subterranean domicile, as the nest was some distance below the level of the ground. In Sussex, on two or three occasions in remote country districts, I met with nests placed in wooden dwelling-houses and also in sheds. In one case a knot had dropped out of the timber and afforded an entrance to the spot selected; but usually a rotten or defective plank supplied the means of ingress. Their nest is not elaborately put together; but is usually a warm and cosy collection of grass, wool, and feathers, screened by its hidden position from all effects of wind and weather.

* A wall built without mortar.

GREEN WOODPECKER.

PICUS VIRIDIS.

In the forest district of Sussex I have met with considerable numbers of this species. It also appears very generally distributed over most of the southern and eastern counties: I cannot, however, assert that I have observed it further north than Norfolk. In the dusk of a gloomy October evening, some twenty years ago, I caught sight of two birds much resembling Green Woodpeckers in the Tyninghame Woods on the coast of East Lothian. It was impossible to identify them with certainty, owing to the rapidly increasing twilight and the momentary glimpse I was able to obtain as they dashed across the road. From inquiries I have made among keepers and foresters in the North, and also from my own observations, I am of opinion that this species must be of very unfrequent occurrence in Scotland. The call of the bird is so remarkable that it is almost impossible they could be residents in any district without attracting attention. The note must be heard to be thoroughly understood; and I can only describe it as a high-toned scream of laughter. I have no evidence that this species is migratory, or that the British Islands are ever visited by flights from the continent.

It is only in Sussex that I have met with opportunities of closely studying the habits of the Green Woodpecker. I particularly remarked, in both the eastern and central parts of the county, that, with but few exceptions, these birds resorted to beech trees for breeding-purposes. Deserted and recent borings may be found in all quarters of Balcombe Forest, wherever their favourite trees are situated. Large beeches are scattered over the greater portion of that wild and picturesque locality; and though the majority are still sound, the birds appear to have but little difficulty in selecting any number they may require in which decay has already set in. Many of these forest giants measure from five to seven feet in diameter; and the immense quantity of chips that this Woodpecker throws out while boring into such ponderous stems often presents a most curious sight, if examined when the work has been recently executed. I have repeatedly come across heaps of at least from one to two bushels of chips piled up at the roots of the tree; and in two or three instances I have arrived on the spot while the boring was being carried on. Every few seconds the head of the bird is seen at the entrance of the hole with a chip in its bill; this it immediately drops, and at once returns for a fresh supply. Where the wood is soft, it appears that the holes are very rapidly excavated; I have noticed large heaps of débris accumulated in a short space of time. It is, I believe, usually supposed that the boring is a straight entrance or hole and then takes a downward course till the depth at which the bird desires to deposit its eggs is arrived at. This is not invariably the case, as, in a boring I cut out near the western extremity of Balcombe Forest, I discovered the bird had constructed a most curious winding passage. Luckily the tree was particularly rotten, so the labour was slight, or I might have had an undertaking of some hours to follow all the curves and turns that the architect had fashioned. For between two and three feet the hole was cut straight into the stem, next turning downwards for some eight or ten inches, then brought for about a foot in the direction of the entrance, and finally carried downwards to the depth of fifteen or sixteen inches. In trees where only a small portion of the timber was unsound, I discovered the borings extended but a short distance into the stem.

I noticed on several occasions that the male takes part in the duty of incubation and also of feeding the young. In order to ascertain this fact I captured four birds while on their eggs; and in three instances those I secured were males.

The sexes may be easily distinguished, as the black mark that stretches like a moustache from below each side of the beak contains a small patch of red feathers in the male; these are absent in the female. Before the young birds quit the nest a few of these bright feathers have already made their appearance. The eye of the nestling I remarked was a dirty greyish white. The hissing and snapping noise emitted by a brood of young Woodpeckers while in the nest would most probably deter any one unacquainted with their note from exploring the hole in which they were concealed without due caution, as the sound could hardly be expected to proceed from a bird.

Among the food which this species conveys to its young I have found small insects of various kinds, spiders, ants and their eggs. The mouth and throat of an old male (killed accidentally while shooting specimens of the young) were greatly distended by a large quantity of two different kinds of ants' eggs, as well as numbers of the insects themselves.

GREAT SPOTTED WOODPECKER.

PICUS MAJOR.

THOUGH this species is occasionally observed in considerable numbers on the north-east coast of Scotland at the time of migration, I am of opinion it is by no means plentiful at the present date in the Highlands. The remains of the old timber in the valley of the Spey, and in many other parts of Inverness and the adjoining counties, indicate that Woodpeckers were formerly numerous in those districts. From reports I have gathered from keepers and foresters in the various glens, I conclude the birds must have belonged to this species. On some of the largest and oldest trees I have counted from twenty to thirty holes bored right into the centre of the stem. According to the statements of my informants, it appears that these Woodpeckers commenced to decrease in numbers about 1845 or 1850. In many parts of the country only an occasional straggler was seen for nearly thirty years. I discovered, however, on passing through several of these localities in 1878 and 1879, that a few pairs had lately taken up their quarters in these long-deserted haunts. The cause of their disappearance in the first instance was perfectly unaccountable to all those with whom I conversed on the subject.

Squirrels were accused by the keepers of destroying the nests of Crossbills and Siskins in some of the districts where the Woodpecker had previously been abundant. I perceive these animals are supposed by more than one writer to be responsible for the scarcity of *Picus major*. This is a subject on which I will not venture an opinion. Though I have frequently trapped squirrels by means of eggs, I never saw one in the act of preying on either young birds or eggs, and am consequently unable to give any information concerning their predatory habits on my own authority.

In Cumberland and Yorkshire I met with a few pairs of Larger Spotted Woodpeckers during the summer months in districts where large timber abounded. Norfolk appears to be the most northern county in which this species is to be found in any numbers. Occasionally, during the autumn and early winter, I have come across a few birds in the plantations near the coast. These, in every instance where I obtained a chance of examining them, were in the immature stage and, I believe, migrants from the north of Europe. I can find no evidence among my notes of having received wings from the lightships off the east coast; so I conjecture it is most probable these birds were stragglers from some flock that had first made the land on the inhospitable shores of Shetland or Orkney, Caithness or Eastern Ross, and then gradually worked their way towards the south. In the vicinity of Norwich this Woodpecker is by no means uncommon; and there are also residents in various other parts of the county. Throughout Kent, Sussex, and Surrey this species is very generally distributed. I have observed a few specimens in several other counties in addition to those named; and I believe the bird is more common than is usually supposed.

The food of this species is composed of insects of various kinds, for the most part extracted from the rough bark of trees. I have observed the young fed on the flying ant, also a mixture of flies, grubs, and other small insects. Should the old bird be shot while carrying this description of food, it will be found that the greater portion of the insects are alive—a black heaving mass, about the size of a Blackbird's egg, completely cramming the mouth and throat, and at times even forcing apart the upper and lower mandibles to a considerable extent.

Although this Woodpecker, like others of the family, makes use of many varieties of trees for breeding-purposes, I remarked in certain districts almost every nest would be found in the same description of timber. In the Highlands (though few nests now occupied have come under my observation) I noticed this bird breeding in Scotch fir and birch. With scarcely a single exception the old borings I examined in the forests were in Scotch fir. Elm and oak appear most frequently resorted to in the more southern counties; but I have also met with broods in several varieties of fruit-trees as well as willow and fir. The last nest I examined was in a remarkably high Scotch fir in one of the Sussex forests. The tree was rotten in the heart; and the bird appeared to have first taken up its quarters at the time when the decomposition set in. The highest boring was near the summit of the dead limb; and at short intervals a fresh entrance had been made as the decay progressed. Nine holes were counted in a space of about fifteen or sixteen feet, the young birds being discovered on their usual bed about a foot or fifteen inches below the level of the lowest boring. The diameter of this hole was exactly 2¼ inches; it was impossible to judge the size of the others, as decay had already set in round the edges.

Towards the end of September 1868 the north-east coast of Scotland was visited by a large flight of Woodpeckers, scattered birds being noticed in the district for at least ten days or a fortnight. Those that came under my own observation were, in several instances, in most unusual situations. I noticed a few on the coast near Dornoch; and in the dusk of a misty evening, with the wind blowing strong from the east, I passed numbers fluttering along the sandy links, and sheltering among the rough bushes on the Ross-shire side of the Dornoch Firth. They were especially numerous along the narrow strip of sand leading towards the Meikle Ferry. Judging by the worn and ragged condition of two or three I shot, and others that were picked up disabled, I imagine they must have met with rough weather on their passage, and also that the portion of the coast on which they had been driven was unsuited to their habits and requirements. From reports received from keepers and others in the neighbourhood, I learned the flight extended along the coast-line for many miles. Several of the birds that had been shot were brought or sent to me in order to be identified, a few from remote districts arriving in the shape of skins*. All I examined were in immature plumage and, for the most part, in very poor condition. From those I shot and picked up I did not reserve a single specimen, owing to the ragged and dirty state of their feathers. In consequence of the excessive weakness of the greater number met with, it is probable that but a small percentage would regain sufficient strength to enable them to continue their journey. A dozen or so of dead bodies were passed during one morning along the shore; and for a week or two longer I noticed a few single birds in the woods on both sides of the Firth. These cannot have remained long in the district, as after the end of the first week in October I did not observe any specimens in the vicinity of the coast, although I remained a year longer on the shores of the Firth.

The cry of the male is two or three notes of a low whistle, uttered most commonly in the spring, just before the breeding-season. I have, however, heard it on several occasions after the young were hatched. Whether the female has the same note I am unable to state. I remarked that the only sound produced by one I prevented for several hours from visiting her brood was a sharp klick, something resembling the noise by

* Although I am unable to record with certainty the fact that I have obtained the White-backed Woodpecker (*Picus leuconotus*) in the British Islands, I consider it may not be out of place to state that this species has, without doubt, occurred on our shores. Some years after returning to the south, I happened to discover one of the skins previously mentioned in a box of nests and other materials brought from the north. I was immediately struck by the appearance of the specimen, and, on comparing it with a skin of *P. leuconotus*, there was not the slightest doubt as to its identity. At the time the birds were killed I had no works that alluded to this species, and consequently imagined all those that came under my notice were simply immature specimens of *P. major*. I should not have mentioned this fact, had I not considered it highly probable that one at least of those I shot (and failed to preserve, owing to their ragged condition) also belonged to this northern species.

which impatient horsemen are supposed to urge on their unwilling steeds. Flying to the topmost branches of one of the adjacent trees, she uttered this note once or twice at short intervals, and speedily dashed off into the depths of the forest, returning again from time to time to discover if it was possible to make her way to her nest, which was placed in a large Scotch fir. On one occasion during her absence my attention was attracted by a Coal Tit, who was diligently searching for food to convey to his brood, cunningly concealed in a rotten stump at no great distance. While closely inspecting the limbs of the fir, he became aware of the holes in the trunk, and instantly popped into the very one in which the young Woodpeckers were quietly reposing. Startled by his unexpected appearance, or mistaking him for the shadow of their absent parent, the whole family at once broke out into full cry; and I never saw a bird make a hasty retreat with greater signs of alarm than poor *Parus ater* exhibited as he dashed from the hole and disappeared in the thickest of the surrounding cover.

If taken when young, these Woodpeckers are easily reared in confinement. Those I secured as specimens were procured in Sussex, the brood having been hatched in a large Scotch fir. The loud cries they emitted from the inside of the tree led me to believe (though unable to obtain a glimpse of them) that they must be ready to take their departure. On cutting an opening into the stem, I was surprised to discover my supposition was entirely wrong. Though the quills were plainly showing, there was not a single feather opened on any of the young birds. As I had shot both male and female, it was useless to leave them longer; so giving each of the four that composed the brood a good feed from the immense ball of insects I found in the mouth of one of their defunct parents, together with some pieces of raw beef, which I had brought with me in case it might be needed, I was enabled to satisfy their wants for the time. Being regularly supplied with raw beef, as well as a few worms, insects, and ants' eggs, their feathers rapidly expanded.

The following dates, taken from my notes jotted down at the time, will show the rate at which their plumage was assumed :—

"June 3rd. Young Woodpeckers taken from the nest; only pin-feathers visible. There was but little difference in the size of the brood of four; two, however, were slightly larger, as well as decidedly more vigorous.

"June 4th. All grown considerably, and feathers expanding rapidly. The two largest pecking and hammering round the woodwork of their cage.

"June 8th. The tail-feathers making their appearance.

"June 9th. One or two commenced to call, the note being similar to the whistle of the old male.

"June 14th. As the two largest and strongest persisted in knocking the smaller and weaker birds from their perches, they were killed today, being now full-fledged, and in the state in which they were required as specimens. Eye dark hazel. Beak dark slate. Feet and legs pale slate. These two I conjectured were males, the crowns of their heads being entirely covered by crimson feathers, while the smaller birds exhibited but an exceedingly minute patch of this colour. One of the weakest of the brood showed a pale pink mark on the feathers in the centre of the breast.

"June 21st. The two remaining birds were now full-fledged, and consequently shared the same fate as their companions. These were both faintly marked with pink in the centre of the breast. By this time I discovered the small patch of crimson on the head had increased, and there was not the slightest difference in the plumage of the four young ones that composed the brood, with the exception of the pale pink spot in the centre of the breast of the two more backward birds. From this evidence I think we may fairly state that, in their first feathers, the male and female of the Great Spotted Woodpecker show the same amount of crimson on the head."

LESSER SPOTTED WOODPECKER.

PICUS MINOR.

It is only in Sussex that I have met with the chance of closely studying the habits of the Lesser Spotted Woodpecker. With the exception of two or three pairs in Norfolk, and a stray bird or two in Middlesex, Surrey, and Kent, I have never positively identified this species in either England or Scotland. In the southern and eastern counties, I am of opinion that this Woodpecker is of much more frequent occurrence than is generally supposed, its small size and common habit of seeking its food in the upper branches of large trees enabling it to escape observation unless closely searched for.

I noticed that these birds, during winter and early spring, appear to have a regular course which they pursue from day to day. I repeatedly timed them arriving at certain trees from the same direction almost to the minute, and, after remaining their usual time among the branches, departing, if undisturbed, in the very line they had taken on the previous day. During the breeding-season the cares of providing for their young probably compel them to shorten their wanderings; and I have never noticed at that season the same regularity with regard to the course they follow. This custom is, I believe, common to all our British Woodpeckers, though I have not so frequently observed it in the two larger species.

Borings of the Lesser Spotted Woodpecker are to be met with in several varieties of forest timber, and also in apple-, plum-, and other fruit-trees. The breeding-quarters these birds resort to vary considerably in height. I have often both heard and seen them excavating holes near the uppermost parts of some tall poplars in the well-wooded district just north of the range of the South Downs; and on two or three occasions I observed their nests at no greater elevation than from five to six feet above the ground.

Though usually somewhat shy, and, as a rule, selecting their breeding-stations in some quiet spot where they are free from constant observation or interruption, I discovered a brood of young in a pear-tree standing not more than four or five yards from the door of a cottage, in a village of some considerable size. On examining the hole, which was placed at such a low elevation as to be easily inspected without mounting the tree, the young (though unable to fly any distance) hurriedly made their escape, climbing rapidly to the upper branches, where the old birds were fluttering round in the greatest consternation. Being in want of specimens at this particular age, I had little difficulty in capturing the whole brood, consisting of four. There was not the slightest difference in the size and plumage of the three largest, the crowns of their heads being strongly marked with red; one was somewhat smaller, and exhibited but few red feathers on the head. From the observations made while rearing the Great Spotted Woodpeckers, I have not the slightest doubt that in a few days this bird would have assumed the same plumage as the rest of the brood. It is, I consider, quite clear that there is little or no difference between the immature males and females till after the first moult. The food brought by the old birds appeared similar to that procured by the Greater Spotted, viz. flying ants and other small insects, with a few grubs and caterpillars. This garden appeared to possess some peculiar attractions for the Woodpecker tribe. The previous season a pair of the Great Spotted Woodpeckers had reared their young in an adjoining tree, the two limbs being within a few feet of one another. When examined side by side, it was easy to distinguish the difference in the size of the holes cut by the two species, the entrance to the nursery of *Picus minor* being about half an inch smaller in diameter than that required by his larger relative.

The note of the male is a low whistle, repeated two or three times in succession.

I was assured by a gardener in the interior of Sussex that this species was destructive to peas. He showed me two or three he had shot while protecting these vegetables from the attacks of Hawfinches and Sparrows. There was not the slightest doubt as to the identity of the birds, and I fully believe they were killed where the man described (I have repeatedly seen a pair or two frequenting the garden); but that the peas were the object of their visit I can scarcely credit.

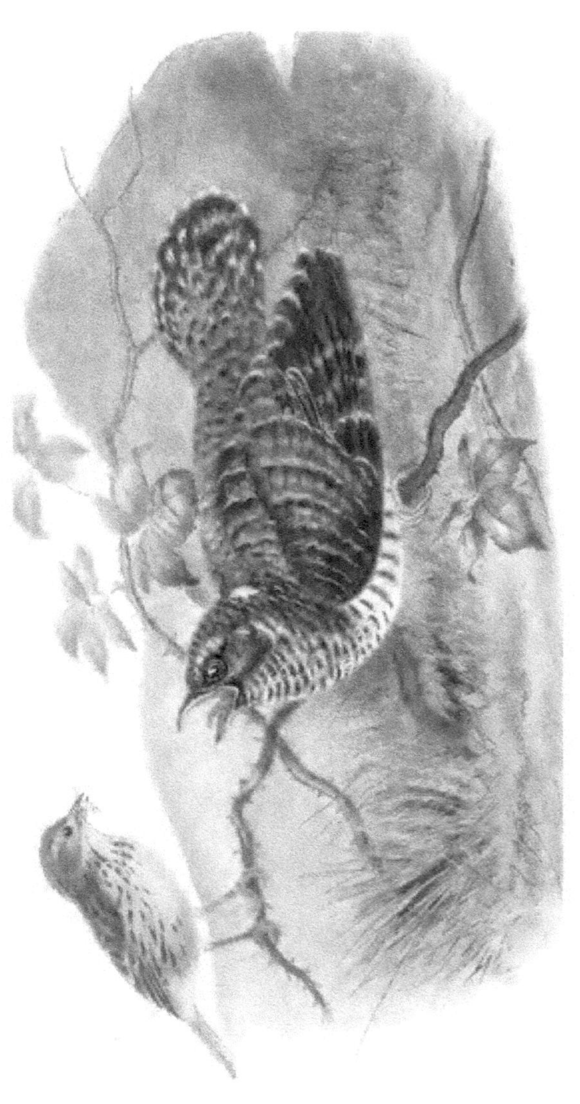

CUCKOO.

CUCULUS CANORUS.

There are few parts of Great Britain to which the Cuckoo is not a well-known summer visitor, being especially numerous in some of the wildest districts of the north of Scotland. The rocks and heather of the Highland glens are fully as attractive to this singular species as the plantations and extensive reed-beds of the east of Norfolk or the furze-covered downs of Sussex. After reaching our shores in spring, Cuckoos apparently proceed with but little delay towards their haunts, few remaining for any length of time in the neighbourhood of the coast. For a day or so they may be seen flitting along the hedgerows, invariably attracting attention as they flap slowly over the bushes (their manner of flight somewhat resembling that of the smaller Hawks); the wanderers, however, speedily pass over, and the vicinity of the shore is deserted, except by an occasional straggler, till the return journey is entered upon early in autumn.

It is probable that Cuckoos return regularly to their accustomed haunts, from which during the season they seldom stray any considerable distance. Though failing to catch a glimpse of the bird, I was frequently informed a few years back, by keepers, shepherds, and others, of a Cuckoo exhibiting red or tawny plumage, that was seen for two or three seasons resorting to a well-sheltered valley in the South Downs. During the latter part of May and early in June 1870 I repeatedly observed a male of this species, showing a broad patch of white on the wings, skimming over the marshes and round the reed-beds about Hickling Broad in Norfolk; in the following year a bird with much the same markings was again seen frequenting the same localities.

Though several facts still remain to be ascertained, the breeding-habits of the Cuckoo have been so fully described by many authors that most of the peculiarities of this singular species are now generally well known to all who take an interest in bird-life; the extraordinary manner in which the young eject their companions from the nest has also been accurately depicted. The observations that I have been enabled to make on this subject threw no further light on the habits of the bird, and may consequently be passed over.

The following extracts from my notes for May 1872 tend to prove that the egg is laid on the ground and then conveyed to the nest. Having marked down a Green Sandpiper, in a dyke in the Potter-Heigham marshes, I followed the bank round towards the spot where the bird was lost sight of. On looking cautiously over a thorn bush which had effectually concealed my approach, the Sandpiper rose and was at once secured. At the report of the gun a Cuckoo fluttered from the sloping bank within a yard of where I stood, and on examining the spot (a bare patch among brambles, weeds, and rough grass) an egg was discovered lying on the ground. There could not be the slightest doubt as to its identity, and the bird was evidently a female; in all probability, unless so suddenly alarmed, she would have removed it on rising on wing.

I am inclined to believe that whatever may be the position of the nest, the egg is invariably laid on the ground and then transported to the spot selected. In May 1873 I happened to catch sight of a female Cuckoo skimming slowly over a rush-marsh in the east of Norfolk; a Pipit was following closely in attendance, and while for a few moments she swooped down into the grass the poor little bird hovered round with quivering wings exhibiting the greatest distress. Under the impression that the Cuckoo must at that moment have deposited her egg in the nest of the Pipit, I was proceeding to examine the spot, when it was discovered that a plank forming the footway across a marsh-dyke had been removed, and my visit was deferred till another day. Again and again I passed the marsh, occasionally noticing one or other of the Pipits, though the plank still being absent the small drain in which the old Cuckoo was lost sight of remained unexplored. It was not till some weeks later, when a young Cuckoo attended by a Pipit was observed on the marsh wall *, that I made my way towards the spot previously mentioned, when a nest, evidently but lately deserted, was at once detected. There were undoubted signs that a juvenile Cuckoo had occupied the nest; an egg also was lying in the grass near at hand, though I was unable to find the remains of any of the unfortunates that ought in the usual course of affairs to have been ejected. It is very probable, however, that the youngsters when turned out may have been picked up by a passing Rook or Crow; and rats, I also obtained good evidence, were extremely active in the immediate neighbourhood. From the actions of the Pipits and the date of the appearance of the young Cuckoo I am convinced that the egg was deposited in the manner described; should my conjecture prove correct, it is evident that the Cuckoo merely skims down to the nest, inserts her egg, and immediately departs.

No one who has watched the female attended from time to time by her numerous admirers can possibly imagine that Cuckoos pair; while fishing quietly in some sheltered corner among the reed-beds of the Norfolk broads, or resting on the breezy downs of Sussex, I have met with ample opportunities of observing their habits during summer.

A long list of the birds to whose charge the Cuckoo commits its offspring has been given by several authors; the nests in which I have found the eggs are but five in number—Meadow-Pipit, Reed-Warbler, Hedge-Sparrow, Pied Wagtail, and Robin. On the downs of Sussex, as well as on the moorlands of Perthshire and other northern counties, I remarked that Cuckoos most frequently consigned their eggs to the care of Meadow-Pipits. In the broad district of the east of Norfolk the swaying cradles of the Reed-Wren appear to be largely patronized, though I have noticed a few young birds being fed by the Pipits that breed along the rough banks in the drier parts of the rush-marshes.

On the 18th of June, 1875, a Cuckoo that had recently left the nest was watched for some time in one of the sheltered valleys on the South Downs between Falmer and Lewes while attended by a pair of Meadow-Pipits, and a specimen being required, the youngster was shot, when it proved blind in both eyes. I remarked that the foster-parents had at times hovered round their charge, probably in some manner directing its movements, as it occasionally settled among the low twigs of the stunted thorn bushes †.

The note of the Cuckoo may be heard at all hours of the night. I find the following entry in my journal for 1868, under date of May 17th, jotted down while driving through the Western Highlands:—"On pulling up at the Inn at Kenlochewe half an hour after midnight a Cuckoo was calling loudly in the plantations round the building; others were also heard before daylight as we proceeded on our way towards the east." In the neighbourhood of the Norfolk broads these birds are at times exceedingly noisy during the night. While on Hickling Broad an hour before daybreak on the 15th of June, 1873, the continued jarring of the Night-Hawks and the calls of the Cuckoos, coupled with the discordant sounds arising from the Sedge-birds and frogs in the reed-beds, rendered it utterly impossible to distinguish the note of a small Warbler that I believed to be in the locality.

Though the Cuckoo has been repeatedly charged with destroying the eggs of game, I must confess that

* The embankments thrown up to hold back the waters of the broads, meres, or rivers are termed "walls" in this part of Norfolk.

† The interior of the mouth of this specimen was exceedingly bright orange; legs and feet pale lemon-yellow, shaded with a tinge of ochre; the eyes a dull grey tint and evidently sightless.

this habit has entirely escaped my notice. It was recently asserted by a well-known sportsman in the 'Field' that a keeper had watched a Cuckoo carry off the egg of a Pheasant from the nest, and also shot the thief while consuming the plunder. In order to inquire more fully into the matter, I requested the address of the man, and ascertained the facts to be as follows:—The keeper happened to have noticed a Pheasant's nest from which several eggs had disappeared, and imagining that a shepherd boy was the culprit, concealed himself in a hedgerow to watch the spot; almost immediately a Cuckoo alighted in an oak tree and shortly after flew down and carried an egg some ten or a dozen yards on to the open ground. While in the act of sucking it the bird was shot, and close at hand were found the shells of the eggs previously stolen from the nest. In answer to a question as to the manner in which the egg was transported, my informant stated that the bird appeared to have pecked a hole in the shell before taking it in its bill. Two cases in which Cuckoos destroyed the eggs of Wood-Pigeons had also come under his observation, the eggs in both instances being sucked on the nests. It was only in the summer of 1881, when all the smaller birds were scarce, owing to the wide-spread destruction caused by the severity of the winter, that the keeper had noticed Cuckoos attack the eggs of either Pheasants or Pigeons. This man evidently considered eggs the natural food of the Cuckoo—small, perhaps, preferred, as a rule, but the larger taken without hesitation in the absence of the former. More recently he had shot a female Cuckoo which had settled on a rough bank by the nest of a Robin, and devoured in succession the contents of three eggs. He also informed me that he had seen a female Cuckoo sitting on the nest of a Spotted Flycatcher *, where she remained for some time; this latter statement by no means corresponds with my own observations, which would lead to the belief that the egg is laid on the ground and then conveyed to the nest.

If the Cuckoo is as destructive to eggs as its accusers declare, it appears strange that the depredations of a species so widely distributed have hitherto escaped my observation: I have also great doubts as to whether the beak of a Cuckoo is sufficiently powerful to break the egg of a Pheasant. Many years ago I frequently assisted the keepers in killing down Jays, Magpies, and Crows during spring in a densely wooded district in the east of Sussex. These robbers were captured in traps baited with the eggs of Thrushes or Pigeons; but though Cuckoos were exceedingly numerous not a single bird was taken.

Letters also appeared in the 'Field' during the first quarter of 1882 asserting that the Cuckoo had been discovered to feed largely on the eggs of small birds. The only instance I ever met with in any manner corroborating this supposed habit occurred many years ago in Sussex. While passing a thick clump of holly bushes a Cuckoo blundered out within a yard, and on examining the spot I discovered the nest of a Hedge-Sparrow containing one egg, the shell of which exhibited two small slits or cuts apparently caused by the beak of a bird. On further search being made, another egg, entirely uninjured, was detected on the ground below the nest.

Within the last few years I ascertained from the natives in a remote district of the eastern counties that the belief still exists that the Cuckoo turns into a Hawk during winter.

* The Flycatcher was referred to as a "Hay-builder" (a name not unfrequently bestowed on the Whitethroat in Sussex); there was, however, no doubt as to the species, the nest being built on the limb of a trained fruit-tree, and the habits and plumage of the bird accurately described.

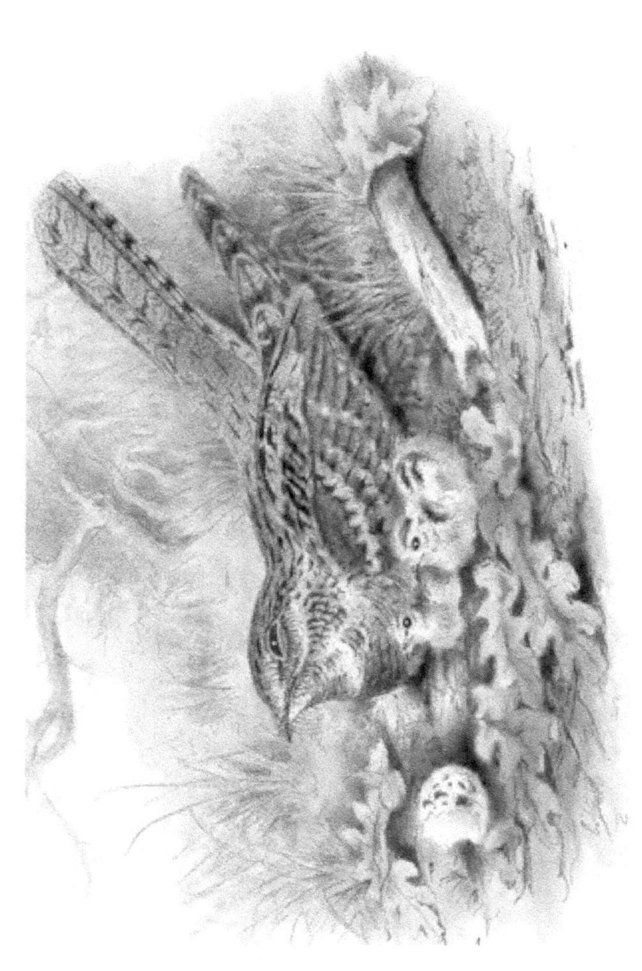

NIGHTJAR.

CAPRIMULGUS EUROPÆUS.

I have met with this singular bird in every county in which I have passed the summer months, from Sussex to Sutherland. Though I failed to notice the species in Caithness, it is probably to be found in the southern or more wooded portion, the barren and treeless moors of the central and northern parts of the county being perhaps unsuited to its habits. Throughout the Long Island I never observed a single specimen, though often crossing the hills at all hours of the day and night. In the east of Ross-shire it appears as numerous as in the south of England; indeed I am acquainted with no part of Great Britain where the bird is so plentiful as on the hill of Tarlogie near Tain.

The Nightjar is only a summer visitor to our islands, and is rarely seen before the end of the first week in May. If met with at sea on a fine still morning, while making the passage of the Channel, its curious flight would mislead any one unacquainted with its habits at this season. I have known several instances where this species has been mistaken for a large Petrel—its flight, as it turns and twists over the water, now hovering for a moment over a submerged butterfly or moth, and again dashing rapidly after some passing insect, much resembling that of the wandering sea-bird that is supposed to be the harbinger of storm and tempest. Every other migrant I am acquainted with pursues its course with but slight deviation from the point for which it is making; this species, however, may frequently be observed hawking about over salt water in much the same manner as a Swallow or Martin over a pond or river. On one occasion I carefully noted the movements of a party of two or three of these birds skimming round the steamboat from which I was watching them. The sea was without a ripple; and every action, as they rose or fell in the air or darted over the surface, was plainly visible; and I was easily able to keep them in view for at least a quarter of an hour, though now and then at a distance of three or four hundred yards. To the best of my recollection I have never noticed one of these birds at sea after eight or nine o'clock in the morning; and I believe they generally reach the coast at a still earlier hour. It is a singular fact that, although they by no means hasten their journey over the Channel, and remain (as previously described) for a considerable time either searching for food or sweeping in a sportive manner over the surface, I have never noticed one so engaged over any of the inland waters in the neighbourhood of their summer haunts. I have studied their habits in the vicinity of highland lochs and the larger broads in the eastern counties, and have been unable to record a single instance where they followed their prey over the surface of either loch or broad.

The Nightjar (as its name implies) is never heard, and seldom seen, by day, unless disturbed from the spot where it is resting. It is usually flushed from the bare ground in a ride through a wood or an open space on a moor or down, usually at only a short distance from some bush of ferns, rank heather, or other mountain plant. If cautiously approached, the bird may be noticed squatting almost flat on the ground, with the head drawn back between the shoulders, and the eyes either entirely or partly closed. It now and then takes up its quarters for its daily rest in somewhat curious situations: I have repeatedly started one from garden-seats or chairs, and more than once from flower-beds, as well as garden-paths. This has usually occurred soon after their arrival or shortly before their departure in the autumn.

On fine still nights the Nightjar may often be seen rising from the centre of a dusty road, dashing out of sight for a moment or two, and again coming into view as it settles at a short distance further ahead. This curious performance is supposed to be induced by the habit of dusting itself, in which the bird is said to indulge. It is quite possible that this may be the case, though, owing to the darkness, I was never able to ascertain its actions on the ground.

During the autumn months the Nightjar may frequently be observed at dusk darting round the chimneys and up and down the streets of towns in the neighbourhood of the sea-coast. I distinctly watched one of these birds, through the gloom of an impending storm, alight on the roof of a house in Yarmouth; the position it took up was lengthways on a ridge-tile.

The remarkable serrated claw on the centre toe of this species is frequently supposed by country people to assist the bird in clearing the scales or down of the moths it captures from its mouth and bristles. For my own part, I am of opinion that the true use of this singularly formed claw has not yet been discovered.

As the sun disappears the well-known whirring note of the Nightjar may be heard resounding far and near through its haunts. Perched on the limb of a tree in the outskirts of a dense covert or a straggling plantation, the bird gives utterance to the strange jarring sounds that, even when listened to at a short distance, appear as they rise and fall in the silence of the wood, now loud and then almost imperceptible, to spring first from one quarter and the next moment from an entirely opposite direction. A warm still evening in June is the time to study the note of this singular bird; in cold, wet, or stormy weather, when the wind whistles through the trees, the note of the Nightjar may be awaited in vain, or, at most, a single whirr will be detected in some sheltered corner.

The food of this species consists, I believe, entirely of moths, beetles, and other nocturnal insects. It is not only perfectly harmless, but most useful in clearing off a superabundance of destructive insects. Five-and-twenty or thirty years ago I have heard one or two keepers in the southern counties declare they were allied to the Hawk tribe, and the poor birds suffered in consequence. This exceedingly mistaken idea has, I believe, now entirely disappeared, and for years I have never, either in England or Scotland, met with a single guardian of the preserves who was not perfectly acquainted with their habits.

Nightjar and Goatsucker are the commonest of the titles by which this species is known. In some localities it is styled the Nighthawk, Eve-jar, and Fern-Owl. The reason for the appellation of Goatsucker is too ridiculous to need a word of explanation.

The two curiously marbled eggs of this species are placed either on a clearing in the wood or thicket the bird frequents, or on an open spot on a moor or down. There is usually some shelter from bush, bank, or low shrub within a few feet of the spot where they are deposited. With the exception of a dead leaf or two, or a strand of grass carried by the wind and lodged in the slight natural hollow the bird makes use of, there is not the least suspicion of a nest.

The Plate shows a female with two young ones newly hatched. It is taken from a rough sketch made of the group in a grassy valley among the South Downs between Lewes and Brighton. The eggs had been laid on the slope of a hill facing the south, and were sheltered from above by a thick and spreading furze bush.

SWIFT.

CYPSELUS APUS.

The Swift may be observed in most parts of England and Scotland, being distributed more or less plentifully over the country from north to south. This species appears, according to my own experience, to fall off in numbers in the Northern Highlands; there is, however, a large colony, which has been established for many years, in the Cromarty rocks, overlooking the Moray Firth. I also noticed a small party, early in May 1869, near Durness, in Sutherland; and a week or two later my attention was attracted by a couple of pairs which were screaming over the road between Castletown and Dunnet Head, on the north coast of Caithness.

The time that the Swift passes in these islands does not extend over a longer period than between three and four months. Though its visit is so limited in duration, this species appears able to withstand sudden changes of temperature far more readily than either the Swallow or Martin, both of whom arrive in this country at a considerably earlier date. I am aware that some authors have recorded instances where this bird has been captured in a helpless condition during cold and stormy weather; but not a single Swift has ever come under my observation exhibiting the slightest signs of being incapacitated by wet or cold, though Swallows and Martins might be seen on all sides sheltering from the force of the storm. I particularly remarked this fact on June 8, 1871, at which date a gale of wind and rain (succeeding several days of cold and cutting breezes from the north and east) broke over the Norfolk coast.

The food of this species is composed entirely of insects. As a rule, the Swift captures its prey at a greater elevation than Swallows or Martins.

I have never observed a Swift settle on the ground; and it is probable that its nesting-materials (straw or grass and a few small feathers) are collected while on wing. Incommoded by its long wings and the shortness of its legs, this species seems unable to rise from the ground. I never tried the experiment but once; and then the bird was either incapable or unwilling to make its escape till lifted a short distance into the air.

For breeding-purposes the Swift, for the most part, resorts to cavities under the eaves of houses, or any accessible niches and apertures they can discover in churches and other large buildings. In wild localities, where situations of this description are wanting, they do not hesitate to make use of fissures and cracks in the face of cliffs or precipices. In several localities round the northern coast, and in one instance in a remote and rugged Highland glen, I have watched these birds flying up and down the face of the rocks without being able to detect any of their nesting-quarters. So rapid are their movements, and so instantaneous the evolutions they go through while turning and twisting to and fro in front of the cliffs, that it is almost impossible to keep any single specimen in sight. As I previously stated, there is a large colony in the Cromarty rocks; here they may be easily watched from the sands at the foot of the cliffs.

SWALLOW.

HIRUNDO RUSTICA.

The Swallow is without doubt one of our most familiar British birds, being well known in every county from north to south. I have not observed it in the Outer Hebrides, though I am of opinion stragglers must occasionally make their appearance in those barren islands, as I have seen a bird or two fly past when half across the Minch, in the beginning of May.

In many cases, I believe, the early Swallows so frequently reported are simply Sand-Martins, of which but an imperfect view has been obtained. The Greenfinch, however, as I am well aware, has misled several observers who were not thoroughly acquainted with the singular flight of the old male at that season. This species is usually supposed to arrive early in April; but although numbers are observed shortly after that date, these birds continue crossing in small parties till the end of May. While noting the arrival of birds of passage during several years, I remarked large quantities making their way to land on various dates, May 17th and again the 21st, 22nd, and 25th being days on which numerous arrivals were recorded.

I have never seen Swallows crossing the Channel in large compact flocks; scores, or possibly even hundreds, might be in sight at the same time; but they would be flying in small scattered parties. Occasionally there might be a break in the stream of travellers, when only a single bird or two would fly quietly past; and again, after an interval of perhaps an hour or more, fresh comers would appear in view. Though I have watched Swallows while making the passage of the Channel on many occasions, I do not remember having seen large numbers on wing after midday. Single birds and small parties may continue crossing till late in the afternoon; but the main bodies apparently make an early start, shortly after daybreak. Some years back an unfortunate Swallow was transfixed on the point of the arrow forming the vane to the signal-pole on the centre pier at Shoreham Harbour. The bird, I conclude, must have been making its way to the shore during the night, and was probably attracted by the harbour-light, which stands at but a short distance inland from the signal-pole.

All my observations concerning the arrival of the Swallow were made in the English Channel. From the numbers constantly seen during favourable weather crossing straight from the French coast to our southern shores, I imagine that the short sea-passage is the favourite route, the remainder of the journey to the northern counties being probably made over land. It is, however, clear that a few, at all events, must pass over some portions of the North Sea, as in the spring of 1873 I received the wings of several Swallows that had struck against the light-ships off the east coast.

In the last week of April 1874 I watched for some time an immense concourse of Swallows collected together by the side of a pool of brackish water, just over the sea-beach near Shoreham. The wind was blowing in strong gusts from the west, with drifting rain; and the whole of the birds were sitting facing the gale. Hundreds were closely packed on the ground at the water's edge; but the greater number were perched on the points of some slightly exposed faggots and stakes which had been driven into the mud to keep back the tides. Those that were settled on the twigs covered almost every available spot for a distance of at least a quarter of a mile. When disturbed they speedily gave evidence that, though attempting to shelter from the force of the wind and rain, they were by no means incapacitated from flight or suffering from the effects of the storm. It was between 9 and 10 o'clock in the morning when I observed this gathering; and on passing the same spot late in the afternoon, by which time the weather had moderated, there was hardly a Swallow to be seen. As there had been but a light breeze in the early morning till a few hours after daybreak, when the wind freshened, it is most probable these birds had only managed to make the land after the commencement of the gale. Then finding it too rough to continue their journey, they had brought up in the best shelter available to wait for a change of weather.

Swallows are speedily affected by a sudden change of temperature. I have on several occasions noticed them much cut up by storms of wind and rain. At such times they may be observed sheltering from the cold and drifting squalls behind banks and hedges, and apparently utterly incapable of the slightest exertion.

There is but little doubt that, as a rule, they leave our shores in the autumn in companies larger than those which arrived in the spring. I never met with these on the return passage, but have frequently noticed the gatherings that take place as the time for quitting our shores draws near. I believe it is usually admitted that the majority have taken their departure before November. Large numbers, however, remain after that date in suitable localities. On several sunny days during the first and second weeks in November 1880 I watched a constant stream of Swallows flitting up and down under the shelter of the rugged cliffs that stretch from the Logan Rock to the Land's End. Though a cold and cutting wind from the north-east was blowing at the time, the atmosphere below the level of the moss-grown headlands was warm and pleasant; and here the birds were able to escape the effects of the wintery blast.

On looking over my notes, I can find several instances where small parties of two or three, as well as single birds, have come under my notice up to within a few days of Christmas. These were generally observed on fine hot days hawking up and down in some warm spot, either under the shelter of a row of houses facing the south, or below the level of some range of cliffs where the exclusion of the wind and the heat of the sun enabled the poor birds to pick up a few insects, and prolong their lives till a continuation of rough and stormy weather would put an end to their existence. These late stayers are probably, with but few exceptions, the young of backward broods too weak to attempt the passage of the Channel when the main body take their departure. I consider it extremely doubtful if a single individual ever survives the winter. When discovered half-starved and numbed by cold in some crevice to which they have betaken themselves to die, they have frequently been described as hibernating. These ridiculous reports have led to the belief, in some remote country districts, that Swallows always retire on the approach of cold weather to some convenient spot (either under water, into the mud, or a cavity in some tree or building) and there sleep away the winter. Even as lately as the present summer (A.D. 1882) I have been gravely assured that such was the fact.

There are few parts of the British Islands where Swallows are not welcomed and protected. It is seldom that the troublesome habit of placing its nest, with all the accompanying dirt and filth, in undesirable situations, which is so frequently laid to the charge of the House-Martin, can be ascribed to this species. The interiors of chimneys are perhaps most frequently resorted to for breeding-purposes. It also makes use of the rafters and stays in boat-sheds, farm-lodges, and wooden bridges, to place its cradle on. I have seen numbers of nests in the roofs of the oast-houses or barns in which hops are dried. In country districts in the southern and eastern counties where the hop is cultivated, such quarters appear to have some peculiar attraction for these birds. In the summer of 1866, when in Glenlyon, in Perthshire, a pair of Swallows placed their nest on the head of a red deer, which was nailed on a small wooden porch that formed the entrance to the lodge. The nest was built on the upper portion of the skull, between the bases of the antlers. The birds were perfectly fearless; and while the female was sitting, the favourite perch of the male was on one of the brow-antlers.

Swallows and Martins may frequently be observed, when flying over a river or pond, dipping down to the water either to drink or seize a submerged insect. This operation is generally easily effected. Several hundreds of these birds, however, lost their lives in this manner a few years back in the east of Sussex. The water had been drawn off from a large pond in order to thin down the fish; and although the surface still retained its usual appearance, it was in reality nothing more than a thick black mud of about the consistency of treacle. No sooner had the wing of one unlucky bird been caught by the mud while skimming too closely over the surface, than the struggles of the sufferer brought scores to the spot; and within an hour or two the mud was dotted all over with hundreds of dead and dying victims. Some of those nearest the shore were reached with landing-nets, and after being cleansed from the mud in fresh water, and placed in the sun for a short time to dry their feathers, made good their escape.

Though it is now some years since I observed the performance, professional birdcatchers are well aware how readily Swallows can be attracted by a decoy of their own species. The brace-birds they employ are perfectly untrained, and simply flutter helplessly in the air when the twig or perch* to which they are attached is lifted. I have watched numbers captured in this manner—almost every Swallow that appeared in sight being drawn to the spot by the struggles of the dangling prisoner, and flying straight for the fatal nets. Two or three are often taken at a single pull while skimming rapidly past or hovering for a moment over the lure. As the object in capturing these unfortunate birds may possibly seem a mystery, it may be as well to state that there was at one time a considerable demand for the skins by plumassiers. Dozens and dozens were supplied for trap-shooting, though the numbers procured for this purpose were limited, as the hapless captives were supposed to show no sport if they had been any length of time in confinement. Like Starlings, if crammed in the villanous store-cages, Swallows soon become incapable of flight, and refuse to rise when liberated from the trap. Their wretched bodies were also often to be detected among the rows of Wagtails and other small birds that, plucked and neatly ranged round a dish or impaled on a wooden skewer, were hawked as Wheatears about the streets of towns on the south coast by females of far from inviting aspect.

Insects of various kinds captured on the wing form the food of this harmless and useful bird. I watched a pair or two of Swallows flying close over the trees and shrubs in a garden near Brighton at half-past eight one evening during the last week in July; and though it was impossible to see clearly, in consequence of dull and gloomy weather and rapidly approaching darkness, I was almost forced into the belief that the cockchafers, which were swarming round the trees, must be the object of their search. I should imagine, however, these insects would prove too large and tough a prey.

These birds may often be observed collected in great numbers on the limbs of trees; and they have no more favourite resting-place than the wires of the telegraph: here they may at times be seen gathered in immense flocks; I have watched occasionally an almost unbroken line of birds stretching from post to post. Towards the end of summer large flocks, composed for the most part of young, resort at roosting-time to the reeds and willows overhanging streams, or the large beds of water-plants, reeds, rushes, and other rank-growing vegetation that are found in marshy districts. In the latter end of July 1881 I discovered a favourite haunt of some hundreds of Swallows, in the midst of a dismal swamp in the east of Norfolk. Passing the spot on several evenings, we disturbed the birds on each occasion; and it is singular that

* Known as the "swish" among professionals.

they should return so persistently to a spot that must have been at least two or three miles from where the majority were hatched. As we quanted* quietly up the narrow and almost overgrown channel that led through the reed-bed, it was easy to obtain a view of the whole colony before they took wing. I remarked, on two or three consecutive nights, that about half a score of Pied Wagtails kept company with the Swallows. These were running about on the flags and water-plants, and appeared to resort regularly to the same spot at roosting-time.

A specimen of the Swallow has now and then come under my notice so richly tinted with chestnut on the breast, as almost to approach the colouring of *Hirundo savignii*.

* To work a boat with the long setting-pole or quant used in the eastern counties is, in that district, termed quanting.

HOUSE-MARTIN.

HIRUNDO URBICA.

The remarks concerning the distribution of the Swallow might equally be applied to the Martin. There is, however, one addition—viz. that I have good evidence a few now and then make their appearance in the Hebrides, having watched a pair skimming over the harbour of Stornoway in the spring of 1875. I could obtain no information concerning their nesting on the island; so it is possible they were only resting for a while on their way to more northern summer-quarters.

I frequently remarked that these birds, like Sand-Martins, are more punctual in the time of their arrival than Swallows. After the main bodies have taken up their quarters, it is seldom stragglers are noticed on the passage in any thing approaching the numbers of the dilatory Swallows.

In the same manner as the majority of the family, this species is readily affected by protracted storms of wind and rain; it is, I believe, the greatest sufferer from these causes. On two or three occasions I have known almost the whole of the birds in certain localities either destroyed or forced to take their departure, owing to want of food. From observations made in various parts of the country, I should be of opinion that this species has greatly decreased during the last few years.

Previous to leaving our shores for the winter, Martins often collect into immense flocks. I have witnessed these gatherings as early as the 16th of August. On that date in 1874, the rocks to the east of Canty Bay, on the coast of the Firth of Forth, were perfectly alive with thousands of these birds, clustering in swarms along the face of the cliffs. The small colony of Martins that have their summer quarters in the rocks in this neighbourhood do not exceed a few hundreds in number. It is evident that the greater part of this multitude must have been strangers from the interior of the country or the towns and villages along the coast. Though all signs of the visitors had disappeared on the following day, there was no diminution in the number of the residents; and I observed they remained for some weeks longer in their usual haunts. On September 27th, 1879, immense flights alighted on some large buildings near Brighton, the roofs being completely covered. After remaining three or four hours in the vicinity, the whole body took their departure in a south-westerly direction. These birds remain in considerable numbers as late as the second week in November. I watched hundreds flying, in company with Swallows, under the shelter of the rocks near the Land's End at that date in 1880. Compared with Swallows, I have often remarked that but few late stayers are noticed after the main body have left our shores. Martins, I believe, more commonly than others of the Hirundines, desert their young if these are unable to accompany them at the time of migration. About the year 1855 or 1856, I remember several nests, under one building in the east of Sussex, being left with the broods utterly unprovided for. So sudden and simultaneous was the departure of all the birds, that I should almost be of opinion that disease or some unavoidable mishap must have been the cause of such unnatural behaviour.

The situations in which this species principally delights to fix its nest are against the brick or stonework above windows (the sides in some instances adhering to the glass, and entirely preventing the opening of the frame), under the eaves of houses, and occasionally under porches and other inconvenient positions. No wonder careful housewives frequently call out against the dirt and filth, to say nothing of the extra work caused by the pertinacity with which this persevering bird will return to some undesirable spot, after all traces of the offending materials have been carefully removed and effaced. In the spring of 1878, I noticed these birds so eager to obtain quarters against the west face of a house in East Norfolk, that their mud-formed cradles (some occupied and others either incomplete or deserted) stretched in an almost unbroken line from side to side. Two or three nests I remarked were commenced immediately below others, and were built up in such a manner that it was evident, if continued in the same style, they must effectually block the entrances of the two above them. The progress was unusually slow, as the structures were at least twice the ordinary size; I discovered, however, as the work approached completion, that they were contracted towards the upper portion, and in not the slightest degree interfered with the neighbouring domiciles. Several of the adjoining nests were also of greater length than those usually seen, the entrances being placed, in almost every instance, about the centre of the edifice. The small sketch will give an idea of the manner in which some of these curiously fashioned nests were constructed.

To show the rapidity with which this species now and then decreases in numbers in some localities, I may state that while in 1878 there were seventy-five occupied nests round this house, there was but a single one in 1879. Though several more nests were built in the following year, and they have now slowly increased, the birds have by no means reached their former numbers.

In many wild localities where houses are scarce, Martins resort to rocks and cliffs for breeding-purposes. There are two or three small colonies along the rocks below the ruins of Tantallon Castle, on the coast of East Lothian. A far larger number may be found during the summer frequenting the Cromarty rocks (the same range occupied by the Swifts). In many of these situations it is extremely difficult to detect the nests—the height at which they are placed, and the materials with which they are constructed, rendering their appearance almost identical both in colour and outline with the cliffs themselves.

The ignorance often displayed concerning the difference between the two species Swallows and Martins is certainly astonishing when it is considered in what universal estimation these birds are held in most parts of the country. An author, who is often quoted by ornithological writers, gave some interesting information concerning a Sparrow who had appropriated a Swallow's nest being built in by the rightful owners. It is, of course, obvious that the birds must have been Martins. Though I never noticed the usurper served in this well-merited fashion, I have seen the unfortunate Martins driven from their nests on numberless occasions. Only a few weeks back, one of the illustrated weeklies favoured its readers with an engraving entitled the return of the Swallows. In this work of art a number of birds, evidently intended for Swallows, were represented hanging in graceful attitudes on some Martins' nests suspended under the eaves of a house.

When authors and artists who profess to describe and depict the habits of the birds exhibit such a scanty amount of knowledge, the ignorance of the general public is scarcely to be wondered at.

Like the rest of the family, this species is not only perfectly harmless to gardeners and farmers, but it confers an inestimable boon on all by ridding the air of millions of noxious insects.

The movements of the large bodies of Martins and Swallows that collect on the south coast previous to their departure in the autumn are extremely perplexing: one day a continuous stream passes towards the east, and on the following it is quite possible the greater number may be making their way towards the west. Their flight, like that of the Pipits and a few other small birds, is usually supposed to be governed, to a certain extent, by the wind. I noted down the direction taken by the House-Martins and Swallows while passing over the marshes along the coast between Shoreham and Worthing on half-a-dozen occasions during the first three weeks in October 1882. The wind and weather at the time the observations were made are also recorded. This extract from my notes will give some slight idea of the movements of the birds:—

"October 2nd. Strong wind, west south-west. Immense numbers of House-Martins and Swallows flying due east before the wind; thousands continued passing till 3 P.M.

"October 3rd. Wind west and north-west; weather fine. House-Martins and Swallows noticed on wing all the morning. These birds were not pursuing any settled course; some east, some west, and others out to sea.

"October 9th. Wind south; weather fine. House-Martins and Swallows flying east during morning and midday. Numbers observed making their way out to sea between 4 P.M. and 5 P.M.

"October 10th. Wind south-east; weather dull and fine. A few House-Martins and thousands of Swallows flying east.

"October 13th. Wind north-east; weather fine. House-Martins and Swallows flying east.

"October 20th. Wind south; weather fine. After midday, wind strong from south-west. In the early morning a few House-Martins and Swallows flying east. After 10 A.M. the numbers increased, and a continued stream kept passing before the wind up till 3 P.M."

It will be seen that on five days out of six the greater number of the birds were passing from west to east. On former years when I noted their movements in the same locality, the course they followed while on flight was in exactly opposite directions on several consecutive days.

SAND-MARTIN.

HIRUNDO RIPARIA.

According to my own observations, Sand-Martins are met with in most parts of the British Islands, wherever localities suitable for their breeding-operations can be discovered.

Severe weather in the spring is by no means uncommon after the arrival of this diminutive traveller; the Sand-Martin, however, proves itself a remarkably hardy bird. I have more than once noticed hundreds winging their way through a heavy snowstorm in the month of April, and apparently none the worse if the sun broke through on the following day. These birds are the first of the family to make their appearance in the spring. The greater number of those that visit the British Islands probably reach their quarters within a fortnight after the first arrivals. With the exception of a few single birds and some straggling parties, I have never remarked this species while on their passage towards our shores. On the 28th of August, 1882, I observed some hundreds of Sand-Martins at sea, a few miles off the Sussex coast. The day was fine, with a light breeze from the south; and a continued stream of these birds passed the boat, flying due south. Towards the afternoon, numbers were noticed a few hundred yards at sea; these were keeping a course along the shore, and, as far as I was able to judge, were not then intending to make the passage of the Channel.

Hickling Broad in the east of Norfolk, owing to the extent of surrounding marsh-land and the large beds of reeds and other aquatic plants, is a favourite haunt of the Sand-Martin. During fine and bright weather large numbers are constantly to be seen hawking for insects over the surface; while here and there small parties may be observed perched on the stems of the reeds. At times large flocks settle on the grass-marshes, where they remain resting for hours. In stormy weather they are usually absent, particularly if the gale should continue for any length of time. On their first arrival I have watched thousands huddled together on low reeds facing a blinding snow-squall. It is seldom they are much affected by the weather; but the severe storm of June 8th, 1871, cut them up considerably. I collected between forty and fifty perfectly helpless from the effects of the cold, and brought them indoors. With but few exceptions they all recovered, and were able to take their departure towards evening, when the weather moderated. On the 9th of August 1881, during a strong southerly breeze, I noticed immense numbers of these birds sitting on the ground on one of the hills* on Hickling Broad. The whole body were facing the wind, and endeavouring to obtain shelter behind the patches of flags and rushes, as well as the low turf bank built round the marsh to keep back the water during high tides.

In the choice of breeding-places this species is influenced by the nature of the soil, being forced to select situations in which it is able to excavate to a sufficient distance to form its nursery. Sand-pits are frequently resorted to; and in many parts of the country their borings may be observed in railway-cuttings. I have also seen large colonies in river-banks at times but a few feet above the level of the water. In 1865 and 1866 I

* A "hill" in the fen and broad country is simply a piece of open marsh-land. It is not necessarily of any elevation, and is frequently below the level of the surrounding broad or river, the water being kept back by a turf bank, usually termed a "wall."

noticed numbers of these birds rearing their young in the banks of a small island in the river Lyon, in the north-west of Perthshire. The following year I was surprised to find their accustomed quarters entirely deserted; though I searched the island on two or three occasions, I never detected a single bird. Early in June, however, we were visited by a terrible downpour of rain, which caused a heavy spate all over the district. Swollen by the storm, the hill-burns rushed down like mountain-torrents into the river, carrying before the flood a floating mass of débris that swept the shores and destroyed the whole of the crops in its course. Cattle, in two or three instances, were overtaken and drowned; and I well remember landing, by a cast of the phantom minnow, the carcass of a fine ram, which was coming down the river with the first of the spate. The island on which the Martins bred was entirely covered to a depth of three or four feet, the very banks being in some parts torn away by the force of the current and the stumps and roots hurled against them. Though I occasionally noticed a few of the birds in the glen during the summer, I was unable to discover where they had found fresh quarters. A few returned the next spring to their old haunts; but since that date I have been absent from the locality, and I am ignorant whether it is still a resort of this interesting and useful species.

PIED WAGTAIL.

MOTACILLA YARRELLI.

The Pied Wagtail is well known in most parts of the British Islands, more plentiful perhaps in the south, but certainly a summer visitor, if not a resident, in the north. I occasionally remarked several pairs along the banks of the Ness as early in the year as the beginning of April; a few of these probably pass the winter in the district. They may be met with on the stony shores of the river where it flows through the town of Inverness, as well as along the various burns and streams in the neighbourhood. Scattered pairs are also to be observed during the winter on the east coast of Ross-shire.

Though it is a well-known fact that our native birds receive large additions to their numbers early in the spring, I have been unable to learn from personal observation at what date our summer visitors take their departure for the continent. The first and by far the largest arrivals may be looked for on the south coast soon after the beginning of March. Straggling parties continue to cross during the whole of the month; and occasionally a few make their appearance as late as April. On still mornings they may be observed landing by hundreds. They seldom show the slightest signs of fatigue or exhaustion when the passage of the Channel is accomplished. After alighting for a time at some brackish pool in the vicinity of the shore or on newly ploughed land, they invariably continue their journey direct to the quarters they intend to take up for the summer. Although hundreds may have been observed within a mile or two of the coast during the early morning, it is seldom that more than a pair or two will be met with after two o'clock in the day, the whole of the birds of passage having made their way inland. Should the weather set in cold and stormy, few, if any, will make their appearance; but with a change of temperature their accustomed haunts will again be alive with fresh arrivals.

During the summer months these Wagtails may be found scattered over the country, a pair or two here and there wherever suitable localities are procurable. While engaged in their nesting-operations they seldom stray far from the neighbourhood of the farm-buildings, quarries, chalk-pits, or other situations that offer them a home. A low-lying patch of marsh-land, the banks of a horse-pond, a gutter, or a mountain-stream are usually the rendezvous where the largest meetings may be noticed; and to such spots the young make their way on leaving the nest. As autumn draws on they gather in flocks and betake themselves to the river-side, the salt-water mudbanks, or flooded meadows, collecting towards evening in large parties often at a considerable distance from their usual haunts.

These birds may commonly be seen roosting in company with other species. I repeatedly disturbed a party that had taken up their quarters for the night with a number of Swallows in a reed-bed in the east of Norfolk during the months of July and August 1881. The Wagtails appeared, while I observed them, either running on the water-plants or perched on the dead and floating roots of the reeds. I also remarked an assemblage of from twenty to thirty resorting with Reed-Buntings to a patch of rushes in the marshes between Shoreham and Beeding, during the first week in March 1879. By 6 P.M. large numbers of

Buntings were collected among the stems of the reeds, many when they had taken up their positions being entirely lost to sight in the thick cover immediately above the surface of the water. The Wagtails for the most part gathered on the floating weeds and some balks of decayed timber. I noticed a few old birds in perfect plumage, though the majority were evidently young of the previous year, still exhibiting the yellow tinge round the head and a general dull plumage.

The heavy sea that caused so much damage along the Cornish coast on October 7, 1891, broke over and completely flooded some grass-meadows and fields in the outskirts of Penzance. As the waters subsided, immense numbers of Pied Wagtails and a score or so of Grey were to be seen daily feeding round the pools. The former species were still numerous in the district as late as the second week in November. One of their favourite roosting-quarters were the cracks and crannies among the large slabs of rock in the cliffs overhanging the sea between Porthleven and Rinsey. By about half-past four in the afternoon they were gathered in hundreds along the ledges. On being disturbed from their quarters they scattered over the patches of grass in the vicinity, but speedily collected again and returned to the position they had selected. During fine still weather they paid but little regard to the aspect of their roosting-place, though a gale of wind and a threatening sky caused them at once to seek the sheltered side of the gullies that ran down the cliffs. The greater part of these birds showed immature plumage.

The nest of this species is often found in close proximity to buildings—a hole in a thatched roof, an old farm-lodge, or a dilapidated wall being frequently made use of. When breeding in the open country they resort to disused quarries, old lime-kilns, or even any inequalities in hilly ground or the face of rough banks. I have more than once noticed these Wagtails breeding at some height in large trees, the nest being usually placed in some convenient hollow in the main trunk where two or three large limbs branched out. A favourite situation of this description, which I often inspected, was thickly shaded by a luxuriant growth of the Common Polypody (*Polypodium vulgare*).

The food consists of flies and insects, collected while on wing and also on the ground. These birds are excessively fond of glow-worms. A pair were observed to clear off great numbers of these insects which had been collected and placed among the rough grass and creeping plants on a small grotto in a garden in Sussex. Scarcely an insect would be seen on the night following their capture, till the rockwork was covered by netting, when the thieves were kept at a distance. While boating on one of the Norfolk rivers my attention was attracted by a female Pied Wagtail fluttering on the ground, tumbling over and over and apparently unable to rise. At length I discovered she was making an attack on an enormous dragonfly, which eventually succumbed, though the bird evidently had a rough tussle before her object was accomplished.

While conversing on the subject with my puntsman, I learned that the local name of the dragonfly was the "Tom Breezer." A few years later, when again in the same district, I was refreshing my memory as to the local names for various birds, insects, and reptiles, such as "pishemeers" for ants, "hopping-toads" for frogs, &c., &c. The man assented to all the titles I bestowed on the subjects of our discussion, stating that my naming was perfectly correct. He concluded by gravely remarking, "and the things you call wopses* we call wasps—W-A-S-P-S (spelling it slowly over); I looked in a book and found it."

* By this name these abominable pests are invariably spoken of in some country districts in the south.

WHITE WAGTAIL.

MOTACILLA ALBA.

I HAVE never met with the White Wagtail during the winter; and, according to my own observations, those that visit the British Islands in the spring are considerably later in making their appearance on our shores than the Pied Wagtails that pass the winter on the continent. I cannot record a single instance where this species has been observed before the second week in April. During fine weather at that period, these birds may commonly be noticed in Sussex, within a short distance of the sea-coast. As a rule, they appear to be making their way from west to east, and seldom remain in the locality for any length of time. I have watched them seeking for food along the banks round brackish pools, as well as on the muds of Shoreham harbour. A few were also occasionally remarked frequenting the salt marshes between Lancing and Worthing. Further east I found a single specimen feeding along the muddy shores of a dyke in the level near St. Leonards, in the first week in May. When disturbed, the bird took a short flight; but after alighting two or three times on the floating weed and searching closely over the surface, it rose in the air and made a straight course along the shore towards the east. The water in the dyke was partly salt; and the tangled weed that grew in profusion contained a number of minute shells. I am ignorant whether scientific authorities allow that this Wagtail will feed on such apparently unpalatable morsels. Though the bird was not shot in order to ascertain the fact, I was considerably mistaken if it did not swallow several of these small shells.

During the latter end of April, when passing through the district, I repeatedly noticed several pairs of White Wagtails feeding along the shores of the Ness. The birds were not met with farther inland than the town of Inverness, being most frequently seen about the small drains running down to the water, or gathered round any refuse thrown out on the shores. A few Pied Wagtails also resort to the same spots, and a pair or two often intermingle as they chase insects round the puddles or run rapidly along the stony bed of the river. The difference between the two species was most striking when closely examined side by side, the extra size and length of *Motacilla alba* being particularly conspicuous.

Though I never detected the nest or even came to the conclusion that the birds were then settled in the district, numbers of these Wagtails were met with in the island of Lewis, early in May 1877. I did not recognize a single specimen, except in the immediate vicinity of dwelling-houses or round the various outbuildings and enclosures. A severe gale of wind, with hail and rain, from the south-east swept over the island on the 6th of May; shortly after midday the storm moderated, and by 3 P.M. the weather was bright and mild. During the afternoon I remarked at least five pairs of White Wagtails about the gardens and landing-stages round a shooting-lodge on the shores of Loch Shell. On the following day, which was fine, not a single bird was noticed; and it was not till the 9th that I again observed them, a pair or two remaining for several hours in the gardens. On many occasions when watching this species on these islands, I was particularly struck by their confiding nature—eagerly searching for food and actively chasing insects within four or five yards of where I was inspecting their movements. This was especially the case after the gale of May 6.

Up to the present time I have not met with the nest of this species in the British Islands. The bird itself has only been observed during April and May.

GREY WAGTAIL.

MOTACILLA SULPHUREA.

I cannot call to mind a single instance of having noticed this species in the Outer Hebrides. With the exception of a pair or two about Golspie, Lairg and Altnaharra, I never met with the Grey Wagtail further north than the east coast of Ross-shire. In the neighbourhood of Tain these Wagtails were by no means uncommon, most numerous perhaps in the spring and summer, though a few pairs were to be found in certain localities during the winter. I repeatedly noticed these peculiarly clean and elegant-looking birds frequenting the open drains and other repulsive spots that still remain in some old-fashioned Highland towns. They were to be observed at most seasons actively snapping flies and other insects off the heaps of filth and refuse liberally scattered in the public streets. In the town of Inverness a few pairs are to be seen along the banks of the river. Stragglers now and then penetrate the thickly populated parts of the town; but their favourite haunts are the shores between the bridge and the islands. These birds are also to be met with in various parts along the canal towards the west.

In Perthshire the Grey Wagtail is common in many districts; I find, however, in my notes that in some localities they disappear during the winter, and do not show themselves till well on in April. The dust-heap at the back of a shooting-lodge that does not rejoice in (or rather, as prejudiced natives would declare, suffer from) drains is the happy hunting-ground of these birds. As a rule they are of a sociable disposition, and appear to prefer quarters at no great distance from human habitations. In several of the southern counties of Scotland these birds were noticed. On one occasion I detected a pair on the island of Fidra, in the Firth of Forth; and they are also common during the autumn along the shore from North Berwick to Dunbar. Along the hill-burns and river-banks in Cumberland, and also on the coast of Northumberland, I remarked several pairs. During summer and autumn a few may be met with in the wildest parts of the rocky glens on the Yorkshire moors, through which the hill-streams make their way towards the North Sea. In Norfolk I did not recognize the species, except in three or four instances where stragglers made their appearance in autumn in the neighbourhood of Breydon mudflats; these, doubtless, were working their way south for the winter. To the best of my recollection, I never caught a glimpse of a single specimen in the broad-district.

In Sussex, these birds are to be met with during autumn, winter, and early spring, frequenting streams and river-banks. A few remain in the neighbourhood of Brighton at these seasons, resorting to open drains or pools, and in some instances visiting the gardens adjoining the town. In the west of England I did not penetrate their haunts during the breeding-season, though a few specimens were now and then observed in the autumn.

The nest is most commonly placed in a hole among stones on the rough bank of a mountain-stream or in the cavities of old masonry. These birds frequently return during many successive years to the same situations. While fishing one spring in Glenlyon in Perthshire, I noticed a fine male of this species running along the riverside, apparently somewhat uneasy at his haunt being invaded. On inquiring of the keeper if he had ever remarked the nest of the species, he stated that he well remembered a nest being found in a hole in the bridge close to which we were standing, when some repairs were made nearly twenty years previously. After pointing out an aperture where a stone was wanting, he held up the landing-net, and immediately captured the female, who at that moment issued from her nest.

GREY-HEADED WAGTAIL.

MOTACILLA FLAVA.

THE Grey-headed Wagtail, if looked for with care, may be met with every spring along the coast of Sussex. I never detected this species alighting on the salt-water mudbanks, or in such close proximity to the sea-shore as the White Wagtail, all that came under my observation in this locality being noticed a short distance inland. As far as I have been able to judge, the Grey-headed closely resembles the Yellow Wagtail in its habits and the localities to which it resorts. I am well acquainted with certain spots about a mile from the sea-coast, between Brighton and Shoreham, where a pair or two might be found at almost any time during May.

In Norfolk I have also recognized two or three males of this species in the marshes within a short distance of Breydon mudflats; occasionally I remarked the same birds, or others closely resembling them (when carefully examined through powerful glasses, the variations in the grey of the head or the clouded markings among the yellow feathers on the breast can readily be distinguished), frequenting the pastures in the vicinity of the wall on several consecutive days. As I returned from Yarmouth at the end of the month when the flocks of Waders, which then claimed my attention, had ceased to fly, I was unable to ascertain if they remained and bred in the neighbourhood. According to my note-books, I recognized this species in either the north or south marshes every season while awaiting the spring flight on Breydon muds.

It is only in Sussex, Kent, and Norfolk that I positively identified the Grey-headed Wagtail. There is little doubt this species breeds not uncommonly within a few miles of Brighton. I repeatedly observed males frequenting two or three of the sheep-ponds that are scattered over the downs at seasons when it was most probable the female was sitting close at hand.

An adult male and female are figured in the Plate. When first killed, the head and upper part of the neck of the female exhibits a strongly marked grey shade. Though the colour is fainter, it appears, when seen in certain lights, almost as conspicuous as the clear bluish-grey tint on the head of the male. I mention this fact, as it is highly probable that females of the Yellow Wagtail (if showing a rather whiter line than usual over the eye) have been occasionally mistaken and figured for this species. The male represented in the Plate was shot April 17, 1871, about a mile west of Brighton; and the female was procured within a short distance of the same spot ten days later. This female was in company with an exceedingly brightly marked male; and the pair had, I am of opinion, taken up their quarters for the season. On passing the spot during the second week in May, a pair were again discovered frequenting the same locality; and I conclude the male had already consoled himself by a fresh partner for the loss of his former mate.

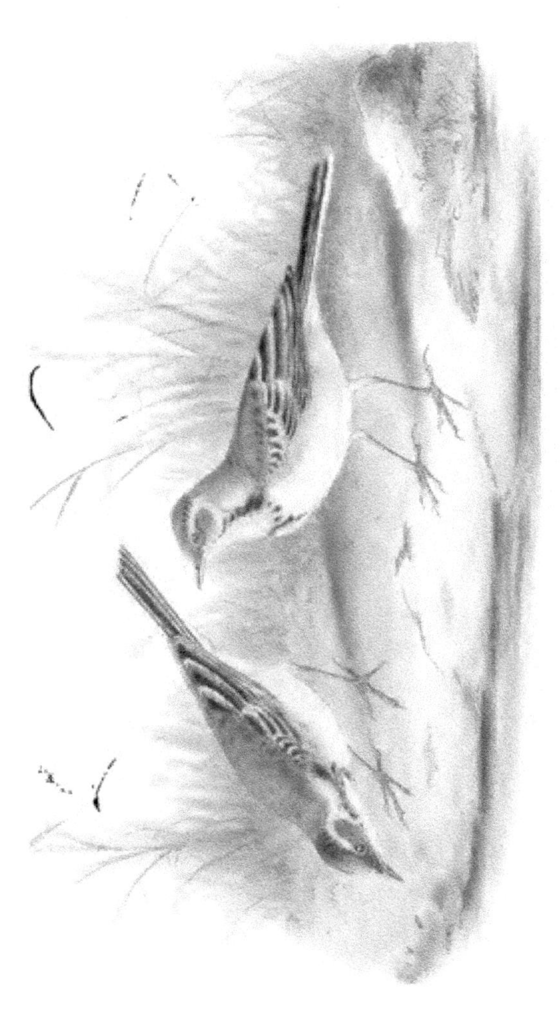

YELLOW WAGTAIL.

MOTACILLA RAYI.

LARGE numbers of this attractive bird make their appearance on the south coast early in the spring. For at least a month, from about the second week of April till well on in May, they may be noticed landing on the shores of Sussex when the wind is light and the weather favourable. At this season they are to be found following the plough or scattered over the grass-meadows in the vicinity of the coast as far as a mile or two inland. By the end of May the majority have taken their departure, and all that remain are the few pairs breeding in the district. In no part of the British Islands have I met with this species so numerous during the summer months as in the Norfolk marshes.

The counties north of the Humber do not appear so suitable to the habits of the Yellow Wagtail; and though stragglers are to be met with in many localities, I have never observed these birds in any thing approaching the numbers that frequent the flat districts on the east coast. In Scotland I remarked a few pairs at various times near Dunbar, and again on Gullane links. The species was also recognized near the sea-coast within a short distance of Nairn and Inverness, and once or twice on "the fendom," a remarkably flat sandy stretch of low-lying ground to the east of Tain, in Ross-shire.

In not a single instance have I detected the nest in Scotland. I have no wish to state that the bird does not breed in considerable numbers so far north, as I gave but little attention to the species in this locality, being well acquainted with its habits from constantly observing them in the south. The situations chosen by the Yellow Wagtail for breeding-purposes vary considerably. In Norfolk, where I have had the most opportunities of observing them in their summer haunts, they frequently resort to holes in the banks of the water-dykes intersecting the grass-marshes, the spot being usually well screened by long grass or overhanging plants. In the southern counties I have occasionally found their nests in situations almost similar, in the levels towards the east of Sussex and also in Kent. Throughout the arable portions of Sussex, in the immediate vicinity and to the west of Brighton, these birds commonly rear their young in the cornfields, some small inequality in the side of a grip or bank or even an open furrow being selected.

Early in August the young birds collect in numbers in the Norfolk marshes. At this season considerable flocks now and then make their way to the farm-buildings, and may be seen eagerly searching for insects among the beasts in the yards. I have remarked as many as fifty or sixty busily engaged among the litter, flying up, when disturbed, to the roofs of the sheds, but speedily returning when the cause of their alarm had vanished. In Sussex I noticed both old and young gathering in the marshes near the sea-coast previous to migrating.

The nestling plumage of this species is totally different from that assumed after the first moult. In its earliest feathers the Yellow Wagtail bears a strong resemblance to the Pipit tribe. Before the end of August a complete change has come over them; and by that time it is difficult to distinguish the old birds from their broods, both being arrayed in their autumn travelling-dress.

The Plate shows the young birds in their first feathers. This plumage is worn for only a few weeks.

MEADOW-PIPIT.

ANTHUS PRATENSIS.

There are few birds so generally distributed over the country from north to south as the Meadow-Pipit. The salt marshes and furze-covered downs of Sussex seem as well suited to its requirements as the moors and stony hillsides of Sutherland.

In many parts of the British Islands this species may be met with during the winter; a considerable number, however, take their departure towards the south during September and October. There is little doubt that the majority making this movement cross the Channel towards the continent, though at what point they accomplish the passage I am unable to state. I have watched the migration in many parts of the country and for a number of years. In the north of Scotland I remarked immense flights of these birds passing from north to south over the east of Ross-shire from the 15th to the 20th of September 1868. These, I believe, must have been migrants from across the North Sea, as Blackbirds and Thrushes in thousands were passing at the same time, and Redwings also showed themselves in small flocks. I noticed a week or so later that the usual natives of the district had not disappeared from their accustomed haunts, and were to be met with in about the same numbers as previously. For several consecutive days after October 20, 1872, small scattered parties of Meadow-Pipits continued flying in a southerly direction along the denes near Yarmouth, and also at times penetrating among the houses and up the streets towards the east of the town. During a squall of wind and rain, one poor bird, evidently worn out by a long journey, was blown against the glass of a window and fell in the garden below, where it was immediately attacked by a Robin and driven into some thick bushes. Annually during September and October large bodies make their appearance in the vicinity of the Sussex coast. At this season I repeatedly noticed them approaching and hovering for a few moments round the Lark-glasses which were some years ago so commonly seen in the neighbourhood of Brighton.

For at least six weeks, countless Meadow-Pipits may be met with almost daily in this locality: their numbers, however, vary considerably, according to the weather. After the beginning of November, though flocks occasionally show themselves, it is evident that the greater part of the birds composing the autumnal flights have taken their departure. Having observed but a few stragglers at sea in the autumn, I should be of opinion the main bodies commence the passage before it is fairly light. While the flight lasts, large flocks and single birds may be noticed on fine mornings with a light breeze steadily making their way along the coast. One day the multitudes pass west; and on the following it is quite possible they may be flying towards the east. After carefully watching and noting down their movements during several years, I consider it impossible to state with certainty the course these small birds may follow; but, as a rule, it is most frequently either against or across the wind. The flight of Pipits, Wagtails, and the Swallow tribe is at this season exceedingly confusing, and much concerning their movements still remains to be learned. Though Swallows and Martins desert our shores entirely, a certain number of Pipits and Wagtails are at all times to be found; and not unfrequently, as previously remarked, a considerable body of Pipits may be detected harbouring in some open spot where food is obtainable during severe weather. From observations made in various parts of the country, I conclude that numbers of the Pipits landing on our coasts in March and April are on their way to more northern breeding-grounds.

A few extracts from my notes for 1882 will shew the line of flight followed by these birds along the coast of Sussex and the wind and weather at the time the observations were made:—

"Sept. 12. The morning was still and fine, with a light breeze from the north. Meadow-Pipits continued flying in large and small bodies for several hours along the coast between Shoreham and Brighton. The whole number pursued a course parallel with the shore from west to east. I watched these flocks of Meadow-Pipits streaming past for several hours, and detected but few strangers in their ranks besides an occasional Pied Wagtail. Swallows and Martins were also making their way east.

"Sept. 13. Weather excessively cold; fresh north-west breeze. I did not notice a single Pipit on the move, though several small parties were harbouring in the stubbles and in some of the fields of coarse grass near the coast.

"Sept. 14. Wind changeable from south and west. A few Pipits continued to pass east. During the day a severe thunderstorm broke over the district, accompanied by hail and heavy rain.

"Sept. 17. Light breeze from north-west; weather fine. Immense numbers of Pipits seen along the coast from Lancing to Newhaven, the downs on the summit of the cliffs in some parts perfectly swarming with this species. The birds were mostly stationary; but a slight movement from east to west took place."

During the next week there was no general flight, though the numbers met with on certain days varied considerably.

"Sept. 29. Strong wind from the south-west. Small flights of Pipits making their way towards the west.

"Oct. 2. Strong wind west-south-west. Very few Pipits seen; those recognized were moving both east and west. There were, however, numbers of Larks and thousands of Swallows flying east before the strong wind.

"Oct. 3. Wind west and north-west; weather fine. Numbers of Pipits flying west.

"Oct. 9. Wind south; weather fine. Small parties of Pipits flying west.

"Oct. 10. Wind south-east; weather fine. A few Pipits flying east.

"Oct. 13. Wind north-east; weather fine. Some Pipits making their way due east, and others following an exactly opposite course; many small flocks stationary in the stubbles.

"Oct. 20. Wind south; weather fine. Numbers of Pipits moving east.

"Oct. 28. Wind east; heavy rain. Large flocks of Pipits harbouring in the stubbles and rough meadows near the coast; none seen on flight.

"Nov. 6. Wind south; fine still morning. A flock of from forty to fifty Pipits were pecking about on the shingle-banks between Shoreham and Lancing. At times they would fly down to the large heaps of sea-weed recently cast up by the gales, and then betake themselves to the scanty vegetation on the higher portion of the beach or some brackish pools on the opposite side of the sea-wall. Small parties of Chaffinches and Greenfinches were in company with the Pipits; the finches, however, did not follow them down to the sea-weed, but remained searching for food among the various seed-producing plants on the higher ridges of the beach. These Titlarks appeared remarkably sociable, as when disturbed from the shore they joined a large flock of some hundreds of Twites, and after a short flight settled with them on the saltings.

"Nov. 10. Wind west. But one or two Pipits seen along the coast from Shoreham to Lancing.

"Nov. 11. Wind west; weather fine. I remarked a good many single Pipits on the highest portions of the Downs, near the Dyke; there were also a few scattered along the sides of the hill roads."

During the winter months, Meadow-Pipits not unfrequently resort to localities that are damp or flooded.

When all but running water is frozen, they betake themselves to the edges of the saltings or any open springs. These residents seldom appear much affected by the cold, and may be seen in any ordinary weather running actively over the ground in search of food. The extraordinary violence of the wind during the terrible snow-storm of January 18, 1881, however, proved most disastrous to the feathered tribe, and utterly incapacitated almost the whole of the small birds in its course. Thousands must have perished through cold and want of food after the buffetings they received during the force of the gale. On the 26th of January (eight days after the storm) I happened to be in Shoreham harbour shortly before high tide. This was the first time the water had entirely covered the mudflats since the hurricane; and I remarked hundreds of dead bodies of small birds (Larks, Pipits, Linnets, and many others) washed out from the weeds growing on the banks. These unfortunate birds must have sought shelter from the cutting blasts among the stems of the plants, and perished from the long-continued inclemency of the weather.

When the large flights of Blackbirds, Thrushes, Fieldfares, Larks, and other small birds pass along the coast from east to west on the approach of snow-squalls during the winter months, it is seldom any considerable bodies of Pipits make their appearance. I have seen small parties searching for food in sheltered spots at the time the general movement was taking place, but cannot call to mind an instance of meeting with more than a few specimens working their way west at this season.

Towards the middle of March these birds commence to return to our shores. Any still foggy morning, from about the 10th of the month till well on in April, they may be noticed landing on the south coast, singly and in small flocks, from shortly after daybreak till nine or ten o'clock. For a day or two they may be observed in numbers about the banks of streams and salt-water pools near the sea-beach; but with a change of weather they soon proceed inland, and scatter themselves over the country. Under the date of March 27, 1878, I find in my note-books that hundreds of Meadow-Pipits had now returned and taken up their quarters on the marshes and round the broads in the east of Norfolk. These birds made their appearance simultaneously with large flocks of Starlings, which continued flying east for three or four days. Several parties composed entirely of male Chaffinches also passed over. I remarked the Grey Crows were then gathering previous to taking their departure. Light easterly winds appear to bring all these birds (both those that are leaving our shores and our own summer migrants when on their return journey in the spring) to this part of the coast. It is seldom that any addition to the numbers of these birds is observed in the Highlands before April; this fact was noted for a couple of seasons in the east of Ross-shire.

The persecution that this unfortunate Pipit undergoes from the various smaller Hawks in the Highlands ought to tend to keep down its numbers. Merlins, Sparrow-Hawks, and Harriers all appear to have a special fancy for feeding their young broods with this particular bird as long as any are to be met with in their neighbourhood. I am aware my own experience in this respect differs considerably from that of a well known writer on Highland sports, who remarks that this species suffers from the attacks of ground-vermin, such as stoats and weasels, but is seldom molested by Hawks.

For breeding-purposes the Meadow-Pipit resorts to a great variety of situations. On the south coast I have found their nests in the long rank grass growing round the pools of brackish water within a short distance of the sea-shore. The pairs that nest in this locality are, without doubt, residents that have passed the winter in the district. In many instances I recognized the three or four pairs that have their quarters round a certain piece of water near Shoreham, on every occasion when visiting the spot during autumn, winter, and early spring. These stationary birds are remarkably early breeders; their nests are usually built, and their eggs not unfrequently laid, before the greater number of the migrants have arrived. Many pairs of Pipits may be seen on the furze and heath covered ranges of the South Downs during the summer months. Their nests are usually placed under the shelter of the heather or other coarse vegetation on a grassy bank, or even in some slight inequality in the ground or on the bare hill-side. Among the broads and rivers of the eastern counties these birds seldom resort to particularly marshy situations in which to rear their brood, choosing, as a rule, a dry spot on a turf-wall or a rush-grown mound rising above the general level. On the grouse-moors and on the steep mountain-sides in the northern counties, this Pipit is plentifully distributed, being occasionally seen at an elevation considerably over one thousand feet in height. A ledge of rock or a tuft of grass serves to ward off the cutting winds from their unfledged young.

The eggs of this species vary greatly, though not to the same extent as those of the Tree-Pipit, many shades of red, brown, and grey being frequently met with. On June 1, 1870, I drove a bird off her nest in the long grass on the marsh-wall round Heigham Sounds, in Norfolk. On examining the five eggs on which she was sitting, I discovered they were unlike any I had previously met with. There was not the slightest doubt as to the identity of the bird, as she rose at my feet; and the nest was unmistakable. In order, however, that there should be no possibility of an error, I approached the spot again after a short interval, and captured in a butterfly-net a female Meadow-Pipit. The eggs were utterly unlike those of any British bird. The ground was a pale blue (the same shade as the egg of the Wheatear), spotted with moderately sized markings of a pale violet or bluish grey, a darker spot of the same tint showing here and there. The whole five were much alike, the size of the markings and the thickness and regularity of the spots on each individual shell being almost precisely similar. In shape they were somewhat longer than the usual egg of *Anthus pratensis*. On examining them again today (August 31, 1882) I find their shades have but very slightly faded during the lapse of eleven years and a quarter.

The nest of the Meadow-Pipit is frequently chosen by the Cuckoo as the cradle in which it deposits its egg. I have noticed this fact repeatedly on the downs of Sussex, and also on several occasions in the Highlands.

TREE-PIPIT.

ANTHUS ARBOREUS.

In the valley of the Spey, particularly throughout those parts of the forest of Glenmore where the timber is composed of old though moderate-sized Scotch fir, this Pipit may be met with in numbers during the breeding-season. I have also observed a few scattered pairs on somewhat similar ground in Ross-shire. In the more northern counties I failed to meet with it, and was also unable to learn any tidings from keepers who, I was aware, were well acquainted with the species. Perthshire is probably visited by the Tree-Pipit; but I cannot find in my note-books any record of its having attracted my attention. In suitable localities in the south of Scotland this species may be seen, though, according to my own experience, it is far more uncommon than in the southern and eastern counties of England.

The Tree-Pipit is only a summer visitor to the British Islands, usually making its appearance towards the end of April, and frequently being observed in considerable numbers scattered over the country in the vicinity of the south coast for some time previous to its departure in the autumn.

The note of this Pipit, which is lively and pleasing, is uttered in the air, the songster rising from the topmost branches of a tree and slowly dropping with extended wings. It is known to bird-fanciers as the singing Titlark. This species may readily be distinguished from the Meadow-Pipit by its superior size and the shorter hind toe.

The nest is most commonly placed beneath the shelter of some small shrub in a plantation or the edge of a clearing in a wood. I have, however, observed it in the open in such a situation as might have been chosen by its relative the Meadow-Pipit. On June 25, 1875, while examining a colony of the forester-moth on the South Downs, between Brighton and Lewes, I disturbed a Tree-Pipit from her nest. This was placed among the grass on the bare hillside, the nearest timber being a plantation of Scotch fir and beech on the opposite side of a road, at a distance of some fifty or sixty yards. The female was eventually captured in a butterfly-net, and is now in my collection.

The eggs of this species vary considerably, all shades between a deep red-brown and a dull grey being occasionally met with, streaked, scrawled, and spotted in every conceivable manner.

ROCK-PIPIT.

ANTHUS OBSCURUS.

The name of Rock-Pipit is by no means misapplied. Every part of Great Britain, from north to south, as well as the adjacent islands, where the coast-line is formed by rocks or cliffs, appears to be frequented by this species. In many of these localities the bird may be found as a resident. When observed where the shores are flat or at inland waters, its visits are usually only short, and made during autumn, winter, or early spring.

At any season, with the exception of the height of summer, I have occasionally observed a few of these Pipits along the flat portions of the Sussex coast, from Pagham to Brighton. The muddy edges of the pools of brackish water inside the shingle-banks are their favourite haunts. The chalk cliffs between Brighton and Eastbourne, and in the neighbourhood of Fairlight near Hastings, are resorted to during the breeding-season, though those that nest in these localities are by no means so thickly dispersed throughout the range as over many parts of the more northern coast-line. Pevensey Marsh, Winchelsea Level, and (across the Kentish border) Romney Marsh are each and all visited by this species at the same seasons as the flat districts to the west of Brighton. It is seldom that the birds are observed at the inland parts of these marshes, the particular food (minute worms and small insects) that attracts them appearing to inhabit only those pools that are slightly impregnated by salt. On the Suffolk coast and marshes, and also in Norfolk, I have only recognized this species as a visitor. Breydon Wall and the grassy edges of the mudflats (locally known as the rondes) are the spots on which the bird is usually observed. I frequently remarked it was most numerous in this locality during wet and stormy weather. I repeatedly noticed a pair or two resorting to the grass-marshes round Hickling Broad, though they are seldom seen in this district unless the tides are high and the hills flooded. They may then be watched flitting round the shores of the broad, alighting here and there on any exposed spot, and eagerly searching for insects and small flies, which they capture among the rotten stems of any heap of decaying reeds. These marshes are perhaps four miles in a direct line from the coast; this is the furthest inland that I have ever observed the Rock-Pipit. I find the following note in one of my journals:—"October 16, 1873. Noticed soon after daybreak several Rock-Pipits along the walls round Breydon, and also in the afternoon on the South Denes. Hundreds of Larks were landing on the sea-beach just before dark." It is possible, I imagine, that those observed on the Denes were migrants that had crossed the North Sea, as it was seldom they frequented these dry sandhills. I met with a few in the cliffs and among the rocks on the Yorkshire coast, both north and south of Whitby. This Pipit nests on several of the larger of the Fern Islands off the coast of Northumberland, and also on a few of the detached rocks. I have seen their nests close to the old lighthouse and the surrounding buildings. At Dunbar, on the coast of East Lothian, numbers of these birds breed in the ledges of the rocks in the immediate vicinity of the town. They are also to be met with all the summer along the sea-shore as far as North Berwick. On the islands in the firth, the May, the Bass Rock, Craig Leith, and Fidra, they are particularly plentiful. On the Bass Rock I have known of as many as ten or a dozen nests at one time; and there were doubtless others I failed to detect. Many were placed among the fallen masonry in the old fortifications, and in parts of the buildings where stones had been dislodged from the walls. I stumbled upon one or two among the accumulation of old rubbish in the passages in the ruins, which had been built in almost total darkness. They also resort to the cracks and ledges on the face of the rock, especially on the south side.

On one occasion I discovered a brood, just ready to fly, on a small exposed rock that formed part of the ledge on which the beacon stands, a short distance east of Tantallon. In this instance it was certainly a marvel how the young had escaped destruction from the waves. The whole of the rock that was above water at high tides was but ten or a dozen yards in circumference; and I watched the seas washing up within a foot of the bottom of the nest. The bird had made a most cunning choice of a situation. The nest was placed in a slight hollow in the side of the rock that looked towards the shore, from which it was distant about one hundred yards. An overhanging slab of stone formed a covering towards the north-east, from which quarter the heaviest swells rolled towards the land. But one small tuft of vegetation struggled for existence on this diminutive islet; and behind its scanty shelter the nest was located. A few days after I discovered the young birds they quitted the nest in safety, a result that could scarcely have been anticipated had a heavy gale from the north or east set in. I repeatedly remarked that on this part of the coast the birds appeared to have a preference for the islands; possibly the number of rats along the shores of the mainland may have influenced their selection.

Along the flat shores of the east of Ross-shire I occasionally noticed this species during autumn and early spring on the shores of the firths and the numerous marshy pools. They frequent the Cromarty rocks overhanging the Moray Firth and many points along the rocky coasts of Caithness and Sutherland; but I never spent any time in searching out their nests in those localities. On the small islands off the west coast of Ross-shire, it was almost impossible during the spring to wander any distance among the heather and rough stones without disturbing several of these Pipits from their nests.

The bird to which the name of Scandinavian Rock-Pipit has been given is merely, in my own opinion, a variety of this species*. Early in March I have shot numbers of specimens which plainly showed that the winter dress was identical with that of this bird, only a few of the vinous feathers being visible at that period; on several I procured, only one or two of these feathers could be found. I also obtained specimens exhibiting the change in every stage. In two or three instances the plumage closely approached that of the Water-Pipit (*Anthus spipoletta*); a few spots or clouded markings, however, were always visible among the feathers on the breast. As spring advances the vinous tint gradually spreads over the whole of the breast, and the back of the head and neck becomes a bluish grey. The numbers of this variety that appear on our shores are very uncertain. I have met with them during some seasons in great abundance, while the following year hardly a bird would be recognized. The first arrivals may be looked for—or rather, I ought to say, might have been looked for (as I have not identified a single specimen for the last ten years) soon after the beginning of March; and for about a month or six weeks from that date they would be seen making their way along the coast. As a rule, they appeared to fly against the wind, and were mostly observed on thick foggy mornings. On the 16th of March 1866 (a light wind from the west and weather dull and cloudy) I watched a party of between twenty and thirty of these Pipits collected round a pool of brackish water just inside the sea-beach at Portslade, near Brighton. Immense numbers of Meadow-Pipits, as well as these birds in all stages of plumage, were continually landing till nine or ten o'clock, after which hour they ceased crossing. In the spring of 1867, though I kept a constant watch on all the likely spots along the same range of coast-line, I did not meet with above a dozen specimens. These were particularly backward in their plumage, and but one

* I conclude it is the Pipit known to continental naturalists as *Anthus rupestris*. It comes also, in certain stages of plumage, greatly to resemble *Anthus spipoletta*. Possibly these two scientific names have in some instances been bestowed on one and the same form, which is in reality only a variety of *Anthus obscurus*.

or two showed the vinous tint to any extent. In 1868 and 1869 I was away in the north; and on again visiting their haunts in 1870 I found their numbers had considerably fallen off. Two or three fine specimens, however, were obtained between the 20th and 25th of April, which is the latest date on which I have met with them.

On many occasions during the past ten years I have closely searched these parts of the coast, but not a single specimen was identified. By carefully examining the footmarks on the soft mud round the pools, it was easy to learn if these favourite spots were frequented by any number of the Pipit tribe. As far as I am able to judge, these birds seem now to have entirely changed their line of flight. The only specimen I ever obtained or even observed beyond the borders of Sussex was shot on March 14, 1871, on the Norfolk coast, at a marshy pool near Hersey: for the season of the year it was far advanced in plumage.

As stated previously, the winter dress so closely resembles that of our common Rock-Pipit, that I have been unable to detect the slightest difference, a careful search being needed in order to discover the one or two vinous-tinted feathers on the breast that formed the sole distinguishing marks in the specimens obtained during the early part of the season. I have, however, been favoured with a view of preserved specimens, declared by scientific naturalists to belong to this form of Pipit, in the winter plumage. I must confess that, though unwilling to question the decision of those eminent authorities, I was utterly unable to learn from what outward and visible signs they had formed their judgment. I have closely watched the genuine Rock-Pipit of the British Islands and also the Scandinavian form; and in flight, actions, manner of feeding, and note the two birds seemed identical.

According to my own observations, the Scandinavian Rock-Pipit does not remain and breed in the British Islands. I never remarked the birds frequenting situations where it was probable they would select a site for a nest.

The Plate shows the Scandinavian form of the Rock-Pipit. The figures are taken from specimens obtained between Shoreham and Lancing towards the end of April 1870.

SHORE-LARK.

ALAUDA ALPESTRIS.

A glance at the pages of the older works on ornithology will show that the Shore-Lark was in former days considered a rare wanderer to our shores. It is quite possible the writers may have been correct in their supposition; but I should rather be inclined to believe that the species must have escaped notice, owing to its similarity to the Common Sky-Lark. Unless carefully watched, the two birds would scarcely be distinguished by the majority of observers. At any distance over thirty yards the dark markings and bright colours round the head are not sufficiently conspicuous to the naked eye to attract attention. Those, however, who have once had an opportunity of studying the actions and general habits of this handsome bird would be unlikely to overlook the species. The Shore-Lark appears fond of company; on one occasion I recognized a male and a couple of females associating with a party of Sparrows in the roadway towards the south end of Yarmouth; they also join for a time the flocks of Sky-Larks and Snow-Buntings frequenting the denes along the coast. Unfortunately for their own safety, these birds are remarkably unsuspicious of danger, paying little regard to either net or gun.

It is only in Norfolk, Suffolk, and Sussex that I met with this Lark. The earliest date in any season on which the species came under my observation was the 20th of October; and not a single specimen was ever noticed later than the second week in March. Towards the latter end of October 1879 a flock numbering between twenty and thirty, as well as several small scattered parties, frequented the South Denes at Yarmouth. These birds repeatedly made their way among the buildings in the outskirts of the town, a favourite resort being a few acres of ground adjoining the Naval Hospital recently laid down for grass. From this spot, when disturbed, they made their way either to the upper portion of the sands by the drive or to the open denes further south. Numbers of Snow-Buntings put in an appearance about the same time, and were invariably to be found either along the roadway of the drive or among the sandhills. At times I remarked the two species intermixed while feeding, though, if alarmed, it was seldom they kept company for any distance. Fresh comers joined the first arrivals early in November, and were still more confiding than those previously noticed. Small parties might be watched feeding on the sandy links within twenty yards of the drive, utterly regardless of the traffic. In this locality I observed the Shore-Lark in larger or smaller numbers during the winters of 1871, '72, '73, '79, '81, and '82. The more lonely and unfrequented coast-line between Blakeney and Salthouse is better suited to the requirements of this species; and here they were to be met with collected into large flocks on the few occasions when I visited the district. The rough banks bordering the marshes, interspersed with pools of water and coarse grass, were their haunts. If driven up while feeding, these birds were far less easily alarmed than the Sky-Lark, for the most part merely hovering round the intruder for a few minutes, and again settling close at hand.

The first specimens I obtained were a pair shot in December 1862; these birds were in attendance on an immense gathering of Snow-Buntings on a marsh near Hunstanton. In November 1872 I noticed a small flock along the shore near Benacre Sluice in Suffolk; from their disinclination to rise and quit the beach, it is probable they had only recently made the land. Shortly before dusk the same evening, while steaming along the coast inside the Newcome Sands, I noticed a straggling party of a score or so of small and weary travellers fly past the vessel and disappear in the haze. One poor bird, worn out by its journey, hovered across the deck for a moment and attempted to alight on the paddlebox; here it was unable to gain footing and fluttered helplessly down to the water. The main flock, as far as I could judge, was composed of Sky-Larks; but the unfortunate wayfarer who had failed to board us was a Shore-Lark.

During severe weather in Sussex I often remarked a fresh-captured bird or two of this species in the store-cages of the professional bird-catchers when meeting with them along the downs near the coast. But one small flock of three or four individuals has (with the exception of the above-mentioned captives) come under my notice in this county; these birds were on the shingle-banks between Shoreham and Lancing.

According to my own observations the Shore-Larks are regular winter visitors to several portions of the east coast from Hunstanton to Lowestoft; but it is only occasionally that they show themselves in the southern counties. The seeds of the various grasses and plants growing on the rough banks and uncultivated ground they frequent are doubtless the main food of this species. From closely watching their actions I should also judge that small insects were taken; in that case their prey is so minute as to escape the observation of the naked eye, and a post mortem examination would be needed to establish the fact.

WOOD-LARK.

ALAUDA ARBOREA.

KNOWLEDGE concerning the distribution of this species throughout the British Islands appears somewhat limited; and I regret my own observations can throw no additional light on the subject.

In Scotland I failed entirely to identify the Wood-Lark with any degree of certainty, two or three localities in the south of Yorkshire being the furthest north at which this admirable songster was met with. As far as I am able to judge, the bird is exceedingly local during summer; and, with the exception of the above-mentioned northern county, I have only observed the Wood-Lark about Harrow-on-the-Hill in Middlesex, and in the well-timbered portion of the east of Sussex.

I am ignorant whether any emigrants from the north of Europe arrive on our coasts during autumn or early winter. Wood-Larks have never come under my observation while making the passage of the North Sea; neither were any of their wings recognized among the many hundreds of those of the Sky-Lark received from the light-ships off the east coast *.

As winter approaches there is, during some seasons at least, if not annually, a general movement of this species from north to south along the east coast, and from east to west on the shores of the English Channel. In the latter end of November and early in December 1879, snow fell for several days on the coast of Norfolk, and I remarked a few stragglers of this species passing south over the sand banks near Yarmouth. Numbers of Sky-Larks were taking the same course, moving southward in continuous streams for several hours daily. The severe snow-storm in January 1867 drove countless Larks and other small birds along the coast of Sussex for several consecutive days. Many Wood-Larks also appeared, the whole of these birds on this occasion being obviously far more affected by the cold than their relatives. While the Sky-Larks flew westward in clouds from shortly after daybreak till between 2 and 3 P.M., the unfortunate Wood-Larks were repeatedly settling and gathering together in small flocks on any spot that was free from snow. Here they would remain huddled together till disturbed by a near approach, evidently worn out by want of food and exposure to cold, and retaining scarcely sufficient strength to get on wing and resume their weary journey. Some idea of the numbers of the Wood-Larks in this locality may be formed from the fact that I counted between six and seven dozen in the possession of one bird-catcher alone, who was working his net on the downs between Rottingdean and Newhaven. Many others of the fraternity had from three to four dozen; and a dealer secured forty dozen at the price of three shillings the dozen.

In open winters it is probable that there is but a small accession to the residents in the vicinity of the

* There could be no chance of confusing the wings of the two species. Though the rule as to size would hardly hold good (I have seen an occasional Sky-Lark, probably a young bird, quite as small as the Wood-Lark), there is an unmistakable difference in the colouring, the white markings on the wings of the Wood-Lark being far more plainly defined than in the Sky-Lark. In old skins or stuffed specimens this distinction is not particularly clear; but in fresh-killed birds it is most conspicuous. In addition to this the length and shape of certain of the feathers at once indicate to which species the wing belonged.

south coast. There are, however, a few spots on the downs, some two or three miles inland, where a bird or two may be observed at almost any time the species is looked for between November and the end of January. During the snow-storms in the first and second weeks of December 1882 I did not recognize a single specimen of the Wood-Lark on wing, though considerable flocks of Sky-Larks were moving west. I discovered, on consulting one or two of the professional birdcatchers, that my experience was much the same as their own. I could learn of but one bird having been noticed; this was captured near Seaford.

When watched on wing against a background that shows up the bird, the difference between this species and the Sky-Lark is easily recognized. As it flits past the observer, the plumage on the upper portion (back and wings) of the latter appears of a uniform brown tint, while the dark brown and white markings on the Wood-Lark at once attract attention.

LARK.

ALAUDA ARVENSIS.

There are few parts of the British Islands in which the Lark is not a resident; immense flocks also arrive in this country during autumn from the north of Europe. On almost every occasion when meeting them at sea, I remarked that they flew in compact bodies of several hundreds, seldom showing signs of fatigue, though a few now and then fell out from the ranks and, after hovering for a short time round the steamboat, at length settled on board; then, creeping into the first quiet corner, they puffed out their feathers and speedily dropped off to sleep.

During the years I was in correspondence with the light-ships off the east coast Larks were by far the most numerous of the birds taken on board the vessels*; Starlings were next; and from the crews I learned that Wheatears, in certain states of weather, proved frequent victims—none, however, were captured during the autumn of 1872 or the following spring.

While steaming in company with the herring-fleet in the North Sea during the autumn of 1872, I fell in with Larks in large numbers, flying direct for the Norfolk and Suffolk coasts, almost daily from the 7th of October to the 9th of November. At the same time that these birds are making their way in such swarms across the North Sea, they are also landing on the shores of the Channel or passing along the coast. My notes for 1882 and the following year contain frequent references to the movements of this species along the south coast, between Shoreham and Lancing, as well as the occasional landing of large bodies. The course followed by these birds during autumn is decidedly uncertain; one day the whole of the flocks proceed west, and on the next the direction is probably reversed. On the approach of winter storms, and during the continuation of severe weather, they invariably make their way towards the west.

"1882, September 29. Wind south. Larks continued flying west during the greater part of the day.

"October 2. Strong wind, west-south-west. Larks in considerable numbers flying east before the strong wind.

"October 3. Wind changeable, west and north-west. Larks in large flocks making their way towards the west.

"October 10. Wind south-east; weather fine. The whole of the Larks flying east.

"October 13. Wind north-east. Larks flying east.

"October 20. Light wind from the south; after midday the wind freshened from the south-west. Larks flying west. On this day the whole of the Pipits moved east.

"December 9. Wind north-east, cold, and snow three inches deep. After 9 A.M. wind shifted north-west, when Larks commenced flying west in immense numbers."

* It is recorded that during foggy weather in autumn, many years ago, at least one thousand small birds, mostly Larks, were captured one night on board the 'Newarp.' Several of the crew having been at once set to work, six hundred of the slain were stripped of their feathers, and an immense sea-pie, a three-decker (three tiers of birds with an intervening layer of crust between), was built up and proved a great success.

A head wind appears to draw Larks towards the land, though it is impossible to hazard an opinion as to the point from which the birds arriving on the south coast had started on their journey. On the 8th of October it will be seen that they landed before a light favouring breeze.

"1883, October 5. Wind north, strong. Larks crossing against the wind all day.

"October 6. Wind north, strong. Immense numbers of Larks crossing all day and landing till after dusk. In order to ascertain their condition I fired one shot into a dense flock sweeping low over the shingle-banks just after dark, and on examination their crops proved perfectly empty.

"October 8. Light wind, south; fine. Large quantities of Larks still landing.

"October 10. Wind south-east; fine. Larks flying west."

A heavy fall of snow and a cold wind from the north-west is certain to bring myriads of Larks and other land-birds along the south coast, intent on making their way from east to west; occasionally they pass in continuous streams from daylight till dark. Larks are usually the first to show, a slight covering of snow being sufficient to put them in motion, while it requires a few days of severe weather before Fieldfares, Redwings, or Blackbirds appear in any numbers. The storm of January 1867 caused by far the most extensive migration of small birds I have ever witnessed in Sussex; from the summit of the cliffs between Rottingdean and Newhaven, as far as one could see inland over the Downs, these endless swarms extended; for at least a mile at sea also clouds of Larks and Starlings intermixed with other species were working west, sweeping closely over the water to avoid the force of the wind.

At such times the whole of the bird-catching fraternity of Brighton are engaged in the work of destruction. Should a strong cold wind from the north-west be blowing, the course of the birds is close to the ground, and thousands are captured in the nets. There is great competition for what are considered the best pitches, numbers of men leaving Brighton before midnight and depositing their packs on the ground they intend to occupy, to reserve the spot; they seek what shelter they can till daylight behind some brushwood or stack. From thirty to fifty dozen are commonly captured, and the takes not unfrequently reach as high as eighty dozen. I have often seen over two hundred clap-nets at work on a favourable day; and as scores of drag-nets are out as soon as dusk sets in, some idea of the number of birds taken may be formed.

When pressed by want during continued snow-storms, Larks are forced to put up with green meat in order to sustain life; the leaves of the winter-cabbages in the fields are at times entirely consumed, the veins alone being left, presenting a most singular appearance; turnip-greens also suffer considerably from their attacks. The terrible hurricane of drifting sleet and snow in January 1881 inflicted great suffering on all the various species of small birds in Sussex. On the 25th several Larks in an exceedingly weak and helpless state alighted on our lawn to feed on the bread and scraps provided for the usual pensioners; on the following day I watched hundreds of their dead bodies swept out by the flood-tide from the weeds on the mud-banks in Shoreham harbour in which they had sought refuge at the commencement of the gale.

A scarce bird not unfrequently falls into the possession of one unacquainted with its value, and the occurrence consequently remains unrecorded. Towards the latter end of the flight-time in January 1867, while Larks were still passing over the south coast, I drove along the road between Rottingdean and Newhaven to make notes on the various species moving towards the west. After watching the passage for several hours I pulled my conveyance up at the roadside, as the daylight was commencing to fade, and proceeded to discuss a well-earned lunch: while so employed a roughly clad individual, armed with an antiquated muzzle-loader, drew up alongside, and after loafing around for a few minutes, making some remarks as to the weather and other subjects, at length broke the ice by inquiring if I would buy a French Partridge. Not satisfied with my answer, he produced the bird, which I immediately identified as a female Little Bustard in fair plumage. On informing him that any naturalist in Brighton ought to give him far more than the price he had asked (first eighteen pence, finally dropping to a "bob"), he became suspicious and resolutely refused to carry his prize in its present condition into the town, where he imagined he might be deemed liable for killing game without a licence. The stupid fellow evidently distrusted the advice tendered; and finally sitting down on the roadside bank he plucked his bird with the greatest satisfaction, remarking, when his work was completed, that it would "make a good supper for the missus and me."

Some five-and-twenty years ago the fields in the neighbourhood of Brighton were resorted to during the autumn flight by quantities of gunners who indulged in the sport of shooting these birds while on passage. For this amusement the well-known Lark-glass was made use of, the reflection of the sun on the twirling glass being supposed to prove the attraction*; anyhow, the infatuated birds when once in view made hastily towards the lure, skimming round on extended wings and offering a succession of the easiest shots. Though the numbers of shooters have greatly increased, this old-fashioned custom has gradually fallen into disrepute; I do not remember to have seen more than one or two Lark-glasses in operation during the last half-dozen years. Meadow-Pipits are also attracted by these means if the flights, as is usually the case, happen to be passing over at the time. In October 1875, having placed a glass some hundred yards or so from the back of our house near Brighton, in order to watch the actions of the Larks when undisturbed, I shot an immature Black Redstart that darted down. Whether it was attracted by the glass or was on the point of settling in the garden close at hand (a favourite resort in those days for that species), I had no means of ascertaining, the bird having been killed the moment it was identified.

In June 1870, my attention having been attracted by a couple of Larks hovering in the greatest state of excitement over a rough bank near one of the Norfolk broads, I ascertained, after a few minutes' watching, that a stoat carrying one of their newly fledged brood in its mouth was the cause of the disturbance. Thinking that the group would afford a good chance for the taxidermist to exercise his skill, I procured the whole party with one shot, and much regret that the plates in "Rough Notes" are too small to depict the scene. Some of the lesser Falcons as well as Hawks also prey upon this species, and to rats they not unfrequently fall victims. A few winters ago I discovered that one or two of these destructive brutes had taken up their quarters in the vicinity of my boatsheds in the east of Norfolk. They commenced operations by devouring holes in the men's oily coats, and next turned their attention to the decaying carcases of some Grey and Carrion Crows hanging on a vermin-pole. A dog that accompanied me soon pointed out their whereabouts, below the hatches of one of the gunning-punts lying on the bank. From this shelter they were soon forced and destroyed, and the contents of their domicile being overhauled, it was ascertained that they had carried there a Lark and a Starling, both perfectly fresh; these they must have captured themselves on the marshes, as none had been shot in the neighbourhood. There were also parts of the Crows transported by some means from the pole on which they had been suspended, and a bottle containing a few drops of Rangoon oil. The latter had been flung out the previous day on the bank to the distance of about twenty or thirty yards; and it would doubtless have been amusing to have observed the manner in which the rats conveyed it to their nest.

The tints on the plumage of young Larks in their first summer are much lighter in colouring than in mature birds, the whole of the feathers on the back being edged with a pale straw and the general tone more subdued. None but those acquainted with the species during all its changes would imagine the relationship between an old and young Lark shot in August.

* For my own part I always imagined the Larks took it for a Kestrel hovering close to the ground, which it certainly much resembles.

SNOW-BUNTING.

EMBERIZA NIVALIS.

In July 1876 I made an attempt to reach the ground, on the summit of the high hills in the east of Inverness, where the Snow-Bunting is supposed to breed; a dreadful storm of wind and rain, however, put a stop to our advance and rendered it an impossibility to reach the haunts of the birds. A short extract from my notes will give an account of the attempt we made:—

"July 4th. Having settled to search Ben Muich Dhui for Snow-Buntings, we decided on making an early start, and leaving the lodge at midnight we drove to a bothy on the east side of the forest. Here four keepers and foresters were awaiting our arrival, and an immediate start was made for the high ground. The morning proved dull and gloomy and we were well up the Braemore Pass before it became fairly light. The weather then got worse and the wind increased, the mist and clouds rolled lower down the hills, while the rain drifted in blinding showers, rendering it impossible for us to advance. For two hours we sheltered among some large slabs of rock near the highest part of the Pass in hopes that the storm might moderate. At length, however, we came to the conclusion that it was quite useless to attempt to reach the high ground; added to which the position we now found ourselves in could scarcely be termed pleasant. The terrific gusts as they roared round the crags above us now and then dislodged stones and pieces of rock that came rolling down the side of the hill. Some of these dashed past us at no great distance just after we had quitted our shelter, and I must confess I felt greatly relieved when we emerged from the Pass; the unearthly howling and screeching of the wind among the jagged and pointed rocks was perfectly deafening, and the force of the blasts was such that it would have been the height of folly to have proceeded further. I was much surprised at the presence of a Wren far up on the bleak hill-side; during the lulls in the storm the little bird mounted on the wet and dripping rocks and sang as loudly as if his lot was cast in pleasant places. When first the sound of his note was heard we were unable to make out what bird it could be, and a considerable time elapsed before we caught sight of the diminutive songster strutting about on the summit of a large stone. Towards mid-day the sun broke through and the wind dropped a little, but it continued far too rough to renew our attempt to reach the top of the hills."

In the winter of 1868 I was staying at Tain, in the east of Ross-shire, for the punt-gunning on the Dornoch Firth, as well as Partridge- and Snipe-shooting on the Fendom, the stretch of sandy flats and cultivated land that extends along the south shore for several miles. While returning one evening just after dark over the rough ground covered with coarse grass on the Fendom, we put up an immense number of Snow-Buntings. The birds rose almost at our feet and flitted in thousands low down, the white on their wings resembling the foam at sea when the waves are seen breaking in the dusk. I conclude it is the young birds of the year that exhibit such a warm brown colouring on their first arrival in autumn; there are many different tints to be seen, and scarcely any will be found with exactly the same plumage. In December 1862 I noticed a very large flock on some marshy ground near Hunstanton, on the Norfolk coast; when settled and spread out feeding they must have covered at least a couple of acres. Occasionally during winter I have known a great many taken by the clap-nets on the downs near Brighton, and still more by the drag-nets at night. Though such immense numbers make their way south in winter, the hill-tops in the Highlands are not entirely deserted at that season. When Ptarmigan-shooting on the hills in the north-east of Perthshire, in December 1867, I repeatedly found flocks on the higher slopes of the snow-clad mountains. I was rather amused at the description given by a forester in Inverness of the nature of the ground on the summit of the mountains to which this bird resorted. "The hill-top," he remarked, "was a very vulgar place."

On the 29th of October, 1879, the weather being stormy at the time, there were large flocks of these birds on the denes near the harbour-mouth at Yarmouth; occasionally during the following week I remarked they were intermixed with Shore-Larks. Many small flocks of Snow-Buntings were seen on the south denes near Yarmouth about the middle of February 1882; some were exceedingly light-coloured, with much white showing, and others very dark. Several specimens exhibiting various stages of plumage were shot in a sand-pit near the shore, between the town and the harbour-mouth.

I have a few entries in my notes, taken while staying at Yarmouth in the autumn of 1872, referring to Snow-Buntings, and they are as follows:—

"September 26th. Weather rough, wind south-west. Three Snow-Buntings, the first I had met with this season, were shot on the south denes, and proved to be two males and a female. During the remainder of the time passed at Yarmouth, I seldom went along the denes without observing several along the side of the carriage-drive; they generally showed in the greatest numbers in rough weather.

"October 31st. There was to-day a large addition to the flock of Snow-Buntings on the south denes; most of the fresh arrivals were dark-coloured, being, I suppose, young birds of the year.

"November 1st. Steamed out of Yarmouth harbour, round the Barber Sands off Caister, which were, as usual, covered with Gulls; I noticed a few dark-coloured birds among them, but, on approaching as close as we were able and using the glasses, it was ascertained that they were only Grey Crows. Larks, Rooks, and a few small flocks of Snow-Buntings were the only birds I observed at sea making for land.

"November 5th. Steamed from Yarmouth as far south as Lowestoft, and afterwards back to Caister; no birds of passage seen with the exception of a few Rooks and a small party of Snow-Buntings."

On the 12th of November I was again enabled to make observations on these birds. This was the second day of the terrible storm that, commencing on Monday the 11th of November, continued, with a lull of only a few hours on Friday morning, till Saturday the 16th; then several of the larger fishing-boats left the harbour, but before they could get clear of the sands it came on to blow harder from the east-north-east and they were all forced to put back.

"The gale this morning was blowing from the east-north-east. Several flocks of fowl were still flying north, but the number of Dunlins that passed were not to be compared with those observed the previous day. The Snow-Buntings had received large additions, and the flock must have numbered between two and three hundred. Their favourite haunt and resting-ground seemed to be the carriage-drive along the shore from the town towards the harbour-mouth, though what food they could find there I was unable to discover."

BUNTING.

EMBERIZA MILIARIA.

COMMON in the south, and distributed by no means sparingly over many of the cultivated districts in the northern and western Highlands, this species is well known in most parts of the British Islands. According to my own observations, it is more numerous in Sussex (especially within a few miles of the sea-coast) than in any other county where I have met with a chance of studying its habits.

During summer the Common Bunting is usually to be seen in the immediate vicinity of hay-fields. The male, perched either on some commanding twig along a hedgerow, or on the topmost bar of a post-and-rail fence, is sure to attract attention while uttering from time to time his somewhat monotonous song. Here by the roadside he will await within a few yards the approach of passers by (I have frequently driven past one within six feet without his exhibiting the slightest sign of alarm), and then with drooping legs and an apparently laboured flight, will flutter some forty or fifty yards into the field, and take up a position on any rank plant or strand of grass that will sustain his weight. From this point of vantage he will again continue to drone out his harsh and tuneless ditty.

This species appears to be late in nesting; I have repeatedly seen fresh eggs mown out in June when the hay was cut—the fields of seed-grass being the favourite breeding-quarters of this Bunting in Sussex: their nests are also occasionally discovered under the shelter of coarse herbage on the furze-covered downs. I am not aware of any eggs that vary to a greater extent; at times they differ but slightly from those of the Yellow Hammer, while clutches may now and then be seen blotched and scrawled in every conceivable manner with a rich red-brown. Eggs taken in the east of Sussex, I remarked in several instances, both in shape and colouring, bore but a very slight resemblance to those procured to the west of Brighton.

As early as the last week in August I have noticed these birds especially numerous along the south coast and commencing to flock. Whether those were all natives of the district, or visitors from more northern localities, it was impossible to form an opinion. On the approach of winter large bodies collect and roost in the marine weeds growing on the mudflats above high-water mark in Shoreham Harbour. Soon after 3 P.M. they may be seen flying singly or in small parties from the surrounding country, and, after hovering round a few times, pitching straight down into the thick cover. If disturbed when their quarters are once taken up, it would be discovered that the birds were scattered over several acres of the flats—one, two, or three rising here and there, wherever the cover was most dense. It is not till early in the spring that this situation is totally deserted; I have watched a few scattered birds gathering towards the harbour shortly before sunset as late as the beginning of April.

The upper mandible of this Bunting is furnished with a very prominent protuberance or tooth. This is supposed to assist the bird in shelling the various seeds which form the principal part of its food.

BLACK-HEADED BUNTING.

EMBERIZA SCHŒNICULUS.

The familiar names of Reed-Bunting or Reed-Sparrow, commonly applied to this species, clearly indicate the style of country it frequents. These titles, however, only hold good during summer, as the birds may constantly be observed in autumn and winter joining in small numbers with other Buntings, Linnets, and Finches. In company with these roving flocks, they move from one spot to another—stackyards, waste lands, and any situations where food is procurable being visited.

From Caithness to Sussex this lively bird is to be met with; and even the wild and barren Western Islands are resorted to at certain seasons, if no residents remain all the year round on those inhospitable shores. I remarked a pair or two repeatedly in a few stunted bushes in the garden of a shooting lodge situated on one of the saltwater lochs in the Long Island during the latter end of April and early in May 1877. Their presence at such an early date would lead to the impression that they had passed the winter in this neighbourhood. When I left the lodge (about the middle of May) the birds were still there; and as no suitable nesting-ground could possibly be discovered within a mile or so of their usual quarters (from which they were seldom absent for any length of time), I concluded they had yet to make a move to their summer haunts.

The neighbourhood of rush-grown marshes is the favourite resort of the Black-headed Bunting; and in the Broad districts of the eastern counties this handsome bird may be observed in immense numbers and to the fullest advantage during fine summer weather. The male, with his black head, white neck, and conspicuous red-brown markings on the back, is one of the most attractive inhabitants of these watery wastes. As he flits along the river-bank or the side of the marsh-dyke, by no means disconcerted by a passing boat, there is little difficulty in closely watching his actions. A short stroll across any of the adjoining grass-marshes that are interspersed with thick patches of rushes and other luxuriant water-plants would doubtless start a female, fluttering apparently helpless and injured, from her neatly built nest snugly concealed among the roots of the coarse herbage.

I have no evidence that any migrants from across the North Sea arrive on our coasts during the fall of the year. According to my own experience, this species is decidedly less numerous in many English counties throughout the winter months than during the breeding-season. This local diminution may probably be accounted for by their common habit of joining with other small birds towards the end of autumn and deserting their usual haunts. It is evidently the custom of this species to roost in the neighbourhood of marshes, though whether in winter they separate from the flocks of small birds with whom they keep company during the day I have had no opportunity of ascertaining. As early as the first week in March they may be seen towards evening gathering in the direction of some rush-grown pool or ditch in the levels in the vicinity of the south coast. A patch of reeds in a small water-dyke running through the marshes between Shoreham and Beeding is a favourite resort. I have on several occasions, while passing, watched them approaching their quarters. The birds arrive for the most part singly, flying high and darting down with a sudden swoop, and at once disappearing among the stems of the reeds, appearing to take up a position close above the water. As many as forty or fifty might be counted seeking the shelter of this small patch of rushes shortly before dusk.

In winter, while keeping company with other Buntings and Finches, the food of this species consists for the most part of grain collected from the neighbourhood of farm-buildings and stockyards, as well as the seeds of many grasses and plants. Insects and caterpillars, together with a few seeds, probably form the principal part of their diet during spring and summer. A small white moth which appears among the water-plants growing on the broads in the east of Norfolk early in June is eagerly sought after by this Bunting. The insect is usually found clinging to the stems of the reed; and unless the weather prove too stormy, the birds may be seen daily for a few weeks, flitting from stem to stem, diligently hunting through all the straggling patches of reed that fringe the side of the marshes.

YELLOW BUNTING.

EMBERIZA CITRINELLA.

THE Yellow Bunting is to be met with in almost every part of the British Islands where the country is sufficiently wooded to supply its very modest requirements in the way of concealment for its nest.

Of all our birds, whether native or migratory, this bright-coloured and attractive species is one of the hardiest, apparently more fitted to withstand the severity of the climate than many of our winter visitors from the shores of Norway, Sweden, or Lapland. The Redwing and Fieldfare land on our northern coasts, and pass south as the cold increases, often being found, during protracted storms, helpless from want or frozen to death in the southern counties of England. The swarms of Bramblings which make their appearance in autumn first on the stubbles or in the beech-groves, and finally, as winter draws nearer, in the neighbourhood of the farm-steadings, gradually take their departure, together with the greater number of the Chaffinches, to districts less exposed, leaving the Yellow Hammer to face the cutting blasts and drifting snow-squalls in its native glens. In some of the wildest parts of the Highlands I met with these Buntings, during hard frosts, collected into flocks numbering several hundreds. The sheltered corner of the cattle-yards and the immediate vicinity of any dwelling-houses where food might be procured were their favourite resorts, and, indeed, the only spots where the poor birds had a chance of sustaining life. On one occasion during a heavy snow-storm I observed a large number of these birds, together with a score or so of Chaffinches, clinging to the joints and feeding on the flesh of a dead horse, which had been hung against a dog-kennel at the back of a shooting-lodge in the west of Perthshire. On the pieces being removed and placed on the ground, and the snow swept from them, the half-starved birds came down in hundreds and settled on the meat.

The Yellow Bunting may be found frequenting situations differing considerably in various localities. In Sussex it is distributed over the woodlands, breeding by the roadside hedge or under the shelter of some bramble-covered bank. It is also equally numerous on the furze-clad downs, its nest being concealed in the coarse grass or among the lower branches or roots of some stunted bush. On one occasion (June 18, 1875) I discovered a nest of this species containing three eggs, on the open hillside on the downs to the north of Stanmer Park. The pasture was exceedingly short; and there was not the slightest cover of any description within a distance of five-and-twenty or thirty yards.

The sheltered valleys among this range of hills are a favourite resort during winter, if the weather remains mild. Here I have repeatedly noticed these birds collecting into immense flocks. If disturbed in the evening twilight shortly after seeking their roosting-quarters, the whole hill-side for several acres would appear alive with fluttering wings. Frost and snow soon force them to the farmyards; and in all parts of the country they may be seen clinging to the stacks, or pecking about the yards in company with Sparrows, Greenfinches, and Chaffinches. In the marshes of the Broad districts of the eastern counties, this species is less abundant, its place being taken by its relative the Black-headed Bunting or Reed-Sparrow; on the cultivated lands adjoining the fens, however, it is plentiful. Severe weather, though it usually drives this species from outlying quarters to the neighbourhood of farms and other buildings, seldom causes any general movement from one district to another.

Owing to the breeding-range of this species extending far north, it is probable the British Islands are visited by migrants from across the sea. Only one or two while on the passage have come under my observation off our coasts in autumn; and during the years I received wings from the light-ships no information was gained concerning their arrival.

Throughout the snow-storms early in December 1882, I remarked a few scattered pairs of Yellow Hammers keeping company with Chaffinches, Greenfinches, Pipits, and Wagtails. These birds were fluttering and running busily alongside the roads in the outskirts of Brighton. Wherever the snow had been removed they eagerly scratched the dust-heaps, or any collection of rubbish carted out from the town.

Seeds and insects no doubt form the greater portion of the food of this species. I had previously imagined it was only when pressed by want that meat would be patronized. A female Yellow Hammer, however, was distinctly seen to make a most vigorous attack on a piece of cooked mutton, hung up by a string to a small tree in a garden near Brighton for the benefit of the Titmice. The weather was exceedingly mild at the time, and the sun shining brightly (February 7, 1883); so a scarcity of natural food could hardly have influenced its choice. The wind having twisted up the string round a limb, the Bunting was enabled to reach the meat, which while swinging was accessible only to the Paridæ. A hen sparrow was enjoying the feast in perfect amity with the Bunting. I remarked that while the former attacked the fat alone, the latter was tearing out small strands of meat from the lean.

In the east of Norfolk this species is commonly spoken of as the Goldfinch,—"*Carduelis elegans*" being in that locality termed the "Drawwater."

CIRL BUNTING.

EMBERIZA CIRLUS.

The range of this species is, according to my own experience, exceedingly limited in Great Britain. With the exception of Sussex, where the Cirl Bunting is common in certain localities, I have only met with a chance of observing this bird in the Isle of Wight. That it is an occasional visitor to Norfolk, however, I am in possession of good proof, having discovered a couple of fresh-killed females among a dozen Yellow Buntings and other small birds, shot at my request by a farmer as food for an Owl I kept in confinement. This occurred in the autumn of 1875, at Potter Heigham near Yarmouth. The birds were obtained feeding round a stack that had been thrashed; but though I carefully watched the spot on the following day (being aware the species is considered rare in the district), no other specimens were detected. In the winters of 1879, '81, and '82, I again closely inspected the large numbers of Yellow Hammers frequenting the farm-buildings in this locality, but without recognizing the bird; and doubtless it is but a rare straggler to the east of Norfolk.

In Sussex the Cirl Bunting is a resident, and may be found at all seasons in the country immediately north of the range of the South Downs, being particularly abundant within the distance of fifteen or twenty miles from Brighton. I have seldom, if ever, noticed the bird further inland than eight or ten miles from the coast. During the summer a few make their appearance to the south of the hills, and nest in the immediate vicinity of the seaside towns and villages. I have remarked these Buntings in a few instances as far east and west as Hastings and Bognor.

In autumn they collect in flocks, as many as fifty or sixty being seen at times in company. Yellow Hammers and a few stray Chaffinches are occasionally to be observed in close proximity, though for the most part I have remarked that they appeared to prefer their own society. At this season they feed on the stubbles, resorting for shelter to the hedgerows and coverts. I imagine these birds do not shift their quarters, however severe the weather, beyond paying a visit to the farmyards, having met with them frequenting the slopes of the downs and the adjoining arable land from early in November till the end of February.

The nest much resembles that of the Yellow Hammer, though I have now and then noticed that the structure exhibited a larger quantity of green moss in its composition than is commonly made use of by that species. The quickset edges alongside the London, Brighton, and South Coast Railway are a very favourite breeding-resort for these birds. In the plantations on the sloping sides of the downs, nests may occasionally be seen at an elevation of five or six feet in moss-grown and ivy-covered stumps of thorn. In the foliage of trained rose-bushes, as well as among ferns and creeping plants on rockeries in gardens, the young have been repeatedly reared in the vicinity of Brighton.

The eggs vary to a considerable extent, exhibiting several shades of colour, though in some instances they correspond closely with those of the Yellow Hammer. The young shortly after being hatched are thickly covered with a dull black down, and show a large and clearly defined white gape.

The plumages of the female Cirl Bunting and Yellow Hammer bear a very close resemblance. It is by no seems an easy matter to determine at a glance the identity of a female. All observers of bird-life must, while passing through our country-lanes, have had their attention attracted by the conspicuous warm brown tint of the feathers on the rump or lower part of the back of the Yellow Hammer as the bird flies past or rises to flutter over a hedgerow. In the Cirl Bunting this red-brown colouring is absent, and the plumage is of a pale olive-green tinge. This fact is mentioned because I do not remember to have seen it alluded to by any ornithological writer.

The note of the two species is also very similar; that of the Cirl Bunting, however, is destitute of the prolonged skirl which the Yellow Hammer gives utterance to by way of an ending. In the neighbourhood of the South Downs in Sussex I have heard country people compare the song of the Yellow Hammer to the following words:—"Little bit of bread and no c h e e e s e." The note of the Cirl Bunting is almost identical, with the omission of the long-drawn-out "cheese" at the finish.

CHAFFINCH.

FRINGILLA CÆLEBS.

There are few parts of the British Islands, with the exception of barren and treeless moorlands, where the Chaffinch is not occasionally to be observed at one season or another. In most wooded localities it is common all the year round, though I have met with but a scattered pair or two in many of the dense pine-forests of the Northern Highlands.

Large numbers reach our eastern coasts from across the North Sea during the autumn months. Though immense flocks may occasionally be seen all through the winter in various parts of Great Britain, it is probable that many Chaffinches cross the English Channel, and return to our shores early in the spring. I paid particular attention to all large gatherings of these birds, met with either by sea or land, in order, if possible, to learn whether there is any certain rule as to the separation of the sexes during the winter months. The following notes extracted from my journals will show the date of the arrival of our visitors from the north of Europe, and also the relative numbers of the sexes in any considerable parties that have come under my observation :—

During a heavy snow-storm in December 1865, I noticed several parties of Chaffinches frequenting the farmyards and the dust-heaps at the back of a shooting-lodge in the west of Perthshire. Both males and females were to be seen in about equal numbers.

In January 1867, at the time of the heavy snowfall, when countless myriads of small birds passed from east to west along the coast of Sussex, the stubble-fields between Brighton and Newhaven were, in some parts, almost covered with flocks of Chaffinches. The poor birds, wearied and half-starved, were flying past and dropping wherever a spot free from snow could be discovered. There were both males and females; but after carefully watching them for two or three consecutive days, it was evident the males were most numerous; still one third at least were females.

Towards the end of January 1871, the coast of Sussex was again visited by swarms of fugitives during protracted frost and snow. I remarked that, in the flocks of Chaffinches appearing in the fields, the males and females were in about the same proportion as during the severe weather four years previously.

While steaming in the North Sea between twenty and thirty miles off Yarmouth, on the 7th of October 1872, with a fresh breeze from the south-east, several parties of Chaffinches and Tree-Sparrows were noticed flying towards the land. The Chaffinches that were near enough for the sexes to be identified were males and females in about equal numbers. The other birds seen on the passage during the same day were Rooks, Starlings, and Larks.

On the following day (the 8th), while ten or fifteen miles east of the 'Newarp' floating light, a continued stream of Rooks, Grey Crows, Jackdaws, Starlings, Larks, and Chaffinches were observed making their way towards the land, with but slight intermission, from daylight till dusk. Several Larks and Chaffinches came on board. The Larks were greatly fatigued, and, creeping into any quiet corner, generally went off at once to sleep; while the Chaffinches, though tired, seemed of an inquiring disposition, and pecked about all over the deck, only fluttering a few feet when any of the crew passed near them. One poor little bird, evidently much distressed by its journey, after being a passenger for at least twenty miles, left us as we were entering the harbour, and fluttered on board a fishing-boat just going out. Here he perched himself in a basket hanging over the stern and was carried to sea again. All the Chaffinches that came on board during the day were, without exception, males. In the flocks passing the steam-boat I did not recognize any females; in many instances, however, they were too far off to be clearly examined.

During rough and stormy weather, and, indeed, immediately before a gale, few, if any, small birds are rash enough to attempt to cross. The 10th and 11th of October proved squally with drifting rain from the south-west; and on those days no Chaffinches or Larks were observed on the passage. On the 14th of October, weather still and hazy, the whole of the birds of passage were making good way; and though large numbers of Rooks, Starlings, Larks, Chaffinches, and Tree-Sparrows were continually passing the vessel while about ten miles outside the Cross Sands, the only visitors that boarded us were two or three Tree-Sparrows, who took their departure after a short rest. The males were apparently most numerous in the flocks of Chaffinches, though I clearly recognized one or two small parties entirely composed of females.

On several days between the 21st of October and the 9th of November, I was out at sea in company with the herring-fleet; but not a single Chaffinch was seen crossing, the only birds of passage observed being Rooks, Grey Crows, Starlings, Larks, Snow-Buntings, and Peewits. On Monday the 11th a most disastrous gale of wind set in, with terrific squalls from north-north-east. After continuing blowing all the week from east, south-east, and east-south-east, the wind dropped on the 18th, and on the 20th we were again enabled to steam round the Cross Sands. At the invitation of the master, I went on board the 'Newarp' floating light, and learned they had not yet spoken any vessel since the gale, which they had ridden out with 160 fathoms of cable; and though, naturally, having experienced rough times, every thing, as usual on all the Trinity ships, was in the greatest possible order and brightness. I found on board the only birds that had struck the lights or settled on deck during the storm. These were two Stormy Petrels, one male Siskin, one Tree-Sparrow, one female Blackbird, and one male Chaffinch. This appears a late date for this species to be still crossing; I did not hear of any others till the following spring.

On March 27th, 1873, a fine bright morning, light easterly breeze, I was out on Hickling Broad in the east of Norfolk, and noticed soon after daybreak immense flocks of Starlings flying east, also several parties of male Chaffinches. These Finches were apparently all bound due east, and passed over without halting; as far as I could judge there was not a female among their numbers. Meadow-Pipits were also taking up their quarters round the broad after a winter's absence from the district. A few days later (April 7) I received from the 'Lynn Well' lightship the wings of a few Chaffinches, also several Starlings, and one Meadow-Pipit. This would go to prove that some at least of the flocks observed on the Norfolk coast had continued their journey across the North Sea. After an interval of a few weeks, wings were again sent from the same vessel; and those plainly indicated that Chaffinches had passed over till the end of April. These birds, I was informed, were all red-breasted, and consequently males.

In the spring of 1875 a large mixed flock of Bramblings, Chaffinches, and Tree-Sparrows resorted for several weeks to some arable ground on the downs near Falmer in Sussex. I remarked that the Chaffinches were both males and females, and, as near as I could judge, in about equal numbers.

During the severe gale and protracted frost on the coast of Sussex in January 1881, Chaffinches, like other small birds, suffered excessively. The frozen victims that came under my notice were of both sexes.

Passing on several occasions along the sea-wall from Shoreham to Lancing during November and December 1882, and in January 1883, I repeatedly disturbed large flocks of small birds that resorted for food to the various seed-producing weeds and plants growing on the shingle-banks. Greenfinches, Linnets, Twites, and Chaffinches were constantly to be seen; and here again I remarked both males and females in about equal numbers. By the latter end of February the parties of Chaffinches were considerably reinforced, though at that date a few pairs had evidently taken up their summer quarters along the more wooded portion of the coast-line. The males were singing constantly during the sunshine when the weather was warm and bright. I cannot call to mind having heard the note of this species on previous seasons so early in the year.

On the 5th of March 1883, several straggling parties of Chaffinches, with but few exceptions all males, were noticed flying north across the Downs near Brighton. The weather was remarkably still and fine, with a light air from the north.

During the summer months this handsome species takes up its quarters in gardens and pleasure-grounds in the immediate vicinity of dwelling-houses, as well as throughout the woods and coverts. A few pairs are also to be met with among the scattered bushes and plantations in remote and rocky glens, and even on the furze-covered downs of the southern counties. The neat and beautifully constructed nest is too well known to need description; and the eggs are to be seen in the collection of every schoolboy. Seeds and insects supply the chief items of the food of this useful bird. Destructive it may be at times to the produce of the farm and garden; but the quantities of injurious caterpillars it clears off, atone amply for all its previous delinquencies. In severe weather it will greedily prey on the bones and crumbs provided for Robins and other small pensioners, and if hard pressed will ravenously attack raw flesh, if accessible*.

* *Vide* Yellow Bunting.

BRAMBLING.

FRINGILLA MONTIFRINGILLA.

Though an annual visitor in considerable numbers to our shores, I never remarked this species on passage across the North Sea, and the wings received from the light-ships off the east coast during the seasons of 1872 and 1873 did not exceed a score. It is possible that fine and clear weather may have prevailed at the time of their migration during these years; and under such circumstances but few would be injured by striking the lights. Still, as I was able to gather little or no information concerning this species from the crews of any of the vessels, it is most probable the main flocks of Bramblings make the land towards the northern portion of the Scotch coast. Their early arrival in the Highlands, a month or so at least before any numbers show themselves in England, also points to the same conclusion.

All parts of the Highlands (with the exception of the high ranges) appear to be occasionally visited; I have found large flocks in many of the wildest glens. According to my own experience, they seldom stray far up the mountain-side, resorting on their first arrival to the stubble-fields and being especially partial to the neighbourhood of beech trees. On the approach of severe weather they betake themselves to the farmyards; and by far the greater number eventually move south to avoid the protracted cold and the hardships of a winter in the barren northern glens.

Stragglers and small parties may be seen almost every season on the eastern and southern coast, and, indeed, in all parts of the country, though the immense gatherings that are occasionally met with do not put in an appearance with the same regularity. Hard frost, however, generally brings considerable flocks to the southern counties, where they join company with Finches and Linnets on the stubbles and waste lands. I have now and then observed them moving towards the west with the multitudes of Larks and other small birds that pass along the Sussex coast after a heavy fall of snow. I did not remark that Bramblings were particularly numerous in the severe weather of January 1867, when Fieldfares and Redwings were far more abundant than in any subsequent year. In January 1871 these birds arrived in countless swarms, many of the fields along the coast being completely covered when a flock alighted—their bright colours, shown up as they flew past the snow-drifts, being particularly attractive. During the terrible hurricane in January 1881 large flights again appeared in the south; and on this occasion they suffered excessively from the continued inclemency of the weather. Hundreds collected round the houses, eagerly availing themselves of any scraps of food provided for the starving swarms of pensioners; while here and there a worn-out traveller, numbed and helpless, would creep into some sheltered corner and, puffing out its feathers, quietly await its fate. The numbers of small birds that perished during this storm could scarcely be credited, except by those who witnessed the immense quantities of dead bodies (collected together in many instances to the extent of several hundreds) that were exposed to view as the snow melted.

I obtained a specimen in January 1871 that exhibited a black or rather a dark greyish-coloured throat, the bird (a male) being at that date, of course, in winter plumage. This variety has previously been alluded to by several writers.

A very large flock of Bramblings took up their quarters for several weeks from the end of March 1875 in a beech-plantation on the hill near Falmer in Sussex. Some scores of Chaffinches were among their numbers; and a few Tree-Sparrows also kept company with them. During the day they resorted to the arable land for food, retiring when disturbed to the adjoining beech-woods. Many of the males were in fine plumage; and I secured two or three early in April that showed the perfect breeding-dress; the beaks had also assumed a blue tint. I noticed this gathering, though in considerably reduced numbers, still frequenting the district at the end of the month; a week or so later I learned they had all taken their departure. By May it is probable that all except a few stragglers have left our shores.

I have met with this species during the summer months on but one occasion. While fishing in the west of Perthshire, in June 1866, I was forced to ascend a beech tree to release the line, which had become entangled in the branches; and while so engaged a female Brambling was disturbed from her nest, containing three eggs, which was placed close to the stem of the tree. Being anxious to procure the newly fledged young as specimens, I left her in peace; and on again visiting the spot in about ten days or a fortnight the nest was empty; and, judging by its appearance, I should be of opinion that the young birds had been dragged out by a cat.

This is the only instance I am acquainted with of the Brambling attempting to rear its young in Great Britain. During subsequent years I have both carefully searched the same locality and made many inquiries, but invariably without success, though the bird was well known by those to whom I applied for information.

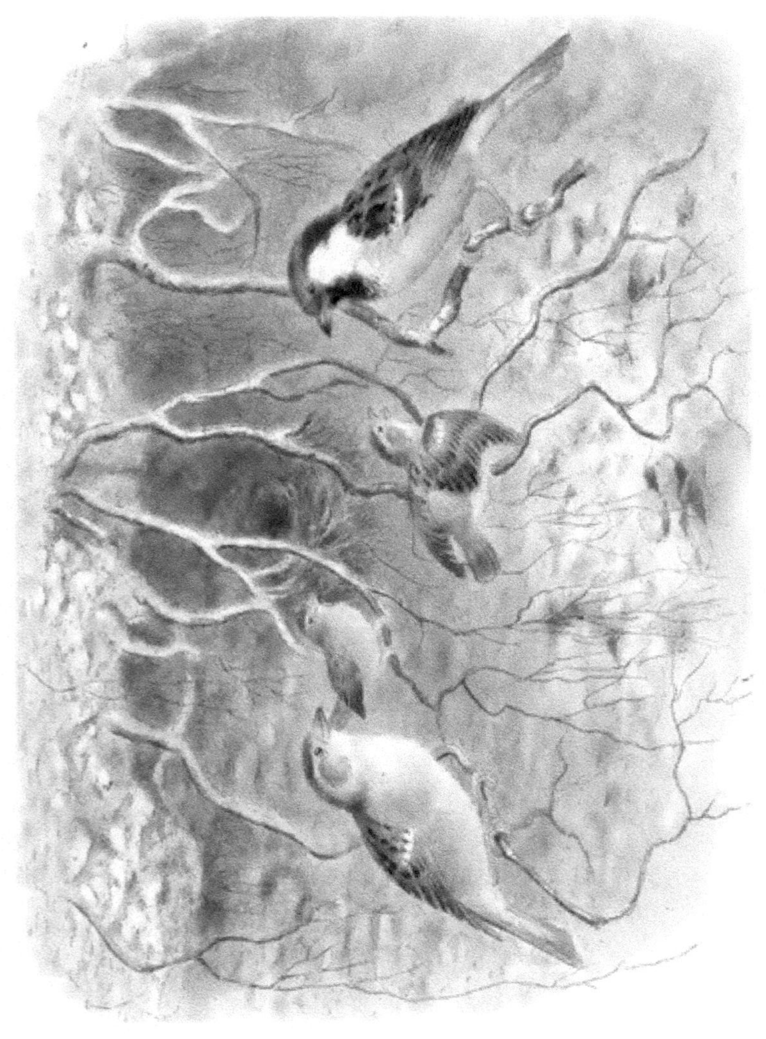

TREE-SPARROW.

PASSER MONTANUS.

Though stated by various authors to be widely distributed over the British Islands, it is only in the southern and eastern counties of England and in East Lothian that I have recognized the Tree-Sparrow.

In some parts of Norfolk this species is almost as numerous as the House-Sparrow, a few remaining in the vicinity of their quarters throughout the year. According to my own observations, this Sparrow is only an occasional visitor to the downs of Sussex, arriving in flocks on the approach of cold weather, passing gradually along the range of hills from east to west, and again making their appearance while on the return journey in the spring. Towards the end of March 1875 I remarked a few of these birds, in company with Chaffinches and Bramblings, resorting to the large beechwoods at Falmer, near Brighton; after remaining in the district till about the middle of April the flock gradually disappeared. On two or three occasions Tree-Sparrows were met with late in autumn flying along the links near Dirleton and also between Canty Bay and Dunbar in East Lothian; in all probability these birds were migrants which had recently crossed the North Sea.

Numbers of this species arrive on our eastern coasts from the northern countries of Europe during autumn. While steaming in company with the herring-fleet, in order to make observations, I frequently noticed these birds while on passage. Occasionally, when weary and worn out, they would alight on board, and selecting some quiet corner, turn their heads over on their backs and puffing out their feathers instantly fall asleep. After resting for a time a few now and then flew down on the deck and pecked about among the crumbs of bread and other food provided for the accommodation of our small feathered visitors; when revived they invariably took their departure before darkness set in, heading straight for the land. The migration appears to be continued through the whole of October, the latest straggler that I heard of being a single bird captured on board the 'Newarp' floating light during the gale that commenced on Monday the 11th of November, 1872, and continued during the whole of the week. On boarding the vessel on the 28th I learned that only seven birds had fallen on deck during the storm, the force of the wind being so great that the majority of those striking the lights were carried overboard.

The scientific name of *Passer montanus* bestowed on this species appears as inappropriate as that of *arboreus*. Though Tree-Sparrows when moving westward on the approach of winter usually pass along the Sussex downs, I never on other occasions met with these birds in a hilly country, their strongholds in Great Britain being evidently the flat portions of the midland and eastern counties. Many of the earlier writers on ornithology (who have been followed, in some instances, by those of a later date) exhibit but little knowledge concerning the habits of this species. The following lines are extracted from a well-known work:—"It is now perfectly clear that this bird resides amongst trees only, and that it makes its nest in holes and cavities of such as are decayed, and never amongst the branches nor in buildings." I took especial pains to hunt out the breeding-quarters of these birds round several farms in the east of Norfolk during the summer of 1873, and in every instance the nests were placed amongst buildings, some in cowsheds, others under the tiles of outhouses, and those or four among the rough stems of some coarse ivy that grew over an old wall. Not one did I discover amongst trees, though House-Sparrows were breeding plentifully both in the branches and the ivy round the trunks. Within the last few years I again visited the district, and noticed the birds still frequenting the same spots; a small colony was also pointed out by one of the natives in the roof of a carpenter's shed.

Occasionally I remarked in the east of Norfolk that these birds were absent from their usual haunts for some months during winter. Under date of Sunday, March 30, 1873, the following occurs in my notes:—"Tree-Sparrows were again numerous round the farm-buildings, this being almost the first day they had put in an appearance, a close watch having been kept for their return." During the winters of 1871 and 1881 they were to be observed continually throughout the cold weather in company with House-Sparrows, Finches, and Buntings round the cattle-yards of several of the farms.

Although it has been asserted that Tree-Sparrows do not inhabit towns in Great Britain, I repeatedly noticed a few pair pecking about in the main road running through the north end of Yarmouth in the autumn of 1872. Whether these were migrants lately landed, or residents, I had no means of ascertaining. A single bird also attracted my attention in a garden rather nearer the outskirts of the town in the summer of 1883.

The newly hatched broods of these Sparrows suffered severely from the fierce heat in the summer of 1873. Several pairs had built their nests under the tiled roofs of some cattle-sheds and piggeries adjoining the Falgate Inn at Potter Heigham, where the space was exceedingly cramped and little or no air could penetrate. Being anxious to procure specimens in the nestling plumage I removed the tiles, when the whole of the young, in all probability suffocated by the tropical heat, were discovered dead in the nests. After their bereavement I noticed three or four pairs of the birds building again between the 7th and 10th of July in some rank ivy overhanging an antiquated wall. This situation had evidently been chosen with considerable forethought, the widely spreading limbs and dense foliage affording ample shade and protection from the rays of the sun.

The male and female of this Sparrow are alike; the young also exhibit the same markings, though somewhat less clearly defined, in their first plumage.

HOUSE-SPARROW.

PASSER DOMESTICUS.

In the appearance of the city-bred and country Sparrow there is always a striking difference; the aspect of the townsman is by no means prepossessing, his worn and shabby attire, frequently black and grimy as the smoke-dried trees and buildings to which he resorts, contrasts but poorly with that of his country relative. The plumage of the latter is for the most part neat and trim, the bright colouring of his cheeks and flanks, as well as the warm red tints on his back, show up conspicuously in the sunlight and render his appearance by no means unattractive; the two birds if seen in company could scarcely be supposed to belong to one and the same species.

From north to south the House-Sparrow is abundant and appears gradually to be extending its range in some parts of the Highlands. Twenty years ago I remarked the absence of these birds about the dwellings in several of the remotest glens; of late years, however, a few pairs have taken up their quarters round the shooting-lodges or the small collections of shealings termed villages in such districts.

Sparrows are decidedly pugnacious, frequently fighting among themselves and occasionally with other species. On the 27th of December, 1883, I happened to be watching a brightly plumaged old male that had settled at some food thrown out for the benefit of the pensioners who regularly collect on our lawn, when a couple of Starlings flew down and attempted to claim a share. Undaunted by the size of his assailants, the Sparrow resolutely defended the portion he had appropriated; with open beak he faced his foes and successfully repulsed three or four attacks, the Starlings eventually drawing off and leaving the plucky little fellow in possession. The encounter appeared exceedingly ridiculous, the two long-legged giants (Starlings when fighting draw themselves up to their greatest height) stalking cautiously round and darting from time to time at the diminutive Sparrow, who, crouching down on his prey with elevated and expanded tail, quietly awaited and repulsed every attempt to approach the food he guarded. When pressed by want these birds become exceedingly daring: the excessive drought early in July 1884 rendered soft food very difficult to obtain, and while the sultry weather lasted I repeatedly noticed one or two cock Sparrows hopping round and closely watching the actions of the Blackbirds while seeking for grubs or worms on the lawn; the moment any prey was secured the Sparrows would dash in, and in almost every instance carry off whatever had been extracted from below the soil. A female Sparrow that attempted to emulate the exploits of her lord and master was assailed by an old hen Blackbird, and having been utterly vanquished was forced to seek safety by flight. As a rule, Sparrows take but little notice of a cat as she creeps stealthily round the stacks while on the watch for mice, neither do they show their enmity when, on maternal duties bent, she makes her way demurely across the yard towards her kittens concealed in the barn; they seem, however, to detect at once the poacher who prowls along the hedgerow or through the plantations in quest of feathered prey. In our gardens we are able to trace accurately the course taken by the feline marauders when stalking through the shrubberies, by the calls and excited actions of the swarm of small birds in attendance. The loud "chuck chuck" of the Blackbird first attracts attention and soon collects a mob of Sparrows, whose shrill notes rapidly draw the whole of their fraternity within hearing to the spot. Last winter I witnessed a most lively scene: at least fifty or sixty birds of various species had settled on the surrounding branches or were flying down and hovering round a vagrant pussy vainly attempting to spring to the top of a wall along which wire netting had been stretched; every time the animal dashed at the wire (invisible owing to the overhanging branches) it was thrown violently backwards, being followed towards the ground by numbers of the noisy rabble. The animosity exhibited by a pair of Wrens, who were by far the most demonstrative of the party, was most amusing; with ruffled feathers these tiny mites fluttered, screaming open-mouthed to within the distance of a few inches, or perched, when wearied by their exertions, for a few moments on the twigs immediately above the object of their hatred, still giving vent to their fury with sharp cries.

Though evincing a partiality for the immediate vicinity of human habitations*, the Sparrow selects a variety of situations in which to rear its young. So well known are the usual nesting-quarters of this familiar species that it is unnecessary to enter into particulars concerning their breeding-habits, which have been described by endless writers; one or two facts referred to in my notes may, however, be worth recording.

The mud-built nests of the House-Martin are frequently appropriated by Sparrows, their rightful owners being turned out and driven to other quarters. These domiciles apparently possess a peculiar attraction for this species, and the rapidity with which they are again occupied after one pair of Sparrows have been disposed of would scarcely be credited. Early in June 1883 I noticed a couple of pair of Martins building under the eves of a farmhouse in Norfolk; no sooner were the nests (which had been constructed side by side) completed than the unfortunate Martins were evicted. For a short time one or two would occasionally return and after circling round skim up to the nest, speedily beating a retreat when faced by the beak of an impudent Sparrow protruded from the opening. The old cocks were often to be seen sitting with their heads blocking the entrances, which in both cases had been at once enlarged to suit the size of the present lodgers. As I was anxious to retain the Martins round the house, I shot down every Sparrow that entered the nests during the hours I happened to be on the spot, four males and two females being killed the first two days. I remarked on one occasion after a male was shot that the female secured another mate within an hour. About five-and-twenty having been cleared off in less than a week, the nests remained vacant for a day or two; as no Martins, however, put in an appearance to claim their old quarters, I left the Sparrows for the future unmolested.

In June 1872, while sheltering from a heavy shower under an overhanging bank on the roadside adjoining a plantation near Falmer, in Sussex, my attention was attracted by a Sparrow endeavouring to approach the spot with food, and turning round, a young brood was discovered in a nest placed in a hole in the chalky soil among the roots dropping through from the thorn-bushes above. Farm-buildings, thatched and slated lodges, as well as ivy-clad walls being within the distance of a couple of hundred yards, the site chosen appeared remarkable. As the crumbling bank overhung considerably, a dark shadow was thrown on the spot where the hole for the nest had been scratched. Within a couple of feet of the entrance a Long-eared Bat (*Vespertilio auritus*) was hanging from one of the twining roots. The hollow excavated in the bank measured about four inches across at the opening, the width of the interior of the cavity being an inch or two more in extent; the entrance to the nest, of which only a small portion was visible from the outside, was placed exactly in the centre of the aperture in the chalk. The birds had constructed their cradle with the usual materials, employing for the exterior strands of hay, rough grass, and fibres of roots, with a warm lining of feathers and small pieces of sheep's wool.

Until the present season, I have always protected Sparrows during summer; at last, however, it became necessary to reduce their numbers, and several nests were lately removed from an ivy-clad wall in my garden

* I cannot call to mind an instance of a nest being placed much more than a quarter of a mile from a dwelling-house.

While examining their composition I remarked that the lining in almost every instance consisted of the down plucked by some captive Wildfowl, while sitting, to cover their eggs, together with a quantity of feathers from the same birds. Some half-dozen nests of these Ducks having recently been cleared away and thrown on a rubbish-heap, the Sparrows had evidently availed themselves of the opportunity for furnishing their own domiciles; small scraps of paper had also been intermixed with these materials in one or two nests.

Though sufficiently hardy to endure the cold to which we are exposed during most winters, Sparrows suffer severely from the effects of the hurricanes that occasionally break over these islands. During the terrific snow-storm of January 18, 1881, the force of the wind and drifting snow was such that thousands of small birds were driven to seek shelter from the cutting blasts in all sorts of out of the way corners and crevices, from which few succeeded in effecting their escape. An instance where at least fifty Sparrows had taken refuge under the shelter of a trug-basket * (containing fish for the captive Gannets) placed in a shed on our grounds near Brighton came under my notice, the warmth from the chimney-stack of a furnace, against which the basket was lying, having probably attracted them to the spot. These unfortunate birds were huddled together in an almost helpless mass, most of them being unable to rise on wing or even stir, as the snow had frozen into solid lumps of ice upon their backs and rendered flight impossible. On the following morning between forty and fifty were found lying dead under the snow-drifts collected round the basket.

A few weeks back I watched a pair of Sparrows amusing themselves in a most singular manner; the two birds were perched on the gutter running round the roof of a conservatory, from which point they kept fluttering some three or four feet up the glass and then sliding quietly back, the performance being indulged in for several minutes.

Though the farmer has just cause for complaint against this species, the Sparrow makes a certain amount of reparation for the damage committed, by the quantities of insects supplied to the young broods. In the immediate vicinity of towns I have repeatedly seen acres of corn where the ears were almost entirely stripped of grain, clouds of young Sparrows rising from these barren patches when alarmed. In such localities it is necessary for the birds to be continually scared, or great loss would ensue, the countless multitudes that find shelter about the buildings in the neighbourhood being entirely beyond the reach of the farmer. A few pence for every score or dozen are often paid by agriculturists in the country to the lads in their employment for young Sparrows taken on the premises. If those who offer these rewards thoroughly understood their own interests, none but full-fledged birds just fit to quit the nest and commence plundering on their own account would be destroyed; it is without doubt while providing for its offspring that this species renders the greatest service.

Numbers of spring flowers also suffer from the inevitable Sparrow; in our small piece of ground near Brighton, the primroses that fringe the paths in the shrubberies are entirely ruined till late in the season. I find the following entries in my notes referring to their depredations:—

"December 29, 1883. Sparrows had already commenced to crop the primroses, every flower or bud that showed having been bitten off.

"January 29, 1884. The bloom of the primroses totally destroyed by the Sparrows.

"February 9, 1884. Hundreds of yellow and variegated crocuses lying on the beds, having been bitten in pieces by the Sparrows. No flowers having appeared on the primroses, owing to their former robberies, the tormentors now attacked the crowns of the plants, tearing out the young shoots.

"March 6, 1884. Violets, both white and purple, scattered about on the paths, having been cut off and carried away by the Sparrows."

Having patiently suffered from the mischievous propensities of the Sparrows the whole of the spring, I

* A "trug" is the local name given in country districts in Sussex to a basket constructed of wide strips of white wood (usually willow) with a handle of ash, and employed, for the most part, for gardening or farming purposes.

still left them unmolested, imagining that some slight amends might be made as soon as their young needed providing for. In this, however, I was soon undeceived: the Sparrows collected in hundreds to prey upon the corn supplied to the Wild Duck, Wigeon, and Teal that were kept in confinement; when the young broods were hatched out, the swarms rapidly increased, the soft food provided for the juveniles being carried off in immense mouthfuls. To such an extent was this pilfering carried on that it became necessary to keep watch within the distance of a few yards while the ducklings satisfied their hunger, otherwise little would have fallen to their share. In order to lessen the numbers of the robbers, I was forced to make use of an air-gun, and at length succeeded in effecting a slight diminution; neither the Wildfowl nor the Thrushes, Blackbirds, Starlings, Robins, Hedge-Sparrows, or Greenfinches that formed the other visitors to the ponds were in the least alarmed by the report of the gun or the effect on the Sparrows, even when turned over within the distance of little more than a foot. Although much has been written extolling their value as exterminators of insect pests, it is evident that Sparrows will shirk the labour of hunting out the larvæ or caterpillars on which they usually feed their young if supplies of soaked bread, mashed potatoes, or other soft provision can be obtained with less exertion. These birds also often make their way (in not the slightest degree intimidated by a wire netting, through which they are able to force an entry) into the coops or enclosures where Chickens or Pigeons are kept, and steal their food, appropriating, in many instances, by far the larger portion.

As the summer draws on, these persevering birds still continue to give trouble in the garden; no sooner are the flower-beds put in order than lobelias, and other tender plants employed for bordering, are cropped off after the manner of the primroses. Red currants also are occasionally patronized to some extent, while for peas, when fit for gathering, they evince an especial taste. My attention was drawn early in the morning of June 17, 1884, to the quantity destroyed in our garden, fully a quarter of the crop of green peas that were then ready for use having been utterly destroyed. The injury inflicted by this species can readily be detected from the well-defined nip given by the Hawfinch; the Sparrow possessing less strength in the mandibles, is forced to gnaw his way gradually to the pea, while the latter leaves the shape of his powerful beak plainly visible on the outside of the pod.

Early in the present year (1885) I again remarked the Sparrows were attacking the primroses, nibbling off the full-blown flowers, and biting far down into the crown to reach the budding shoots. Having been informed that thick white cotton strung up over the roots was a means of scaring these marauders, I resolved to try the experiment, and hundreds of yards were speedily put out, stretched across the ground on twigs inserted among the plants. This proved efficacious to a certain extent, but any exposed roots were still destroyed, and a more forcible remedy was evidently necessary. The air-gun used the previous season was of scarcely sufficient power to do the work thoroughly, so a light 24-bore double pin-fire breechloader with cartridges charged with dust-shot was employed, and after a few days' shooting, some hundreds of Sparrows having been cleared off, the whole of the primroses were saved, the appearance of the thousands of roots bordering some of the paths in full bloom fully repaying the time and labour expended in their protection. As the season drew on, fresh birds were attracted to the garden, some to the pond for water, and others to the food provided for the pinioned Wildfowl; these, however, were kept down by occasional watching and shooting. The peas also were well looked after, several lines of cotton having been stretched over every row; and the intruding robbers meeting with a warm reception, scores being dropped while attempting to settle near the spot, they failed to inflict the slightest damage. A few weeks back I was informed that a large spreading pear-tree in a garden at Shoreham had been almost entirely denuded of bloom by these pests, and on making an investigation it was evident that the damage inflicted had not been exaggerated. A careful study of their habits has convinced me there is not the slightest doubt that Sparrows cause immense losses to both the farmer and gardener, which is by no means repaid by their clearing off the insect pests so injurious to the crops. Should other food be procurable with less exertion, they resolutely refuse to perform their necessary duties, and, increasing rapidly, become an insupportable nuisance, rendering it necessary that their numbers should be diminished and kept within bounds.

In order to aid digestion, or for other purposes, Sparrows occasionally vary their diet: I have often seen them clinging to the newly-built walls in the southern parts of Sussex pecking at the mortar; possibly the salt in the sea-sand used in its composition in this locality may account for this peculiarity. Last February a female was distinctly observed biting off and swallowing some tender shoots of grass on a lawn; as the operation was watched immediately beneath a window at the distance of only six or eight feet, the actions of the bird were clearly visible.

The nest taken near Falmer in Sussex, and previously described, is represented on Plate I., the birds being country Sparrows obtained near the same spot, and differing greatly in general appearance from their grimy relatives, the pair of town Sparrows secured in the vicinity of Brighton, which are depicted on Plate II.

GREENFINCH.

COCCOTHRAUSTES CHLORIS.

The well-known Greenfinch may be found in almost every part of the British Islands—passing the summer only in those districts in which sufficient cover for nesting-purposes is to be met with, though at times a visitor to any wild and open portions of our coast-line where the seeds of various plants afford a supply of food. I have recognized this species during summer and autumn in many parts of the Highlands; with but few exceptions, however, the birds were only noticed in districts where cultivation was carried on. Though strong and hardy, the Greenfinch appears somewhat susceptible to cold, but few, when compared with the numbers of either the Yellow-Hammer or Chaffinch, remaining to face the wintry snow-squalls in the more remote glens.

In all the southern and eastern counties of England with which I am best acquainted this species is common at every season of the year, joining not unfrequently during winter in flocks with other Finches, Buntings, or Sparrows, and resorting to farm-buildings and stackyards. On the 1st of February 1882, during a slight frost, I watched for some time a party of eighteen or twenty clinging to the sides of a stack of oats that had been cut in half; while crawling, after the manner of Titmice, up the even surface they eagerly extracted the grain lying within their reach. Late in autumn and on through the winter Greenfinches may often be seen harbouring about the shingle-banks on the coast of Sussex to the west of Shoreham. Chaffinches, Twites, and Linnets will usually be found in their company, or resorting in small separate parties to the same range of beach, the seeds of the numberless rank weeds that grow on this barren waste proving the attraction to the spot.

Though Greenfinches are usually supposed to commence their nesting-operations so early as April, they may not unfrequently be seen in company after that date. For several days after the 13th of May, 1867, a succession of small flocks was encountered along the links to the east of Dunbar, in East Lothian: as far as I was able to ascertain by watching their movements, these birds were making their way northwards along the coast; a week later others, though in reduced numbers, were noticed on the sandy links near Gullane.

While residing in East Lothian I remarked that Greenfinches nested in considerable numbers, often in close proximity to one another, in the thorn hedges surrounding the plantations of beech near the coast of the Firth of Forth. In the south of England this habit of breeding in company may also be observed; in our garden near Brighton the birds were exceedingly plentiful during the summer of 1883, their nests in some instances being placed so thickly that after the autumn gales had carried off the leaves from the shrubs and young trees at least half a dozen might be counted from one spot. The dense bushes of *Cupressus* as well as privet appeared to be selected in preference to other quarters, though willow, poplar, lime, elm, and red-may were also well patronized. One exceedingly curious nest (the structure being of nearly twice the usual size), placed at the height of about six feet in a privet bush, attracted my attention, the whole of the foundation being composed of a large mass of the common stonecrop (*Sedum acre*), torn up from a rockery close at hand. This nest being subsequently dragged out by a cat, the immense quantity of stonecrop used in its construction was plainly exposed to view. The young birds after leaving these nests joined in small parties, but did not quit the locality in which they were reared for several weeks, roosting at night in some small plantations of sycamore. It was most amusing towards evening, especially when the weather was wet and showery, to watch the forethought displayed by the juveniles while choosing a cosy situation among the thick foliage, their object being apparently to select a position immediately below one of the large spreading leaves, which would evidently afford complete shelter from the raindrops.

A couple of broods are occasionally hatched in the same nest, the second clutch of eggs being laid shortly after the first family have taken their departure. This fact was noted on two occasions (1881 and 1883) in a garden at Potter Heigham, in the east of Norfolk, the nests in both instances being placed in the same yew tree.

In their earlier stages the young birds somewhat resemble juvenile Crossbills; the markings or streaks on the feathers, however, are scarcely so strongly developed. The plumage of both species fades considerably after death, a stuffed specimen giving but a poor idea of either bird when seen in life.

The Greenfinch is by no means an accomplished songster, though its note and plaintive calls in spring, summer, and autumn are sure to attract attention. The old male in early spring-time often renders himself especially conspicuous—rising on wing in the bright sunshine, and, after a short flight, skimming or, rather, floating through the air on extended pinions, with much the same actions as the Swallow or Martin.

After a prevalence of easterly winds during spring, hollies of all descriptions are often attacked by numberless small caterpillars that completely destroy the tender shoots in which they are curled up. In my notes for 1884 it is recorded, under the date of June 17, that Greenfinches were observed for some time busily employed in tearing out these insects. Sparrows are also occasionally to be seen searching diligently over the shrubs affected with this pest.

Large numbers of Greenfinches used formerly to be taken by bird-catchers during spring and autumn, and disposed of with Sparrows for trap-shooting. Among the professional catchers of the south these birds are known as "Chubs," or "Green Chubs."

HAWFINCH.

COCCOTHRAUSTES VULGARIS.

The Hawfinch is said to be distributed over most of our English counties: it is, however, with the exception of two or three flocks noticed in winter in the midland counties, only in Sussex that this species has come under my observation. I well remember a few at Catsfield, Ninfield, and Battle in Sussex, about thirty years ago; though their nests were never detected, I came to the conclusion later on that they were residents in the district.

I should be unwilling to state that this species can with certainty be attracted by a call-bird; the following is, however, my experience on the subject. While at school at Harrow I noticed a fine old male in a store-cage in a bird-catcher's cottage, and, after becoming the purchaser of the bird for a shilling, took it home when the holidays commenced. In a week I captured, in a clap-net, a couple of the Hawfinches previously observed in this part of Sussex. The first flew across my net when set on the lawn at Catsfield House, which my father then hired for several years, and the second settled down to the call-bird in a large grass-field just outside the well-timbered lawn at Catsfield Park, belonging to Sir Andrew Pilkington. There is little doubt that Hawfinches bred at both these places; and their nests could not have escaped observation had the birds been carefully watched among the fruit-trees in the gardens, and the dense cover in the rough plantations adjoining been also thoroughly searched.

On two occasions while staying in Brighton I went and examined the nests of this species, and the following extracts from my notes may possibly give a slight idea as to some of the habits of the birds.

On the 24th of June, 1872, I started from Brighton soon after midnight and drove round by Lewes to Plumpton, where several pairs of Hawfinches were reported to have been inflicting a great deal of damage on the peas in a garden where I had liberty to obtain specimens. Our destination was reached by daybreak, and a few minutes later the old birds were observed feeding their young; the whole party, however, proved exceedingly shy, and the garden being large and surrounded by high trees, it was no easy matter to obtain a shot. I was previously unacquainted with the call-note of this species, which, when once heard, is easily recognized again; had it not been for their shrill whistle I should have had little chance of procuring the birds; their approach was, however, invariably detected as they drew near by the sound before they appeared in sight. After remaining on the watch for eight or nine hours, I succeeded in obtaining the male, female, and three young ones, that had probably left the nest only a few days previously; the juveniles proved to be of about the same size as the old birds and quite as wary. The nest in which they had been reared was placed in a pear-tree in the centre of the garden, and the gardener informed me that the birds had nested regularly in the same tree for the last six or seven years. These destructive finches had devoured or destroyed the whole of the peas that were fit for gathering, the pods being cut to pieces by their broad beaks, and the crop on seven rows utterly ruined. The gardener stated that during the previous season he had set some clams for Wood-Pigeons, baited with hard peas, and in two or three days half a dozen Hawfinches were captured. The following week

I visited the garden at the Manor House at Portslade, and examined the peas to ascertain if there were any Hawfinches in that locality. I discovered that nearly every pod was destroyed, but the peas were extracted in a different manner, and there were no signs of the broad cuts inflicted by Hawfinches, which reveal the shape of their beaks. The gardener informed me that Sparrows had caused the damage in this instance, and after watching for an hour I was convinced that his opinion was correct.

On the 9th of June, 1875, drove over to Plumpton to take a brood of young Hawfinches from the same garden where the birds had been shot in 1872. I happened to be a day too late, five youngsters having been seen by the gardener and keeper in the nest in the early morning, but only three remaining when I reached the spot during the afternoon. These were immediately secured, a landing-net being dropped over the nest, and the pair of old birds were soon obtained while flying round the garden with their mouths crammed full of food for their young; what they had collected was composed of a large mass of caterpillars and chrysalises of various kinds. The nest was in the same pear-tree in which the birds had placed their cradle three years previously, and the three young, which we kept and reared, turned out to be all males. The colours of the soft parts of these juveniles were as follows:—Upper and lower mandibles dull olive-yellow, gape yellow; inside of mouth and tongue a very bright flame-coloured red, shaded here and there with a pale sky-blue and streaked with a beautiful cerise tint. A few lines referring to the three young birds taken from the nest on the 9th of June, 1875, may not be out of place. For a week or two they all required to be fed, but shortly after commenced to help themselves to whatever was provided. As previously stated, they all proved to be males, the two that had left the nest being in all probability females. As they had evinced a disposition to snap at one another, we concluded that a bite from their powerful beaks might be attended with serious results, and consequently kept them separate in three large wire cages, placed side by side, but so that each occupant was just out of the reach of his next-door neighbour's spiteful mandibles. Within a year one of these youngsters was found dead at the bottom of his cage, and, on an examination being made, it was discovered that the skull had been pierced by a broken wire, pointing downwards from the top of the cage, which must have caused instant death. The two that remained went through the regular changes in the colouring of the beak every year; all through the latter part of autumn and early winter the mandibles were a dirty flesh-tint. The change commences towards the end of January, a livid blue gradually showing near the base and the points becoming slightly darker. I find one note entered on the 15th of February, 1883, stating, "beak now quite blue;" again, on March the 6th the same year, "beak now blue with black points." During the whole time they remained in captivity the changes took place at much the same dates; the eyes never varied, the tint of the iris corresponding precisely with the colour of the grey band of plumage round the neck. The seed-tins of the birds were always filled with hemp; but they also received a continuous supply of every description of vegetables, with apples, nuts, hips and haws, and all the plants employed in the composition of salads, scarcely anything eatable coming amiss to them. The long time they lived may, I think, be accounted for by the changes of diet they enjoyed; their excitement (snapping, pecking, and rating at one another) when their dainties were being produced was most amusing. They frequently indulged in vocal performances; some persons might possibly have termed it singing, but the sounds emitted were exceedingly discordant, resembling the squeaking of an ungreased cart-wheel produced with variations. While giving utterance to their quaint melody they occasionally became much excited and danced or hopped on their perches from one side of their cages to the other in a most extraordinary manner; their actions ought to have been seen to be thoroughly understood, as to accurately describe the antics the infatuated birds went through is utterly impossible. Though previously perfectly healthy, one commenced, in May 1883, to exhibit signs of weakness in his right foot; the toes all contracted and remained closed, the poor creature appearing much crippled for some months. At length, however, he recovered the use of his disabled limb and was much the same as ever for a time. The following year he suffered from a second attack, and in the summer of 1885 grew gradually weaker, and becoming still more helpless by degrees, died on the 21st of December. The survivor had for some weeks also been showing unmistakable signs that old age was working its course, and it was now evident the end was drawing near. Once or twice the unfortunate half-blind cripple was discovered lying on his back on the sand on the bottom boards quite helpless, but, on receiving assistance, he came round and kept up till found huddled into a ball, cold and stiff, in a corner of his cage on the morning of the 11th of January, 1886. Nearly eleven years old must be considered a good age for hand-reared birds, as I have frequently heard naturalists, and others who considered themselves good authorities, declare that this species could not be kept for any length of time in captivity. A liberal and varied diet may, however, be supposed to account for their prolonged vitality. After death, the old couple who had spent their lives side by side for so many years were not divided; my gardeners at Brighton, who performed the work of the undertakers, dug up the box in which the first was interred, and inserting the remains of the second, replaced "the chest" * in the long grass, beneath the weeping-willows, that forms the burial-ground for the birds kept in confinement.

Yarrell states, "The bill of the adult male in summer is a deep leaden blue"; this does not agree with observations I made, having remarked, in both wild specimens shot and caged birds reared in confinement, that though the base was of that tint, the points of both mandibles were a dull black, the colour penetrating further back towards the gape of the mouth. One or two of our British authors declare that many of this species leave our shores in winter; the young they consider most probably are the migrants. During all the time I have passed steaming about in the North Sea and the Channel, in the latter part of the year, not a single specimen was ever observed on wing, nor did I hear of their being secured on the light-ships round our eastern or southern coasts. Seebohm, in his beautifully illustrated book on the eggs of British Birds, tells us that the Hawfinch pairs about the middle of April; and this remark agrees with my own experience, as I am of opinion that their nests are usually commenced shortly after that date. The cradles of the Hawfinch are roughly constructed and put together on the outside, strong and prickly twigs being occasionally entwined; the interior, however, is usually finished off with far greater skill, the lining being composed of fine materials, hair, wool, and occasionally feathers being twisted in together. The only two nests I examined were placed in the limbs of the same old pear-tree in the garden at Plumpton, at a height of about eight or nine feet from the ground.

GOLDFINCH.

CARDUELIS ELEGANS.

THANKS to the bird-catchers and dealers, the unfortunate Goldfinches have greatly decreased in numbers during the last thirty years; it is seldom at the present time that a flock of twenty or thirty are observed in the south of England, where formerly they were met with in hundreds. The general call for cage-birds, and the thousands needed to supply the demand, could only have caused this falling-off, as the nature of the country is still, with few exceptions, as suitable to their requirements as it was in days gone by. The extraordinary persecution that this species has undergone may be judged from some statements in the fourth edition of Yarrell, where the following lines occur on page 118, vol. ii.:—"Mr. Hussey in 1860 (Zool. p. 7144) put the average annual captures of this species near Worthing at about 1154 dozens—nearly all being cock-birds—and it would seem that a still larger number used to be yearly taken within ten miles of Brighton. In that neighbourhood, however, it has now become comparatively scarce, owing in part to the fatal practice of catching the birds prior to, or during the breeding-season, and not a hundred may be seen even at the most favourable time of year." Such catches may appear incredible to some readers, but many years ago when a school-boy at Brighton, and also at Harrow, I have often seen, while in company with some of the most skilful and best equipped professional catchers, scores and, on one or two occasions, hundreds struggling in the nets after a pull, and can well understand how the numbers stated to have been taken were reached. I believe that, in those days, these two localities, the country around Worthing and Brighton in Sussex and the unenclosed land (termed "allotment grounds") between one and two miles from Harrow, in the direction of Pinner, were about the best that could be found for this species in Great Britain.

One of the Brighton bird-catchers informed me lately that his best take at one pull had been eleven dozen, and these were captured about five-and-twenty years ago. During the past season he stated he had been out a few times, but no flight had taken place, and his catches had never reached a dozen in a morning.

The grass-fields adjoining the wide-spreading shingle-banks at Shoreham, where my punt and boat-houses are built, were formerly a favourite spot for the netting fraternity, and a few years back a man from London who was well up to his business and provided with an immense stock of call-birds came down regularly every season, and set within a hundred and fifty yards of my station, where I could obtain an excellent view of his proceedings. Although Linnets were plentiful, he met with no great success with the Goldfinches; if I remember right, a single bird was his total catch during one season. I have been in the habit of fishing and shooting on this part of the coast for many years, and have to cross the fields that the Goldfinches formerly passed over at flight-time, but no flocks of these birds have attracted my attention during the autumn, though constantly on the look-out; two or three small parties only, of half a dozen or so, have been observed along the adjoining hedge-rows that border the field during the whole time.

While at home at Catsfield, near Battle in Sussex, for the Christmas holidays during the winters of 1853 and the two following years, I generally amused myself by working a small bird-net every day when the weather was favourable, and caught a number of Bullfinches and several Goldfinches; the former generally moved about in parties of five or six, though never above a pair of Goldfinches were seen, and more frequently solitary cock birds. I had several, perhaps half a dozen, different places suitable for setting my nets, and the morning seldom passed at any of them without one or more of this species being noticed, if not caught. I well remember on one occasion my best male call-bird made his escape, owing to the net becoming entangled in the fastening wire and opening the door of his cage. Though at liberty, he showed no inclination to take his departure, but remained busily engaged in cleaning his plumage in a fence at the side of a plantation about twenty yards distant, and a few minutes after a fresh-caught bird had been placed in the net, he flew down to some thistles and was at once secured again. The numbers found at this season will show that though seldom met with in large flocks, Goldfinches do not entirely desert our shores in winter; I have also observed them in small parties in the plantations round some of the larger Broads in the east of Norfolk. Under the date of December 1882, while shooting at Potter Heigham, it is entered in my notes that at least twenty of this species, in company with as many Siskins, were watched working their way through the woods adjoining Heigham Sounds. Though not feeding together, the Siskins invariably keeping to the alders, while the Goldfinches confined their attentions to the rough bark of the stunted and moss-grown oaks, each party, I remarked, kept the other in sight and immediately joined in company when a lengthened flight to another plantation was undertaken.

The beautiful and neatly built nest of the Goldfinch somewhat resembles that of the Chaffinch; but the materials are finer and more cleverly interwoven, no conspicuous lichens being used in its construction. A brood of five in my collection, taken from their cradle in an apple-tree in a garden at Hickling in June 1873, just as they were on the point of leaving, proved very useful to compare with their parents obtained at the same time. The young in their first plumage appear to differ little from the old birds, with the exception that the black and lovely crimson markings on the heads are wanting. While exhibiting this deficiency the juveniles are generally termed "Grey-pates" by the professional bird-catchers and dealers, that appellation having been bestowed on them on account of the colouring of the feathers on those parts.

In the east of Norfolk I learned that the marshmen invariably spoke of this species as the "Draw-water," evidently bestowing this title on account of the habit it occasionally acquires in confinement of drawing up a small bucket by means of a chain to supply itself with water. While living in Yorkshire many years ago I heard these birds called "Captains" by the country people in the neighbourhood of Doncaster.

SISKIN.

CARDUELIS SPINUS.

Though large numbers of this active species make their appearance in the southern counties of England during autumn and winter, the quarters to which they resort in summer throughout the Highlands are by no means entirely deserted. The weather on Christmas Day in 1865 was remarkably mild and warm for the time of the year, and a flock of from forty to fifty Siskins, their colours shown off to the fullest advantage by the bright sunshine, were noticed busily climbing among the boughs of the alders overhanging the river Lyon in the north-west of Perthshire. This was the largest party I ever met with in the north in winter, and it is probable that the previous open weather accounted for their protracted stay in this usually bleak and inhospitable glen.

On the approach of spring the flocks that have kept company with Redpolls and other small birds about the open commons, groves, and dense hedgerows, where their favourite alder is to be found, gradually take their departure from the southern counties of England. Possibly many of our visitors are from the north of Europe, though there can be no doubt that, if carefully looked for, this species is far from scarce during summer in the large woods of several of the counties of the Northern Highlands.

In the breeding-season I have repeatedly remarked that Siskins, though by no means shy and unapproachable, become more retiring in their habits; it is now less easy to watch their actions closely, unless the birds be detected in the act of building or feeding the young. When once the nest is completed and the labour of incubation commenced, the male, from the many instances that have come under my observation, appears during the midday hours to pass the greater part of his time cleaning his plumage and spreading himself out to enjoy the heat of the sun on almost the topmost branch of some lofty Scotch fir. In several of the straths adjacent to the Beauly river in Inverness-shire, and on the pine-clad hills that slope down to the Dornoch Firth, I had ample opportunities for watching several pairs.

If in quest of Siskins during summer, it is possible to keep moving all day through miles of forest without noticing a single bird, though the haunts of several pairs be passed. When resting quietly or waiting for a view of some other species, I frequently discovered the nest of this bird; indeed it was only by chance that I ever found one. On no single occasion did I meet with Siskins during the breeding-season further south than Perthshire; they appear to nest in the greatest numbers in the eastern portions of Inverness-shire and Ross-shire. In Balnagown and a few localities on towards the east, where these birds were plentiful fifteen or twenty years ago, their numbers have greatly diminished. This falling off is attributed by the keepers to the great abundance of squirrels in the district. I can offer no opinion on the subject; it is, however, a fact that the Siskins have gradually disappeared as the squirrels increased.

Though it is probable, owing to the frequency with which the males may be seen in the depths of the pine-woods during summer, that Siskins commonly breed on Scotch or other firs, it is solely in the birch that I have detected their nests. The light-coloured hoary lichens and pendent masses of *Usnea barbata* that droop from the limbs of the weeping birches in many of the northern glens afford ample concealment for the small and neatly constructed cradle. The nest has been stated to resemble that of the Goldfinch; with the exception perhaps of size, I have noticed little similarity. The outer portion is fashioned with green moss held in position by fibres of roots and strands of grass, finer materials of the same description being used for the lining, in which I have also seen a few catkins of either the birch or alder together with a quantity of the seeds. To the best of my recollection, neither wool, hair, thistle-down, nor the flowers of the cotton-grass were employed in any nest I examined. The Siskin is reported to be an early breeder in the east of Ross-shire: I have seen fresh eggs so late as June 26th; it is, however, quite possible that this may have been a second laying.

It is usually in the neighbourhood of water that these birds may be observed in winter, the alders growing in damp and swampy localities appearing to possess special attractions. A flock of some twenty or thirty, in company with as many Goldfinches, were watched for some time working their way through one of the plantations adjoining the Heigham Sounds in the east of Norfolk in the winter of 1881. Though the two species seldom intermixed, the Siskins busily searching the alder bushes, while the Goldfinches almost entirely confined their attention to the stunted and moss-grown oaks, each party closely followed the direction taken by the other while moving across the open spaces in the wood, and also on starting for a more lengthened flight to the next plantation. A few scattered birds are commonly to be seen in this part of Norfolk in autumn, winter, and early spring; but large flocks are seldom noticed. In Sussex also I remarked their predilection for the neighbourhood of the small streams that run through the wooded portion of the country.

In the spring of 1885, I was much amused at the eccentric behaviour of a cock Siskin confined in a cage with a female of the same species, both being exceedingly tame. Soon after the commencement of the breeding-season the male exhibited an intense dislike to the figure of a bird that he detected in a piece of looking-glass let into the side of his cage. Each time he arrived in front of the mirror, he attacked the supposed stranger with the greatest fury, though utterly unable to drive the intruder from his position. After trying all manner of schemes and working with the utmost activity, he was at last enabled, by inserting his beak below the edge, to dislodge the glass, which then fell from the cage to a table on which it stood. His attitude of defiance on each occasion, craning his neck to ascertain where his adversary had gone, was ridiculous in the extreme. If the glass was returned to its position, he would repeat the performance immediately, dislodging his enemy once or twice in a minute at least; indeed he was never at rest till it had disappeared and the intruder was removed from his sight.

As a warning to those who keep these interesting little birds in confinement, I may state that the horsehair made up in bundles and sold by bird-fanciers as suitable to supply their wants when building is an exceedingly dangerous material to place in their way. A few weeks back on visiting a pair kept in a breeding-cage in one of the conservatories, we discovered the female in a deplorable condition, bound hard and fast by several horsehairs twined round the body, depriving her of the use of both legs and wings. The poor bird was lying utterly helpless on the floor of the cage, and had evidently been in this predicament for several hours, as when released she was almost incapable of moving, being only able to shuffle to the water placed in front of her, of which she seemed greatly in need. The male in his attempts to assist his mate had caught up and entangled three or four strands round his legs, but was still able to make his way from one part of the cage to another, though somewhat cramped in his movements. The female did not entirely recover the use of her legs for some days, but, though completely exhausted at the time, she suffered from no irreparable injuries.

LINNET.

LINOTA CANNABINA

This species has been described by more than one author as of common occurrence in the Western Islands of Scotland; I have no wish to dispute this assertion, though compelled to state that but few, if any, came under my observation in those inhospitable regions. In East Lothian these birds were far from uncommon; I have failed, however, lately to meet with any of the immense breeding-colonies formerly so frequently seen in the southern counties of England.

The Red-breasted Linnet appears at the present time far less abundant than in my bird-nesting days some thirty years ago. Improvements in agriculture, such as the breaking up of waste lands and the wild furze-covered stretches of sloping hill-sides, together with the persecution they annually suffer from the nets of the bird-catchers, have kept on gradually reducing their numbers, till in some parts of the country they have become almost rare birds. Large flocks of Linnets are, however, still seen in the early part of the winter on the downs and along the coast-line near Brighton; I find that the average take for one pair of nets of a morning during the flight-time is between thirty and fifty dozen. The hens are killed at once by their captors; the males, perhaps less fortunate, being sent to London to supply the strange demand for cage-birds so common in some parts of the slums.

It is usually in October that the large flights of Linnets appear on the south coast; I find in my notes for 1882, under date of October 13th (weather fine with a breeze from the north-east), that immense numbers of these birds were passing along in an easterly direction, Larks and Swallows also following the same course. The next season the largest flights were seen on the 9th of the month, when the greater number appeared to be making their way towards the west. During winter, Linnets often join in large flocks with Twites and frequent the saltings along the river Adur between Shoreham and Bramber in Sussex. I have also seen the two species associated about the pools of brackish water near the shore at Lancing; the numberless seed-bearing plants that flourish among the patches of rank moist grass and also on the slopes of the shingle-banks probably prove the attraction to the spot. At times this barren stretch is alive with small birds, Chaffinches, Greenfinches, Pipits, Linnets, and Twites rising singly or in scattered parties at almost every step one takes along the sea-wall.

When heavy falls of snow and cold blasts of wind from north-north-west have brought the clouds of Larks and other small birds to seek shelter in the southern and western counties, I have frequently remarked numbers of Linnets making their way along the downs towards the west. On such occasions, should the frost be severe, this species appears much affected by the weather, seldom flying far, but settling from time to time and pecking about for food under the shelter of banks or furze bushes; after a continuation of excessive cold for any length of time, when the snow lies deep and seeds are covered, they soon exhibit signs of distress and not unfrequently perish in large numbers.

I am aware that scientific naturalists assert that this species visits our shores in considerable numbers from across the North Sea; on no occasion, however, did Linnets come under my observation while on the passage during autumn or early winter. From the light-ships I could gain little information concerning their movements, the only wings received being fifteen taken on board the 'Newarp' early in March 1873. As to which way the poor little travellers were shaping their course when dashed against the lamps, there was no chance of ascertaining.

Furze-clad downs appear the favourite summer-quarters of this species in the vicinity of the south coast; in the more inland portions of the southern counties there are in the wooded districts here and there large fields of furze or gorse to which Linnets resort in numbers during the breeding-season. On one such wild and rugged stretch of ground situated between Catsfield and Ashburnham, known to the natives of the locality as the "borthy field," I well remember Linnets so plentiful about thirty years ago that over three hundred eggs were counted in a single morning's ramble. Three Cuckoo's eggs also came under our observation on that occasion—one in the nest of a Hedge-Sparrow, another in that of a Meadow-Pipit, and the third in the nest of a Linnet containing two pure white eggs. On a certain part of the furze there were for several successive seasons three or four nests in which the whole of the eggs were perfectly white; in shape and size they exactly corresponded with the usual form, and the birds being watched repeatedly there could have been no possibility of a mistake as to their identity. In shrubberies and gardens near Brighton I have occasionally met with the nests of this species in dense bushes of *Cypresses*; when resorting to such quarters the birds become remarkably fearless, paying little or no attention to the presence of those they are accustomed to see round their haunts. Some years ago, when living in East Lothian, I discovered a nest of this bird (which is there termed the Lintie) placed amongst the ends of the straws protruding from the side of a wheat-stack at about the height of fourteen feet from the ground, the young being just on the point of flying. It was somewhat singular that on the thatch of the adjoining stack a Partridge was sitting on fourteen eggs.

The summer plumage of the male Linnet is exceedingly bright and attractive, the feathers on the crown of the head and breast exhibiting a deep carmine tint; in winter these colours change to a dull claret, which renders the bird far less conspicuous. In captivity Linnets, after moulting, never regain the brilliant hues assumed during summer when in a wild state, eventually losing all signs of their former colouring. In the 'Catalogue of the Birds of Northumberland and Durham,' by J. Hancock, it is stated:—"The fact is that the males, from shedding the nest-feathers get a red breast, which they retain only during the first season; they then assume the garb of the female, which is retained for the rest of their lives, as in the case of the Crossbill. This does not seem to be generally understood by ornithologists, though the bird-fancier is quite familiar with the fact that the males never regain the red on the breast after moulting. It is stated by Yarrell that the male assumes the red breast in the breeding-season. This is not quite correct, for just as many are found breeding without the red breast as with it." These remarks do not agree with my own experience; though it is well known that cage-birds never regain their rosy breasts, I have not met with a single instance where a wild male was paired and breeding unless the usual bright tints on the head and breast were fully developed.

LESSER REDPOLL.

LINOTA RUFESCENS.

Large flights of this diminutive species make their way south, as autumn advances, from the northern portions of our islands (if not from across the sea) and remain as winter visitors scattered over the country. The flocks to be seen in the southern and eastern counties from the beginning of October till the end of March are usually far in excess of the numbers passing the summer in this part of Great Britain. The most reliable authorities assert that the Lesser Redpoll is not a native of Scandinavia; it is also stated that the British Islands are not visited by any migrants from the north of Europe. This information, I conclude, must be accepted as indisputable. Considering, however, the fact that, during some seasons at least, their summer-haunts in the Highlands are by no means entirely deserted, the immense numbers spread over England in autumn and winter appear far greater than the entire Redpoll population of the northern parts of Great Britain. With the exception of this large addition to the birds in the south, I have failed to make any observations tending to prove we are visited by strangers from the north of Europe. During the years passed on the north-east coast of Scotland, I did not recognize any large flights in the vicinity of the shore at the time other small migrants were landing by thousands. Though a few wings of the Red-breasted Linnet and one of the Siskin were received during the years I was in communication with the light-ships off the east coast, I could gain no tidings of this species.

At various times in the course of my wanderings I have met with the compactly built and elegant nest of this lively species in almost every county in the north of Scotland. That Redpolls breed in many parts of England has been repeatedly recorded, and in 1869 some two or three pairs nested and reared their young in the immediate vicinity of Brighton. I closely examined the parent birds through the glasses, and all exhibited the worn and faded appearance of those kept in cages. The carmine colouring on the head and breast of the males was also wanting, its place being taken by feathers of a rusty yellow tint. It is probable that the whole of the birds had either been liberated or escaped from confinement, immense numbers being kept in captivity in this locality. On no other occasion have I met with the nest of this species further south than Norfolk. In the neighbourhood of the broads several pairs may occasionally be seen during summer, though the numbers that remain in the district are exceedingly uncertain. In 1873 and 1878 Redpolls were especially plentiful; in 1881 I did not notice a single bird in the locality after the departure of the winter flocks.

I am not aware whether this species rears more than one brood in a season. Young birds were, however, seen on wing in the east of Norfolk in 1878 as early as June 9, and in 1873 a pair commenced building a fortnight later.

With the exception of the Lesser Redpolls near Brighton, whose nests were placed in elder and willow, I have only noticed this species breeding in alder and stunted thorn-bushes. The nests coming under my observation were occasionally placed as low as three or four feet from the ground, and none at a greater elevation than ten or twelve feet have come under my notice. In the eastern counties of England, and also in the Highlands, I repeatedly watched these confiding birds engaged in collecting the materials for building. Under date of June 21, while in the east of Norfolk, the following appears in my notes for 1873:—"A nest of the Lesser Redpoll, about half completed, was observed in a small alder tree overhanging a water-dyke. Both birds proved exceedingly unsuspicious of danger, and paid not the slightest attention while their actions were closely inspected at the distance of only a few paces. The male, a brightly tinted bird, did little or nothing to assist in the work; he, however, on almost every occasion accompanied the female on her short flights of some ten or twenty yards to the adjoining marshy ground where she collected the lining for the nest. Here he usually settled on some low stump or bush, and remained singing and chattering while she gathered the fluff of the cotton-grass. I remarked that the whole of the fluff was picked from the thorn-bushes on to which it had been blown since the grass commenced to seed and shed the flower. This nest was composed externally of dried bent-grass, together with fine strands of roots, lined with the fluff of the cotton-grass and a few small white feathers."

Though no notes were taken on the subject, I am under the impression that many nests have been met with in the Highlands in which a small quantity of green moss had been employed in the formation of the exterior. While lunching during the early part of the fishing-season in the summer of 1866 in a small plantation on the banks of the Lyon, in Perthshire, my attention was attracted by a low twittering note evidently close at hand. On turning round, a nest containing a brood of Redpolls was discovered within a foot of my head on a small twisted alder-stump against which I was leaning. The young birds were but little disconcerted, though the old ones declined to approach within three or four yards. Our quarters being moved a short distance, they flew down without the slightest signs of fear, and fed the nestlings repeatedly during the hour we remained near the spot. I well remember that the colouring of the exterior of the nest corresponded with the green and moss-grown stump on which it was placed; consequently it is probable that living moss was interwoven with the strands of grass and roots that bound together the exterior.

No species responds more readily to the note of the call-bird, immense quantities at times being taken by the clap-nets. Even in the very centre of large towns Redpolls may be captured in small trap-cages placed on the housetops during the season the birds are on flight. I have known many secured in this manner in Brighton and Hastings.

The large flocks that occasionally show themselves in winter resort for the most part to waste lands where the various seed-producing weeds grow rank and strong; plantations and hedgerows of alder also prove attractive, their haunts being almost similar to those of the Siskin, with which species they not unfrequently consort.

A hen Lesser Redpoll which had been kept for some years in a cage in company with a cock Siskin that died in the latter end of March 1885, was much cut up at the death of her companion, for whom she had always evinced a great regard. For several days she called loudly, showing her grief in a most unmistakable manner; and the introduction of another cock Siskin proved of little avail. For the first few days she pitched into the stranger and drove him about in the cage; he then asserted his authority, when she speedily submitted, and after continuing to mope without signs of amendment for a week or two, she pined away and eventually grew weaker and died.

MEALY REDPOLL.

LINOTA LINARIA.

Though several stragglers of the Mealy Redpoll have been observed in the east of Norfolk late in spring, I can learn of no well-authenticated instance of this species remaining to breed in Great Britain. The end of the first week in October is the earliest date at which I met with this Redpoll; and, according to my own experience, the majority have taken their departure early in March. Though a close look-out for the species was invariably kept in the Northern Highlands (where I was under the impression, from information received, that it might possibly be discovered breeding), I have obtained a chance of studying its habits only in Norfolk and Sussex.

The numbers that reach our shores during autumn vary considerably, flights of hundreds being noticed one season, while scarcely a bird will make its appearance the following year. Large flocks were scattered over the greater portion of the east of Norfolk towards the latter end of 1873, and again in 1881 I noticed a succession of small parties among the alder bushes round Hickling Broad; here they were to be seen almost daily from early in November till the end of January 1882. A few specimens exhibiting rosy breasts were obtained on November 19th and again on January 6th; their tints, however, were far from bright. I remarked that but few males showing the slightest signs of colouring on the breast could be detected in the large bodies that arrived in 1873. On this occasion, in order to ascertain their numbers, I made use of three or four call-birds placed in cages among the large alders on the banks of the Heigham River, near Norwich, and during the morning of December 2nd many hundreds of this species as well as of the Lesser must have been attracted to the spot.

By far the finest males that have come under my observation were seen feeding on a thistle-head blown on to our lawn, near Brighton, on October 19th, 1875. A strong gale from the south-west was in full force at the time, and the tiny strangers were carried away with a terrific blast before I had time to obtain a specimen. Even in the plates of the various coloured works on ornithology, I have never seen anything approaching the rich carmine tint exhibited on the breast and head by these two birds.

The Mealy Redpoll appears to become speedily reconciled to confinement, and thrives well in captivity. Two of the males procured in Norfolk in December 1873, to act as call-birds, proved after a few weeks exceedingly tame. For a couple of years they lived contentedly together in a roomy cage, when early in 1876 a female of the Lesser Redpoll, which flew in at the window, was added. Early in June, as several eggs were found at the bottom of the cage, a small box with a nest and other materials was placed inside. A fresh nest was soon constructed and shortly after five eggs were laid. After sitting thirteen or fourteen days three young hatched out, all of which were successfully reared. One, however, when a couple of months old, was accidentally killed, the others living to the age of about six years. In size these birds were between the Lesser and Mealy Redpoll, the general colouring of the plumage being somewhat paler than is usually seen in either; their heads exhibited a well-defined patch of bright yellow, and the same was suffused strongly over the breasts.

TWITE.

LINOTA FLAVIROSTRIS.

Though of necessity somewhat local, owing to the nature of the country suitable to its requirements, the Twite appears to be distributed over the British Islands from north to south. On the dreary flats of moorland that stretch for many miles across the central portion of Caithness, I have met with numbers of this species throughout the summer months; whilst in Sussex, the saltings that border the river Adur, as well as those lying inside the shingle-banks on the shores of the channel, are annually resorted to by large flocks on the approach of winter.

The Twite is a lively and active bird, always on the move, its actions, when in flocks, resembling those of the Linnet, though the localities in which it is usually found during winter point to the fact that this species prefers situations where its feeding-grounds are exposed to the influence of salt, supplied either by the spray from the sea or the overflow of the tide.

This species is usually reported by writers as most abundant in the western districts of Scotland; some twenty years ago, however, I repeatedly met with small parties (numbering from a dozen up to fifty) about the links and waste lands extending along the shores of the Firth of Forth to the east of Dunbar. On the coast of Norfolk the Twite is also a winter visitor; its well-known call-notes attracted my attention while crossing the rough stony banks in the vicinity of the shore near Salthouse, towards the end of February 1872. The birds were eventually detected feeding among the weeds and rough grass growing round the pools of water in the shingle; when first noticed they were intermixed with Shore-Larks, though on taking wing the two species immediately separated. In Sussex these birds occasionally join in company, when on flight, with Linnets, though the immense flocks that resort to the saltings and adjacent rough lands are usually seen alone. Along the sea-coast halfway between Shoreham and Lancing there is a large sheet of brackish water, formed through the removal of soil for raising an embankment; this pool is surrounded by banks of mud and shingle, overgrown by coarse grass, dock, sea-poppy, beet, and numberless other plants. Here in autumn flocks of Twites are to be observed about the latter end of October, remaining in the locality till the approach of spring. On the 6th of November 1882, I remarked these birds in more than ordinary numbers, their favourite haunts being about the patches of rank herbage on the damp and marshy portions of the ground. Meadow-Pipits resorted at all seasons to this waste, and the small parties of Greenfinches and Chaffinches that harboured about the shingle-banks often settled on the drier spots; though occasionally intermixing with other species while feeding over the ground, the Twites appeared to fraternize with the Linnets only.

If watched at its home on the open moors of the Highlands, flitting from one twig of heather to another, it will readily be noticed that the colouring of the Twite is sober in the extreme, the rosy tinge on the rump of the male being by no means conspicuous; the yellow bill, however, at once attracts attention and reveals the species. As far as my own experience goes, the name of Mountain-Linnet is scarcely applicable;

in no single instance were the barren moorlands on which I met with this bird during the summer months at any elevation on the hill-side.

Numbers of Twites were recognised on the mud-flats in Shoreham harbour among the thousands of small feathered victims that perished in the terrible snow-squalls of the 18th of January, 1881; on the 20th (the first day the water had reached the upper parts of the banks) I watched their dead bodies swept out by the tide in hundreds from the weeds in which they had attempted to shelter from the storm, and where they were eventually frozen to death.

BULLFINCH.

PYRRHULA VULGARIS.

Woodlands or country where thickets and dense hedgerows abound being generally looked upon as the situations to which the Bullfinch resorts, I was naturally somewhat surprised, one wintry day in December 1867, to meet with a flock of these birds near the summit of one of the high mountains that form the boundary between Rannoch and Glenlyon in the north-west of Perthshire. A position had just been taken up to await the appearance of the white hares which beaters had been despatched to drive, when my attention was attracted by a party of eight or ten small birds flitting along the ridge of the hill. At the first glance through the mist I thought the wanderers must be Snow-Buntings; a moment later they alighted close at hand, when, in spite of the drifting fog, no doubt could be entertained as to the species. After remaining for a few minutes perched on the large blocks of stone, or searching busily among the heather-stalks and small creeping plants where free from snow, they moved further west, settling on the bare limbs of a straggling patch of stunted and weather-beaten pines. The sexes were equally represented in this small flock, the bright colours on the breasts of the males being shown off to the fullest advantage against the dark rocks and dead stumps from which the snow had drifted.

During summer and autumn I repeatedly observed Bullfinches in the wooded glens throughout this locality, for the most part resorting to the plantations of birch or larch in which their young were reared, and where the families remained till late in autumn. The more sheltered portions of this wild tract of country were seldom deserted even in the depth of winter. While passing through the birch-woods in pursuit of Black Game after Christmas, I occasionally detected their note; and in answer to the call, the whole number, unless alarmed by a shot, would follow along the hill-side, flitting from tree to tree till the end of the cover was reached *.

The Bullfinch appears to be distributed over the British Islands from north to south; owing to the nature of the country, it is more plentiful in the southern counties of England than on the barren moorlands of the north. Throughout the east of Sussex I remarked that this species has of late decreased considerably. In the neighbourhood of Battle there were, some thirty years ago, several extensive plantations of larch which proved a great attraction to these birds, flocks of from six or eight up to a dozen or more being not unfrequently observed clinging to the waving boughs. Even in this densely wooded district it is at the present time unusual to meet with parties exceeding four or five in number.

There is no denying the fact that, during spring, Bullfinches are occasionally guilty of destroying the buds of fruit-trees; it is, however, questionable whether their visits to the gardens cause any great amount of damage. This subject has been so fully discussed by various writers that any remarks I could make concerning the depredations committed, or the benefits conferred, by this species would be superfluous.

* The plaintive note of the Bullfinch is familiar to all; no bird responds more readily to an imitation of its call.

The Bullfinch has been known in several instances to breed in confinement. A pair that were kept by a naturalist at Brighton in a small aviary made their way through a ventilator into the shop and built a nest in an old-fashioned cut-glass chandelier. This was not detected till an egg dropped through the bottom and fell on the counter, the poor birds having been unable to collect sufficient material to complete the lining of their cradle.

CROSSBILL.

LOXIA CURVIROSTRA.

Although this species occasionally makes its way to the south of England (where I remember several to have been shot by my father's gamekeeper during the winters of 1818 and 1819), I never met with the Crossbill except in the pine-woods of the Highlands. I observed a few small parties on two or three occasions in Perthshire, while in Inverness, Ross-shire, and Sutherland I have had repeated opportunities of studying the habits of these singular birds. In many parts of Inverness and Ross-shire I have seen the nests during the last few years, though, according to what I can learn from keepers and foresters in those districts, the birds have entirely deserted several localities in which they were formerly common during the breeding-season.

In some instances squirrels are considered responsible for the absence of the birds, these animals being declared by my informants to have destroyed the eggs. Whether there is any foundation for this charge, I have had no chance for forming an opinion based on my own observations. If there is any truth in the reports I heard, Crossbills were some years back most plentiful in certain woods, where now only a wandering party at times makes its appearance. There is no denying the fact that squirrels are at the present date positively swarming in some of these localities; and it is affirmed that the Crossbills began to fall off in numbers shortly after the increase of the squirrels. That these quadrupeds are frequently taken in traps when the eggs of small birds are employed as bait, I have had good evidence. This is a plain statement of the case against the squirrels; and I leave those who read to form their own judgment.

It has invariably been in March when I have met with the nests of this species; the young, I remarked, were generally hatched towards the end of the month or early in April. On March 25, 1878, there was a heavy fall of snow over the north of Scotland; and while passing through a fir-wood near Inverness, I noticed that the snow appeared to be piled to the height of at least four or five inches on the top of some nests I had seen a few days previously. I did not make a close examination, merely turning the glasses to the nests, which were at about the height of twenty-five to thirty feet from the ground. It is a curious fact that in every instance the birds must have been sitting at the time, as a few days later I watched them feeding their newly hatched young at each nest.

The Scotch fir appears to be most commonly selected by this species for breeding-purposes. The nest is, according to my own experience, placed near the upper portion of the tree. I have noticed them in some cases as low as fifteen feet; but the most common elevation seems to be about double that height.

The brood, after leaving the nest, keep together with the old birds for some weeks. I have repeatedly observed small parties during May and June frequenting pine-woods, in which I was aware the young had been brought out. As summer advances, the birds from adjoining glens draw together and form large flocks. As far as I was able to judge, they seldom stray to any great distance from their accustomed haunts, being usually found within a radius of ten or twenty miles. The largest assemblage I ever met with was on the 7th of July 1868. The birds composing this gathering must have numbered several hundreds, being scattered thickly over at least half an acre of Scotch firs in a plantation a few miles north of Lairg in Sutherland. I was driving past, when my attention was attracted by the bright hues of the males; and I then pulled up and watched their movements for at least half an hour. The whole flock were busily engaged searching the upper branches of the pines, and gradually drew out of sight over the brow of the hill. I remarked that the majority appeared to be birds in red plumage (I was able to distinguish two different shades of colour); and I did not recognize a single specimen showing signs of immaturity.

Though the young are without doubt fed principally on insects, the adults derive a large portion of their food from the seeds they extract from the cones of the fir. When passing through a wood, it is easy to learn if these birds are common in the district, as on examining the fallen cones, those on which they have been feeding can be readily distinguished. In several of the fir-woods in Inverness and Ross-shire, I noticed the ground in certain spots was thickly covered with the remains of broken cones which had been torn to pieces by these birds.

The note is a sharp whistle repeated two or three times. When once heard it is easily recognized: I have frequently identified small parties flying overhead, which I should never have noticed unless my attention had been attracted by the note.

The Crossbill is soon reconciled to confinement, and becomes a most amusing cage-bird. I had many opportunities of watching a fine male in the possession of a keeper near Inverness. This bird, which was captured in a somewhat singular manner (having been knocked down from a tree by a fir-cone which was flung at him), was in the red plumage when taken, but eventually moulted to a dull green.

Two different stages of plumage exhibited by the male Crossbill are shown in the Plate. The principal figure is taken from an adult in the full breeding-plumage obtained in the spring. The bird with a tinge of orange on the feathers is probably immature. This specimen was shot on July 6, 1876.

STARLING.

STURNUS VULGARIS.

In densely populated and smoky cities this familiar species may constantly be seen; it is a native also of some of the wildest and most desolate portions of our islands. According to my own observations, there are few parts of Great Britain in which the Starling is not to be met with at one season or another.

In all agricultural districts this lively and active bird is of the greatest service to the farmer, as he destroys immense quantities of grubs and other injurious insects during the course of the year. Vegetation would suffer severely in many parts of the country were it not for the assistance rendered by the Starling.

Large flocks may frequently be observed on grass or ploughed land, feeding in company with Rooks and Jackdaws; in pursuit of slugs and worms they also resort at times to the marshes; here they may be seen running over the moist ground with Peewits and other Waders; on taking wing, however, the association speedily terminates, each species striking out a course for themselves. The presence of a large number of these birds with Plovers is by no means welcomed by the fowler; the frequency with which they shift their position, sweeping over and putting the unconscious Waders on the alert, often ruins the chance of a heavy shot from the punt gun. On one occasion while watching the actions of a large body which had been flying for several minutes in a confused manner over the Holmes Marshes, in the east of Norfolk, a Peregrine dashed through the flock, and leaving the victims he had struck fluttering helplessly towards the earth, continued his flight without a halt. For some seconds before the swoop of the Falcon, the movements of the Starlings had been most remarkable—one moment they were gathered into a dense mass, and the next were wheeling round and round in a revolving column, resembling in its rapid changes a cloud of black smoke.

The sheepfold is a favourite resort for the Starling at all seasons of the year, the flies and insects collecting about the flock probably proving the attraction to the spot. Large numbers often appear on the short grass of a well-kept lawn, searching closely and vigorously attacking the larvæ of the cranefly (commonly known as the daddy-long-legs), a grub whose ravages are by no means conducive to the well-being of the turf. As early as the 28th of May I have noticed young birds of the year feeding in this manner in the south of England.

During close and sultry weather in summer and autumn Starlings may be observed on wing at a considerable height in the air, capturing flies and other insects with the greatest rapidity. On such occasions their flight is erratic and uncertain, resembling to a certain degree the movements of a Snipe while drumming, though the drop is by no means so prolonged. By the help of glasses I was able to ascertain that a pair nesting annually in the mouth of the stone lion on the Norfolk Bridge at Shoreham repeatedly carried up to their brood a supply of the large water-lice that infest the stonework of the arches just above the water-mark.

While in the Hebrides, early in May 1877, I remarked a small flock of about twenty individuals harbouring round the outbuildings of a shooting-lodge on the shores of a salt-water loch. These birds spent the greater part of their time picking about on the seaweed on the loch-side, retiring invariably when alarmed to the shelter of the buildings. I was unable to ascertain the nature of the food procured, but, from their actions, it appeared to consist of small marine insects. Though constantly observed till the second week in May, the members of the flock had not evinced any signs of separating.

About many of the collections of miserable and dilapidated shealings termed villages in this remote district, Starlings were to be seen in considerable numbers searching over the adjacent ground and paying but slight regard to the natives or the few passers by.

There is a general outcry against this species by the owners of cherry-orchards; and from repeated observations in various parts of the country, I have no doubt their complaints are well founded. To credit the quantity of fruit that one of these gluttons can put away it is necessary to watch the operation.

Immense flocks of Starlings collect and roost in the reed-beds on the broads in the eastern counties; here they cause at times great damage, their weight breaking down the stems and rendering the crop almost useless*. As early as June small parties of young may be seen gathering towards the marshes. From many parts of the surrounding country these birds, as evening draws near, make their way to the chalk-pits on the Sussex Downs, and pass the night in any sheltered niches in the face of the cliff: in the neighbourhood of Brighton large flocks may be seen crossing the hills in November shortly after three o'clock, holding a straight course to their accustomed quarters.

Though Starlings occasionally fall victims to the Falcon, I have repeatedly watched them persisting for some time in following a Kestrel. No attack was ever attempted, the birds simply wheeling round the Hawk, who seemed utterly unmindful of their attentions, though forced occasionally for a moment to check his flight as the flock dashed past. On the 3rd of October, 1882, while driving along the coast of West Sussex, I remarked three or four different Kestrels mobbed in this manner.

The nest of the Starling is placed in a variety of situations, holes or apertures in the masonry or under the roofs of buildings being perhaps most frequently chosen. Decayed trees and crevices in rocky cliffs or chalk-pits are also resorted to; and the borings of the Woodpecker and the Pigeon-cote are at times invaded and the rightful owners displaced. In a plantation on the banks of the Eden, in Cumberland, I found, in June 1876, the nest of a Pied Flycatcher in the cavity of a rotten branch; this was subsequently destroyed, and the spot appropriated by a pair of Starlings.

In the south of England large numbers of this species are captured early in the autumn by professional bird-catchers and sold for trap-shooting, for which purpose they fetch two shillings a dozen. As many as seventeen dozen have been taken by one pull of the nets, the men asserting that at least ten dozen more escaped before the whole of the struggling captives could be secured †. The slaughter of this useful bird is much to be regretted, and the farmer who grants liberty to the poaching rascals to set their nets on his land will doubtless find cause to regret his indiscretion.

It is well known that immense flocks of Starlings arrive on our eastern coast during the autumn from the north of Europe. At what date the earliest flights make their appearance, I have had no means of ascertaining. The following is from my notes for 1879, when shooting in the east of Norfolk:—"October 16, strong wind from the north, weather cold and stormy. Numbers of Grey Crows and Rooks landing, also flocks of Larks and Starlings. The flight was continued till dark, and possibly still later." These observations were made

* In the east of Norfolk the reed is used instead of laths for plastered walls; it is also employed for fencing round small yards and a variety of other purposes.

† It must not be supposed that such numbers are frequently obtained. The seventeen dozen referred to as secured at one haul proved the largest day's catch in the experience of a man who had carried his nets for over five and twenty years; on the following day he took ten dozen, which were shipped to Australia.

on the broads four miles inland. While steaming in company with the herring-fleet in the North Sea, during the autumn of 1872, for the purpose of taking notes on Gulls and also watching the migration, large flocks of Starlings were encountered, making straight for the Norfolk and Suffolk coast, on many occasions between the 7th of October and the 9th of November. The birds usually kept in compact bodies of from one to three or four hundred, flying strongly, with few, if any, stragglers. I cannot call to mind an instance of noticing a single Starling that showed signs of fatigue. I can offer no opinion concerning the course followed by these migrants after reaching our coasts. During protracted winter storms Starlings in thousands may occasionally be observed making their way along the coast of Sussex from east to west; at times numbers are passed at sea heading towards the west; but I have no personal knowledge of their attempting to cross the channel.

Early in spring Starlings again return towards the east coast. While on Hickling Broad, on the 27th of March, 1873, I noticed that immense flocks of Starlings continued flying east during the whole of the morning up till midday, the wind at the time being light and easterly. It is, however, evident that these birds cross the North Sea earlier in the season, as several in company with Larks were taken on board the "Newarp" and "Haisbro'" light-ships during the last week in February, a couple also being secured on the "Lynn Well" previous to the 8th of March*. Throughout March numbers fall disabled on the floating lights off the east coast, the migration appearing to cease about the end of the month.

The young Starling in his first feathers is clad in a particularly unpretending suit of sober grey. The more conspicuous plumage, which is assumed after the first moult, shows itself in somewhat irregular patches, rendering the appearance of the bird for a time exceedingly strange.

But few varieties of this species have come under my observation; the two I met with, however, were especially striking. While watching a large flock passing the steamboat about twenty miles off Yarmouth, on the 7th of October, 1872, my attention was attracted by a bird entirely cream-coloured; the whole body were so close that I could not have been mistaken. On the 20th of October, 1883, a most singularly marked Starling was detected in a flock of some four or five hundred harbouring about the sheep at Buckingham, near Brighton: the feathers of the tail from the rump downwards were of a pure and spotless white, the rest of the plumage being of the ordinary type. I had ample opportunities for examining this specimen, which, on wing, somewhat resembled the Green Sandpiper, as at times it alighted on the back of a sheep, showing itself off to the fullest advantage.

* Being surprised that Starlings were crossing the North Sea so early as the end of February, I made further inquiries, and learned that the birds were taken at the time stated. On this authority I have given the above information.

DIPPER.

CINCLUS AQUATICUS.

A DIFFERENCE of opinion formerly existed concerning these singular birds. Dippers were declared by certain observers to be prejudicial to the spawn and fry of fish, while others asserted they were not only perfectly harmless, but of the greatest service to the rivers, feeding constantly on various kinds of destructive insects.

According to my own experience, water-beetles, as well as minute shell-fish, together with insects of several species and possibly their larvæ, form their chief diet; whether the shells are swallowed to assist digestion or as a means of nourishment I can offer no opinion. At times, during winter and early spring, I have watched single birds by the pools of salt water on the shores of the Scotch firths, and, judging by their actions, there was little doubt they were in quest of food *. A specimen I obtained on the river Lyon, in Perthshire, in the autumn of 1865, was stated by a taxidermist to contain the remains of several beetles as well as a small quantity of other matter, though, owing to decomposition having set in, he failed to identify many minute particles. By those who were desirous of substantiating a charge, I have been assured that these birds have been both seen and shot while in possession of small fish. This, of course, must be taken for what it is worth; there is, however, not the slightest doubt that their presence on the water is beneficial rather than otherwise. As a proof of the ignorance existing within the last ten years regarding the habits of this species, I ascertained, in more than one district, that both keepers and water-bailiffs had received orders to shoot them down, as a means of affording protection to the spawn of the fish.

Though the Dipper is by no means scarce on many of our English streams and rivers in the midland and northern counties, I have had by far the most opportunities of studying their habits along the rocky burns of the Highlands. In this part of the country they are widely distributed, being found in almost every suitable locality. During spring and summer each pair may usually be seen in the vicinity of their accustomed haunts, seldom straying to any considerable distance. Severe frost, however (occasionally, though by no means often), causes them to make a move and shift their quarters; at such times I have now and then caught a glimpse of the dingy little bird while flitting from pool to pool along the shores of the salt-water estuaries. When gunning on the coast of the Dornoch Firth in the winters of 1868 and 1869, a bird or two were passed almost daily near Mounagie; and a couple of pairs (though seldom if ever seen in company) resorted to the mouths of the small burns between that spot and Bonar Bridge.

Along the sluggish rivers and deep muddy-water dykes of Norfolk the Dipper is occasionally to be met with, two or three specimens having come under my observation in the eastern portion of the county in 1871 and 1872. The birds were noticed in every instance late in autumn; and as few spots could be found in this quarter adapted to their nesting-requirements, it is probable they were simply visitors from across the

* In order to ascertain what prey had been secured, I frequently attempted to obtain a shot at one of these birds; the spots on which they were usually observed, however, were too open to permit a near approach.

North Sea. Whether these were the black-bellied form, *Cinclus melanogaster* (the variety most commonly procured in the county), I had no means of ascertaining, as the birds invariably rose out of shot and were not seen again.

From the Bridge of Balgie, which spans the Lyon a short distance east of Meggernie Castle, and looks down on a noted grilse-pool, as well as from many other overhanging spots, I have often carefully watched the actions of the Dipper. Though repeatedly unsuccessful in my attempts, I was determined, if possible, to learn whether there was any foundation for the report that this species is endowed with the power of walking on the bottom while in search of food. The view obtained of the birds while beneath the surface was usually indistinct, owing to the ripple on the flowing water; in every instance, however, where their movements could be discerned they appeared to seize their prey while swimming, or rather hovering on wing among the stones and rocks that formed the bed of the pool. Their mode of progression much resembled that of the Common Guillemot when viewed diving in the tanks of an aquarium: frequent strokes were made with the wings, enabling the birds to retain their position and seek out the insects on which they subsist. On regaining the surface they would not unfrequently swim a short distance to some neighbouring rock or stone; under such circumstances I remarked the wings were almost invariably used to assist in stemming the current. Their actions while partially swimming and flapping forcibly reminded me of the endeavours of a crippled fowl, when hotly pursued, to evade capture*. On numberless occasions I have seen Dippers disappear below the surface; but the ripple on the water prevented all chance of detecting the object of their search.

The note of *Cinclus aquaticus* is more shrill than melodious; possibly its sweetness may be somewhat drowned by the constant murmur of the water in the rapid streams, along which the song is most frequently heard.

The nest is a warm and cosy structure of long and coarse grasses, coated externally with green moss collected from the adjacent burn-sides and swamps. I detected a nest in the spring of 1876 snugly concealed among some roots and twining plants under a slab of rock, over which a hill-stream dashed down the mountain-side from the Crossfell in Cumberland. The bird, on being disturbed, made its escape through the sheet of falling water. Owing to the constant spray, the nest was exceedingly damp and of no little weight. The eggs are five or six in number, white when fresh laid, but for the most part presenting a stained and dirty appearance before hatching.

* I have carefully perused the account given by that accurate observer, Macgillivray, of the subaqueous manœuvres of the Dipper. Though thoroughly agreeing with all his remarks concerning the actions of the bird itself, I should scarcely be inclined to describe its movements below the surface as similar to those of the Merganser or, more especially, the Cormorant. As far as I have been able to judge, the Dipper depends almost entirely on the aid of its wings to capture its prey, and it is a question if these are the tactics of the species with which it is compared.

www.ingramcontent.com/pod-product-compliance
Lightning Source LLC
Chambersburg PA
CBHW021220270326
41929CB00010B/1200